Christianity

Christianity

An Asian Religion in Vancouver

JASON BYASSEE
ALBERT Y. S. CHU
ROSS A. LOCKHART

Foreword by Darrell L. Guder
Afterword by Mi-Jung Lee

CASCADE *Books* • Eugene, Oregon

CHRISTIANITY
An Asian Religion in Vancouver

Copyright © 2023 Jason Byassee, Albert Y. S. Chu, and Ross A. Lockhart. All rights reserved. Except for brief quotations in critical publications or reviews, no part of this book may be reproduced in any manner without prior written permission from the publisher. Write: Permissions, Wipf and Stock Publishers, 199 W. 8th Ave., Suite 3, Eugene, OR 97401.

Cascade Books
An Imprint of Wipf and Stock Publishers
199 W. 8th Ave., Suite 3
Eugene, OR 97401

www.wipfandstock.com

PAPERBACK ISBN: 978-1-6667-5252-6
HARDCOVER ISBN: 978-1-6667-5253-3
EBOOK ISBN: 978-1-6667-5254-0

Cataloguing-in-Publication data:

Names: Byassee, Jason, author. | Chu, Albert Y. S., author. | Lockhart, Ross A., author. | Guder, Darrell L., 1939–, foreword. | Lee, Mi-Jung, afterword.

Title: Christianity : an Asian religion in Vancouver / Jason Byassee, Albert Y. S. Chu, and Ross A. Lockhart ; foreword by Darrell L. Guder ; afterword by Mi-Jung Lee.

Description: Eugene, OR : Cascade Books, 2023 | Includes bibliographical references.

Identifiers: ISBN 978-1-6667-5252-6 (paperback) | ISBN 978-1-6667-5253-3 (hardcover) | ISBN 978-1-6667-5254-0 (ebook)

Subjects: LCSH: Asians—British Columbia—Christianity. | British Columbia—Christianity.

Classification: BL2530.C3 .C47 2023 (paperback) | BL2530.C3 .C47 (ebook)

06/12/23

Scripture quotations marked NRSV are taken from the Holy Bible, New Revised Standard Version Bible, copyright 1989, Division of Christian Education of the National Council of the Churches of Christ in the United States of America.

Used by permission. All rights reserved. Scripture quotations marked (NIV) are taken from the Holy Bible, New International Version®, NIV®. Copyright © 1973, 1978, 1984, 2011 by Biblica, Inc.™ Used by permission of Zondervan. All rights reserved worldwide. www.zondervan.com The "NIV" and "New International Version" are trademarks registered in the United States Patent and Trademark Office by Biblica, Inc.™

Scripture quotations marked THE MESSAGE. Copyright © by Eugene H. Peterson 1993, 1994, 1995, 1996, 2000, 2001, 2002. Used by permission of Tyndale House Publishers, Inc.

Contents

Foreword by Darrell L. Guder   vii

Introduction   1

Chapter 1   A Brief History of Asian Immigration to Vancouver   9

Chapter 2   Ethnic Churches and Denominational Loyalty   17

Chapter 3   Vocation   25

Chapter 4   A New Family   39

Chapter 5   New Hands for the Harvest   48

Chapter 6   "Jook-sing"   57

Chapter 7   The Church God Is Bringing   64

Conclusion—Where Is God Moving Next?   72

Afterword by Mi-Jung Lee   79

Bibliography   81

Foreword

Western Canada has, in recent years, provided rich resources for researching the declining state of modern religion, especially Christianity, within its cultural parameters. Those parameters are widely described with the term "Cascadia," generally used for British Columbia, Washington, and Oregon, and discussed under rubrics that include secularization, Christendom (and especially "end of"), religious skepticism, "spiritual but not religious," and diverse forms of ecclesial inventiveness. The Centre for Missional Leadership at St. Andrew's Hall has, in the last decade, pursued a number of intriguing Cascadian initiatives that are stimulating provocative research. These CML initiatives are leading some of its partners to wonder if the discussion thus far has focused too much on decline when it might be a more sensitive approach to wonder whether we are experiencing something like the possible emergence of Christianity as an Asian religion in Vancouver. The "end of Christendom" tactic, as missionally generative as it certainly is, could actually be developing into a restrictive set of lenses that conceal what is really going on in, say, Vancouver. Could the missional initiatives thus far be defining God's mission too narrowly?

One of the themes that has surfaced in the emerging missional discussion has been migration. The biblical witness to God's missional witness is rooted in the call to Abraham and the movement of an emerging people who are challenged to come out and become instruments of God's promises "for all the nations." Are those promises not to find their fulfillment through the ongoing pilgrimage of

Foreword

the God of Abraham, Isaac, Jacob, and Moses? God's people are a tabernacle community, who betray their vocation when they focus too much on temples rather than glorying in the tents in which God is present and active. Some have argued that Christendom's problem was (is!) its loss of that sense of tent vocation and its replacement with temples. The provocative storytelling of the following chapters may stimulate some course corrections in the missional discussion. It may lead us to recognize penitently how our lenses can continue to be shaped by the legacy of Christendom! It may liberate us as we risk exploring how Christianity may be rediscovered as an "Asian religion."

>   DARRELL L. GUDER
>   Senior Fellow in Residence
>   St. Andrew's Hall, Vancouver

Introduction

Vancouver Chinese poet Jim Wong-Chu describes tradition as being like a bundle of leaves carefully wrapped with a string. A gentle tug and the string gives way as the leaves open to reveal the precious gift of "sweet rice within."[1] Wong-Chu's personal story offers a "tradition" quite different from the dominant narrative of Canada's founding as a European colonial project. Wong-Chu was born in Hong Kong in 1949 before he was brought to Canada in 1953 as a "paper son"[2] to be raised in British Columbia by aunts and uncles. While working in the Chinese Canadian restaurant industry, moving from dishwasher to delivery boy to short order cook, his artistic talents flourished on the side. He enrolled in what is now called Emily Carr University, and while studying photography and poetry, Jim Wong-Chu helped bring Vancouver's Chinatown to life in curated images and words. Wong-Chu's life and work bears testimony to the creation of an emerging civic culture that challenged, and then helped reverse, the default origin story of Vancouver as a tale of ever westward expansion of European power.[3]

From creation tales to family trees to Hollywood studios, origin stories are powerful, compelling, and enduring narratives that

1. Wong-Chu, *Chinatown Ghosts*, 10.

2. Paper sons or daughters refers to individuals who immigrated to Canada as children by adopting the false identities of others at a time when Canada limited Chinese immigration.

3. Of course, the deeper origin story of this land is with the Indigenous people, and we note that the city of Vancouver is built on the traditional, ancestral, and unceded territory of the Coast Salish peoples including the Musqueam, Squamish, and Tsleil-Waututh nations.

1

CHRISTIANITY

help frame our understanding of what it means to be a human being in a particular place. As a city, Vancouver traditionally had a well-known, often repeated and, until recently, rarely challenged origin story itself. The city takes its name from English Royal Navy Captain George Vancouver who first visited the region and met with Indigenous peoples in 1792, a year after the Spanish first appeared in the area. British settlement of the territory began over thirty years later with the establishment of Fort Langley in 1827. New Westminster, which today is a suburb of Vancouver, was the first area developed by the British on the banks of the province's longest river, named for the Northwest Company's famous explorer Simon Fraser. The two British colonies on Vancouver Island and what is now the Lower Mainland were united in 1866 with New Westminster as its capital for two years, until the more established city of Victoria (dating back to 1843) became the home of the legislature and government bureaucracy. Meanwhile, on July 1, 1867, the British North American colonies of Canada (Upper and Lower Canada known today as Ontario and Quebec), along with New Brunswick and Nova Scotia, were united in confederation to form the Dominion of Canada. Four years later the colony of British Columbia joined Canada, with the promise of a railway connecting east and west, and the majority of male, British, non-Indigenous citizens who were permitted to vote did so to join confederation on July 20, 1871.

The railway would take another fifteen years to finally reach the West Coast, but when it did arrive, the city of Vancouver began to take shape, as the Canadian Pacific Railroad found that the Gastown area (now a tourist haven for cruise ship passengers) was a better harbor and terminus for shipping than the original Port Moody site further east. That is the traditional, Eurocentric telling of Vancouver's origin story. But, as University of British Columbia urban geographer David Ley argues, "In the quest to understand society, things are not always as they appear; causes and consequences may be concealed; subtle explanations may on the surface seem implausible."[4]

Indeed, as Vancouver set out plans for Canada's 150th anniversary of confederation, public awareness had turned away from

---

4. Ley, "Christian Faith," 281.

INTRODUCTION

the former origin story of the city and a growing movement took hold of "Canada 150+," recognizing that the Indigenous history of this West Coast territory goes well beyond the century and a half of a modern nation-state.[5] Instead, as the former origin story of the city of Vancouver breaks down, gaps in the Eurocentric narrative create space for the witness of neighbors for whom there has been no bard that others listen to attempting to tell their tale or a statue to commemorate their history. From Canada's First Peoples to more recent newcomers with roots in Asia, Africa, and South America, the lived experience of those who are not of European ancestry are finding voice and sharing their painful and challenging stories of what it is like to be here but not always seen or heard. Jim Wong-Chu captures this in his poem "How feel I do?" where he explores the pain of an Asian immigrant adjusting to an English-dominant culture confessing that he feels at home in the embarrassment of one trying desperately to fit in and adapt to this new Canadian culture.[6]

This project emerged out of earlier research focusing on missional churches in the Pacific Northwest region of North America known as Cascadia, that includes Greater Vancouver with its population of 2.6 million people.[7] That project highlighted the vibrancy of Asian Christian congregations in Vancouver and sparked our curiosity as researchers to move beyond interviews with clergy leaders alone. And so, we began a new project conducting interviews with laypeople who reflected the growth of Asian Christianity in this region where the dominant narrative in media and culture is one of religious decline and irrelevance. The authors, three friends who are pastors preaching regularly in the city, as well as engaged in distinct work on a university campus, listened carefully to these stories of Asian Christian laypeople whose devotion to Jesus Christ often goes unnoticed in the culture around them. *Christianity: An Asian Religion in Vancouver* is meant to surprise and reorient our understanding of religious identity in a context where so often the

5. "Strengthening Our Relations: Canada 150+."
6. Wong-Chu, *Chinatown Ghosts*, 21.
7. Byassee and Lockhart, *Better Than Brunch*.

3

broader secularization thesis is accepted without question. Missiologist Stefan Paas describes the secularized nations of the West today as being characterized by "low and decreasing levels of church attendance, low and decreasing levels of other types of church involvement (baptism, church weddings, Christian funerals, etc.)." For Paas, they have a "widespread lack of belief in traditional Christian doctrines (a personal God, the divinity of Jesus Christ, heaven and hell, etc.), a general indifference towards traditional religious questions and cultural elites that are often quite critical of religion and religious institutions."[8] Canadian philosopher Charles Taylor attempts to describe this shift in the West to secularity as "a move from a society where belief in God is unchallenged and indeed, unproblematic, to one in which it is understood to be one option among others, and frequently not the easiest to embrace."[9] This leads to a dominant cultural narrative, fueled by a media that still attends primarily to (formerly) mainline denominations, that gleefully proclaims the end of Christianity in Canada with a "best before shelf life" of 2040.[10]

And why not? After all, Canada is well-known among observers of secularization for its standout irreligiosity. Our friend Jason's native United States of America is the standard go-to counterargument for secularization theses in general. It has long been observed that as cultures industrialize and grow wealthy, their faith adherence declines. That has been true in western Europe, in Australia and New Zealand, and in Canada, but not in the world's most industrialized and wealthy nation, the United States. Canada is significant in this counterargument as a fellow North American country colonized by the English and French that has, in fact, declined precipitously in its faith adherence. Even the part of Canada colonized by the French has been a standout: Quebec fell from perhaps the most widely Christian place on earth to one of the least in a very short time, in its renowned 1960s "Quiet Revolution."

8. Paas, *Church Planting*, 4–5.
9. Taylor, *Secular Age*, 3.
10. Stewart, "Gone by 2040."

Introduction

In short, Canada is much more like its European forebears in its decline in faith. The United States of America stands out as a counterexample. At least for now.

On a neighborhood level, our neighbors with European heritage here in Vancouver and its suburbs tend to think of Christianity as something their grandparents once believed in. Aside from cultural accretions like statutory holidays and Christmas lights, the cross is not something that shapes their lives, much less those of the children they are raising. As they or their parents moved to the West Coast of Canada, they left behind whatever observation of Christian faith they may have once had. Mark Noll has documented that Canada was once *more* faith-observant than the United States of America.[11] This faith was allied more closely with the English crown and the Canadian government than was ever the case in the breakaway United States. Yet as Christian officialdom declined in Canada, so did church attendance and profession of faith among Canadians as documented by our colleagues at The University of Toronto.[12] If you ally with the government, and the government turns its back on you, what do you have left? Seminarians in denominations that have "Canada" in their title, like those whose seminarians we teach from the United Church of Canada, the Anglican Church of Canada, and the Presbyterian Church in Canada, must wonder what their church is *for* once the Canada in their title no longer cares about Christianity. And yet. Our neighbors with European heritage may think Christianity was something their forebears cared about with no present purchase in their lives, but that's because they are not paying attention. While they dismiss the presence and power of Christian faith, it is likely an Asian-Canadian immigrant Christian who is teaching their children in their local school. It is another Asian-Canadian Christian who is managing their portfolio, making possible their dreamed-for one-day retirement. It is another who is their local family physician, and another who is curing their heart disease, with prescriptions filled by yet another at their local pharmacy. Yet another, as of this writing, was a Member of Parliament in

11. Noll, *What Happened to Christian Canada?*
12. Clarke and Macdonald, *Leaving Christianity.*

5

Christianity

Ottawa representing a Vancouver riding. Another was anchoring the local news on their Canadian Television (CTV) broadcast. Another is leading the research to cure cancer in the country and elsewhere, and others are advancing the medical technology to make their old age more bearable. And each of these Asian-Canadian Christians is engaging in their work *because of their Christian faith*. In short, secularization looks more compelling if we are speaking of white Canadians with European heritage. It looks less so if we think of Christianity as an Asian religion crossing the Pacific with Chinese diaspora and other Asian immigrants. This book is filled with stories that show that secularization is not the only story in Greater Vancouver. It might not even be the most important one.

Jesus Christ promised his followers that there would always be a church. He made no promises about its ethnic makeup (much less any permanent clergy or pension plan, much to the chagrin of these authors!). There may be an ongoing church in North America, even in Western Canada. All appearances indicate that it will be a heavily Asian church in the Lower Mainland of British Columbia. Asian diaspora churches in these lands are celebrating and spreading the gospel. And they seriously call secularization theories into question.

As you read on in this study, you will be invited into conversations with a wide variety of Asian Canadian Christian laypeople who are changing the face and social fabric not only of the city of Vancouver in general, but the Body of Christ in this place. Despite the diversity of Asian Canadian Christian interview subjects, we recognize that any attempt to define what "Asian" means is entering into contested space. For the sake of this study, we followed the definitions of Statistics Canada, which identifies eleven different categories of Canadians by race.[13] Our interview subjects were primarily limited to the four Statistics Canada categories of Chinese, Filipino, Korean, and Japanese. With only a couple of exceptions, the scope of the project did not enable us to include interviews outside those categories in what Statistics Canada identifies as "Southeast Asian (e.g., Vietnamese, Cambodian, Malaysian, Laotian, etc.), "West Asian (e.g., Iranian, Afghan, etc.)," or "South Asian (e.g., East

---

13. Statistics Canada, "Visible Minority and Population Group."

Introduction

Indian, Pakistani, Sri Lankan, etc.)."[14] We are keenly aware of our neighbors from these other Asian communities in Greater Vancouver and look forward to future research projects that will help tell their stories as well.

Despite the limitations of the scope of this study, it has been a remarkable experience to engage in rich conversation and deep contemplation about what God is up to in these Asian Canadian Christians' lives in church and community, seeking the common good in a city that has not always been a hospitable place for newcomers from the Pacific Rim. While the dominant narrative of ecclesiastical decline still looks to European Christian heritage in Canada moving west, this study invites you to turn your gaze to the other side of the globe, as we encounter a transplanted faith and people in this "City of Glass"[15] hemmed in by North Shore mountains and the Pacific Ocean. In chapter 1, we will explore in greater detail the history of Asian immigration to Vancouver to better situate the interviews that follow. In chapter 2, we explore the unique aspects of Asian ethnic churches in Vancouver and their more fluid relationship to denominational identity and loyalty. In chapter 3, we will engage our interview subjects in an exploration of Christian vocation and how their theological values impact the workplace in Vancouver. In chapter 4, we will explore aspects of Asian culture, including the concept of "saving face" and how adopting a Christian identity creates both tension and opportunity for new understandings of belonging. Chapter 5 attends to the understanding and priority of mission within Asian Christian communities in Vancouver. Chapter 6 explores Jook-sing identity of Asian believers in Vancouver who, like the hollow bamboo tree, struggle with the emptiness between Asian and Western cultural realities. In chapter 7, as the project moves toward a conclusion, we will reflect together on what the changing face of Christianity in Vancouver might mean moving forward. As we lean further into God's active dismantling of European heritage Christianity on the West Coast, what does it mean to give way to a Christianity in Vancouver predominantly as an Asian religion. Our conclusion will

---

14. Statistics Canada, "Visible Minority and Population Group."
15. Coupland, *City of Glass*.

be a resting place in this journey of discovery, as we attempt to name together where God might be moving ahead of us in Vancouver, as we prepare for the next, most faithful step of Christian witness in this West Coast region.

Throughout the course of this study, we invite you to remain open to the delightful surprise of Christian faith taking shape in Vancouver in ways that you may not have imagined possible. Along with this surprise, comes the comfort of knowing that we all inhabit this West Coast paradise together, finding new ways to proclaim the reign of God in shared experiences of this urban space nicknamed "Rain City."

CHAPTER I

A Brief History of Asian Immigration to Vancouver

Following a cursory encounter with Spanish colonial power, the region we now know as Vancouver was shaped since the late eighteenth century by the political, cultural, economic, and military influence of the British Empire. Captain George Vancouver first remarked of the land, "the intermediate space is occupied by very low land, apparently a swampy flat, that retires several miles, before the country rises to meet the rugged snowy mountains."[1] From its humble beginnings as the sawmill community of Granville, Vancouver's story bears evidence of the transformative influence of immigration and impact of wider geopolitical influences. Before immigration of any kind to the region, what we now call Vancouver was home to the first peoples of the land including the Musqueam, Squamish, and Tsleil-Waututh Nations. Reconciliation with Indigenous peoples, in light of the devastating impact of colonialism, has only begun in earnest in the twenty-first century and is a significant political issue for Vancouverites today. In the early development of Vancouver, however, non-Indigenous residents enthusiastically reflected the "Britishness" of British Columbia, along with immigrants from continental Europe. For the focus of this study, it is important to note exceptions to this European-focused immigration pattern

---

1. Geddes, *Vancouver*, 29.

CHRISTIANITY

that include the historic Chinese presence (and other immigrants from across Asia) dating back to the gold rush and national railway expansion of the nineteenth century. When the railway connecting British Columbia to the rest of Canada was complete and formally recognized at Craigellachie on November 7, 1885, many of the former Chinese railway workers migrated to the West Coast and settled in and around Vancouver. The Chinese living in Vancouver referred to their new home as "Saltwater City"[2] with the majority taking up residence in the neighborhood bordered by streets bearing the names to this day of Hastings, Pender, and Main, in what quickly became known as "Chinatown."

By the early twentieth century, Vancouver had grown to a population of 120,000 people with Chinatown expanding rapidly to over 3,500 residents, evolving from a few wooden shacks to several blocks of brick buildings.[3] The growth of Chinatown and Vancouver's Asian community is even more remarkable given the widespread racist sentiments and entrenched government policy in place at the time known as the "Chinese head tax," which sought to limit non-European immigrant numbers and influence. In 1885 (a year before Vancouver was founded) the Parliament of Canada enacted a racist policy meant to discourage further Chinese immigration after the completion of the trans-national railway, on which many Chinese immigrants worked in dangerous conditions that led to workplace injury and death.[4] By the 1901 census, 86 percent of all Chinese in Canada declared their home in the province of British Columbia, the majority migrating to the urban centers of Vancouver and Victoria.[5]

---

2. Saltwater City (Hahm-sui-fau) was the name given to Vancouver by its early Chinese residents to set it apart from the older mainland city of New Westminster (now a suburb of Vancouver) on the freshwater Fraser River. The name is no longer common in Chinese communities, who refer to Vancouver as "Wen-go-wa."

3. Yee, *Saltwater City*, 17.

4. It is estimated that as many as six hundred Chinese workers were killed building the railroad to Vancouver through the Rocky Mountains in the late nineteenth century.

5. Ley, *Millionaire Migrants*, 32–33.

A Brief History of Asian Immigration to Vancouver

British Columbians today are often surprised to learn that their inclusive and racially diverse West Coast province historically had the most aggressive anti-Chinese sentiment and punitive provincial legislation. While British Columbians begrudgingly acknowledge that Vancouverites have rioted during Stanley Cup finals when the NHL Canucks lost (not once but twice!) in the last three decades, they are especially appalled when informed of the history of race-based riots in the city's history. Vancouver experienced its first anti-Chinese race riot just one year after incorporation as a city in 1887, fueled in large part by tensions over employment of Chinese labors at cut rate prices and real estate speculation. By 1907, white Vancouverites had formed an organization known as the Asiatic Exclusion League, advertising widely in local newspapers such as the *Sun*, *Daily Province*, and *Saturday Sunset* promoting racist cartoons and providing editorials discussing the "Chinese Problem." Evidence of this deep-seated racism can be found in the highest levels of government with Premier Richard McBride declaring in 1919 the need for a common commitment to "a white British Columbia, a white land, and a white Empire."[6]

In 1923 the Chinese head tax was removed, but it was followed by a more restrictive policy than the original one that prevented Chinese immigration even further before being repealed in 1947.[7] As noted above, racism could be found at the highest levels of government and industry in British Columbia. In June 1922 John Hart, the provincial finance minister, said in opposition to repealing the Chinese head tax, "We want British Columbia to be a white province."[8] At that same time, British Columbia's Attorney General Alex Manson (a Presbyterian layperson) stated his position in the legislature this way,

6. Donaldson, *Land of Destiny*, 65–66.

7. Although the exculsion law was repleaded in 1947, federal Order-in-Council 2115 still restricted Chinese immigration and was only ended in 1956. The federal government of Canada formerly apologized for the Chinese head tax in 2006.

8. Hart's fellow Cabinet Minister Thomas Dufferin Pattullo (for whom a famous bridge in Vancouver is named) said regarding Asian immigrants and Caucasian citizens, "We must trade together, but I think it is sufficient to suggest that we should occupy our own spheres."

11

Christianity

> I have no real objection to the Oriental, but the real objection to him and the one that is permanent, and incurable is that there is an ethnological difference which cannot be overcome. The two races cannot mix, and I believe our first duty is to our own people.
>
> It is a matter of our own domestic affairs that we should endeavour to protect the white race from the necessity of intermingling with Oriental blood, and I think we have every warrant for fighting to prevent a situation that will inevitably result in race deterioration.[9]

This racial discrimination extended to owning real estate, something hard to imagine today in Vancouver where one-third of the $38 billion residential home sales in the area are purchased by Chinese buyers.[10] Just decades earlier these same persons would have been prevented purchasing that property based on their racial origins. Indeed, many homes in Vancouver's wealthier neighborhoods like Shaughnessy or the British Pacific Properties included "white only" clauses in their land titles such as "No person of the African or Asiatic race, or of African or Asiatic descent (except servants of the occupier of the premises in residence) shall reside or be allowed to remain on the premises."[11] Even with such blatantly racist policies in place, immigration from Asia and other non-Western regions continued in earnest throughout the second half of the twentieth century. Today, 54 percent of Vancouverites identify as a visible minority, with Chinese being the largest ethnic group at 19.6 percent in the Greater Vancouver region.[12]

Of the many factors impacting immigration on the city of Vancouver, there are a few seminal events worth highlighting from the last several decades. For example, one hundred years after Vancouver's founding, the city hosted "Expo '86" with its theme of technology

---

9. Anderson, *Vancouver's Chinatown*, 112.
10. Northam, "Vancouver Has Been Transformed."
11. "West Vancouver Makes Racist Land Covenants History."
12. For example, in the 2001 census, immigrants represented 45.4 percent of the city's population. In 2016, Statistics Canada reported the number of immigrants living in Vancouver to be 42.5 percent. See "Immigrant Demographics." See also McElroy, "Majority of Metro Vancouver Residents."

A Brief History of Asian Immigration to Vancouver

and communications and drew twenty-two million visitors from across North America and around the world. Expo gave the city of Vancouver global exposure and brought increased immigration and investment that helped build the modern metropolitan area known as the "City of Glass."[13] This included federal government funding to build a large convention center (where cruise ships dock today) as well as the first line of what has now become Vancouver's Skytrain public transportation system. The site of Expo '86 was sold after the exposition to Concord Pacific Developments, majority owned by Li Ka-shing, patriarch of the wealthiest family in Hong Kong. The land used for Expo '86 on Vancouver's False Creek was transformed by the Li family through the building of 10,000 housing units and seven million square feet of office space beside the new BC Place, a 60,000-seat sports stadium remembered as another Expo '86 legacy gift to the city of Vancouver. Following Expo, the Li family's significant economic investment in the city encouraged other wealthy investors from Asia to also move capital into the region. Social geographer David Ley at the University of British Columbia noted that the Li family were significant models for many other wealthy Asian investors to participate in this "trans-pacific migration" described as "where the big fish swim, the smaller fish follow."[14]

A second notable event was the increase of immigration (including a significant transfer of wealth) to Vancouver in advance of the British handover of Hong Kong to the Chinese government in 1997. This flow of capital was aided by the Canadian government's Business Immigration Programme (BIP) expressly intent upon recruiting wealthy immigrants to advance economic development in Canada, either through active entrepreneurialism or more passive investment. By 2001, almost 330,000 immigrants landed in Canada under the BIP, making the Canadian programme the

13. Vancouver has developed several nicknames over the years from "wet city" to "Lotusland" to "Hollywood North" due to the scale of the movie-making industry here. Internationally recognized author and artist Douglas Coupland has given it another moniker "City of Glass," in reference to its concentration of large business and residential skyscrapers set against the backdrop of the North Shore mountains. For more, please see Coupland, *City of Glass*.

14. Ley, *Millionaire Migrants*, 55.

13

most successful in the global immigration marketplace, far ahead of competing programs in Commonwealth countries such as Australia or New Zealand, as well as the United States.[15] During this period, Hong Kong, Taiwan, and South Korea accounted for over half the business immigrants landing in Canada, three-quarters of these newcomers settling in British Columbia. That arrival of "millionaire migrants" continued to Vancouver into the first two decades of the twenty-first century, bringing not only wealthy investors from Hong Kong but from mainland China as well. Today, for visitors and residents alike, the influence of Asian culture is noticeable throughout Vancouver with 43 percent of the local population claiming Asian heritage making it the "most Asian city outside of Asia."[16]

Another significant event that shaped immigration to Vancouver was the decision to host the 2010 Winter Olympics games, with athletes participating from eighty-two nations around the world. With the world's media focused on Vancouver, the games once again highlighted the livability of the West Coast city, that further fueled the transfer of wealth from Asia to the Lower Mainland of British Columbia. In fact, advocates for affordable housing have noted that the Vancouver Olympic Bid Committee was made up of local real estate developers including the chairperson, Jack Poole.[17] "At the risk of sounding naïve, we had understood the bid was aimed at getting the Games," noted *Western Investor* editor Frank O'Brien reflecting on the Olympic bid, "raising Vancouver's international profile and welcoming elite athletes to one of the world's best skiing locations. Wrong. The real purpose of the 2010 Olympic bid (was) to seduce the provincial and federal governments and long-suffering taxpayers into footing a billion-dollar bill to pave the path for

---

15. Ley, *Millionaire Migrants*, 20.
16. Todd, "Vancouver Is the Most 'Asian' City."
17. Appointed by British Columbia Premier Gordon Campbell, developer Jack Poole led the bid for the Winter Olympics, appointing to the Board of Directors fellow real estate leaders such as David Podmore (Poole's partner at Concert Properties), Canaccord's Peter Brown, real estate giant David McLean, Stanley Kwok (former vice president of Concord Pacific), and Robert Fung (director of Gordon Capital, a firm owned by Li Ka-Shing's son Richard).

A Brief History of Asian Immigration to Vancouver

future real estate sales."[18] In the aftermath of the Olympics, wealthy immigrants continued to purchase property in Vancouver either for investment or to live in, whether together or in what is known as an "astronaut household."[19] Wealthy Asian immigrant investors were courted in Vancouver as "industry and government were aggressively marketing real estate overseas as this fantastic and lucrative investment."[20] Similar to the economic impact of Expo '86, the 2010 Winter Olympics created new neighborhoods in Vancouver (and Whistler) where the former Olympic villages were built for athletes. Often, these condos purchased by overseas owners were left empty and unoccupied most of the year, prompting one critic to describe Vancouver as "a resort city where rich foreigners live a few months per year," adding that the Olympic games were simply a "$6 billion ad buy" for the real estate industry.[21]

In Vancouver, the Olympic Village housing development helped reimagine False Creek, which had previously been an old warehouse district, preserving the 1930s Salt Company building as a brewery and restaurant.[22] Sixteen new Skytrain stations were created for the games (including one at Olympic Village) with the launch of the "Canada Line" further expanding the public transit system from the original Expo line built in 1986.[23] High profile international events like Expo '86 or the 2010 Winter Olympics helped raise the profile of Vancouver's quality of life, especially for those with wealth in Asia seeking a better life for themselves and their families, leading to the slogan within the Chinese Canadian

---

18. Donaldson, *Land of Destiny*, 222.

19. Ley, *Millionaire Migrants*, 230. In an astronaut household the prinicpal wage earner, almost always a male, works in East Asia, often in a business owned prior to migration, and commutes several times a year to join his nuclear family in Canada for a few weeks at a time. See also *New York Times* coverage of astronaut families in Vancouver in Dives, "Astronaut' Families."

20. Blennerhaassett, "Asian Community Blamed."

21. Donaldson, *Land of Destiny*, 224.

22. Atkin, *Changing City*, 195.

23. SkyTrain is the oldest and longest, fully automated, driverless, rapid-transit system in the world.

15

Christianity

community in Vancouver, "Hong Kong for making money, Canada for quality of life."[24]

While Vancouver's Chinatown continues to be a vibrant community of its own, it is increasingly recognized more for its historic significance rather than being the center of Chinese life in the city. As Paul Cheng wrote, "Chinatown has changed, it's only busy in the daytime for tourism, or for people who live close by to get groceries. Historically, it's nice to have it there. But the real functions, the real developments (that formed Chinatown's social and economic hubs) are not there anymore. Now, Richmond is said to be the new Chinatown."[25] From its humble begins as a place of refuge for Chinese immigrants, Chinatown now stands as a landmark from which immigrants from Asia helped shape and enliven Canada's third largest city.

---

24. Ley, *Millionaire Migrants*, 5.
25. Lin, Cho, and Wong-Chu, *AlliterAsian*, 69.

Chapter 2

Ethnic Churches and Denominational Loyalty

When Vancouver resident Hansel Wang first arrived in Canada from Hong Kong as a foreign student back in 1972, he was met in the arrival hall of the Winnipeg International Airport by members of the University of Manitoba Chinese Christian fellowship.[1] Those involved in this fellowship were enthusiastic in welcoming new arrivals, and spotted Hansel as fresh-off-the-plane, gave him a lift from the airport, then helped him acclimatize to a new country (and we do stress *acclimatize* due to the temperature difference!). This group went so far as to introduce him to a host family that he stayed with until he eventually moved into the university residence. It was while he was in residence that a member of the Navigators (an international, interdenominational Christian ministry) shared the Gospel with Hansel, and led him to his belief in Jesus and his baptism the very next spring.

This story became a familiar one described to us by many immigrants to Canada interviewed for the book. New Asian immigrants, refugees, and foreign students to Canada frequently turned to churches and other Christian groups belonging to their same ethnic group to assist in their transition to a new country. These

---

1. Hansel Wang was a recipient of the lifetime achievement award from TransLink transit company for his work in the SkyTrain program.

ethnic churches provide the requisite social networks through which newcomers can acquire jobs, housing, English language schooling, and information about Canadian norms, customs, and government requirements.[2] Not only that, but many of these ethnic churches see new arrivals to the country as their mission field.

Sylvia Leung, who works with the Canadian federal government, and as a literary editor, started attending the Vancouver Lutheran Chinese Church at the age of six with her family a few years after they arrived in Canada as refugees. This Chinese church was a godsend, providing much needed care for Sylvia's family during her mother's battle with cancer, support after her unfortunate passing, as well as assistance in their ongoing integration into Canada. As Sylvia states:

> The Chinese church, or Asian churches, they speak our language, they speak the immigrants' language, they understand the home country, and [the church] is the only home immigrants have. When they come here, it's a completely different culture, and they may not know the language well. It's home. It's familiar. . . . I think that is why a lot of Asians get baptized here, because this is the only help they get, whereas it's prejudice everywhere else.

Sylvia, like others we interviewed, did not feel the same kind of affinity, kinship, or welcome in the non-ethnic churches they tried to attend. The Vancouver Chinese Lutheran Church not only helped Sylvia and her family integrate into a new country, but the church also helped them find a new faith. Over time, Sylvia eventually left the Chinese Lutheran church and started attending a Mennonite Brethren church, but has now found a church home at the Village Church (Baptist) in Surrey.

The important role that ethnic churches play is especially true for those that come to Canada with *some* Christian faith or background. Upon their arrival, many will immediately look to the church for help. They will begin to attend an ethnic church that a

---

2. Our operating definition of an *ethnic church* is any church congregation that indicates whether by name, vision, or mission an emphasis on ministering to a particular ethnic group.

relative or friend attends or knows of, or they will simply go to the nearest ethnic church they can find.

Take for example Winnie Pang, an ESL teacher at the British Columbia Institute of Technology. Her parents were nominal Christians in Hong Kong. Winnie's paternal grandfather had come to faith through the work of missionaries in China before World War II and escaped to Macau after the war due to the Communist revolution in China. Winnie's mother went to an Anglican Christian high school in Hong Kong. Although both Winnie's father and mother had some familiarity with Christianity in their past, it was only after they arrived in Canada that their faith become "more real and solid."

Living close to Chinatown in Vancouver, Winnie and her family began attending the Christ Church of China located on Pender Street in the heart of Chinatown. Christ Church of China was an independent nondenominational church that provided for Winnie and her family "a ready-made community of people with the same language." They began to attend regularly and become very involved in the life and worship of the church. After getting her teaching degree, Winnie went back to Hong Kong and taught English for a time at a girls-only Baptist Christian school and then a Methodist Christian school. Since returning from Hong Kong, Winnie now attends Fraserlands Church.

It comes as no surprise, then, that as immigration from Pacific Rim nations continues to funnel into the Lower Mainland, membership and attendance in Asian ethnic churches continue to grow, while non-Asian churches or Western mainline churches continue their steady decline. Jason once asked an official in the Roman Catholic Archdiocese of Vancouver office what Protestant churches could learn from their growth in the region, to which the official replied, "find a country with lots of members of your denomination and encourage them to immigrate to Canada."

One story that vividly illustrates this development is the story of Pacific Grace Mennonite Brethren Church. Pacific Grace MB Church began on December 11, 1963, as Pacific Grace Mission Chapel in Vancouver. The congregation worshipped in English and German and set out to reach out to the Chinese community that lived nearby in Chinatown. By the late 1960s, most Sunday school children were Chinese, reflecting the changing composition of the neighborhood. By 1977, the Chinese congregation comprised 80 percent of the church. Thus, in April of 1977, the English congregation officially dissolved, leaving the Chinese congregation to take ownership of the church. The church was renamed Pacific Grace Chinese MB Church, and its focus was to serve the ethnic Chinese in Vancouver. As membership grew, fueled by immigrants from Hong Kong in the 1980s and 1990s, the church planted three congregations in the Vancouver area: Burnaby Pacific Grace Chinese Church, South Vancouver Pacific Grace Chinese Church, and North Shore Pacific Grace MB Church. These three churches have further planted the Port Moody Pacific Grace MB Church, Richmond Pacific Grace MB Church, and the Pacific Grace Mandarin Church that has locations in Burnaby and Maple Ridge. As you can tell, the story of Pacific Grace church unmistakably exemplifies the growth of Chinese Christianity, and the giving way of European expressions of the faith in Vancouver over the last few decades.

In a study completed in 2006, there were more than 110 Protestant Chinese churches in Metro Vancouver, operating in Mandarin, Cantonese, and sometimes English. In addition, there are dozens of Catholic congregations filled with ethnic Chinese. Our research suggests that this number has grown further in the last decade and a half. Moreover, this large network of Chinese Christians is served by more than twenty-five Chinese-language Christian newspapers, magazines, radio stations, and theological organizations in Metro Vancouver.[3]

The growth of Christianity among Chinese Canadians is also matched by Korean Canadians. In the past two decades, Koreans have grown to be the fourth largest ethnocultural group in Metro Vancouver, with roughly 200 Korean Christian congregations in the area.[4] In fact, unbeknownst to many, the largest Christian church in Metro Vancouver may actually be a Korean one. Grace Community Church, located in Surrey (it feels more like a campus

3. Todd, "Vancouver's Chinese."
4. Todd, "Metro's 70,000 Ethnic Koreans."

Ethnic Churches and Denominational Loyalty

than a church) has three thousand attendees. In the spirit of those who met Hansel Wang in the Winnipeg airport back in the 1970s, Grace Community Church sends a team to Vancouver International Airport each week to greet newcomers from Korea. Kyung Sook Kim, a deacon at Grace, said church members offer mobile phones to newly arriving Koreans (since they arrive with no quarters or loonies in their pockets), while inviting them to worship.[5]

In reviewing our field notes from this project, we began to see an interesting trend in church attendance among many that we interviewed. In Sylvia's story, she moved from Lutheran to the Mennonite Brethren, and is now Baptist. In Winnie's story, there is mention of six different denominations (Anglican, Independent, Baptist, Methodist, and Alliance) and we don't know of the denomination of those original missionaries in China who led Winnie's grandfather to faith. What we have discovered in our interviews is that when it came to choosing a church to attend, ethnicity is far more important that denominational allegiance.

In 1517, when Martin Luther famously nailed his Ninety-five Theses to the church door in Wittenberg, Germany, he inadvertently lit the match to what is now known as the Protestant Reformation. Luther was not attempting to break away from the Roman Catholic Church, but rather speak to the need for reform in the Catholic Church. Subsequently, the act gave birth to not only the first Protestant denomination, Lutheranism, but many that followed including Reformed, Anglican, and those of the Anabaptist tradition. Since then, Protestants have not slowed down in the ongoing proliferation of denominations. According to some counts, there are well over 45,000 denominations.[6]

Denominations are important. Each of this book's authors are very much involved in and part of the denominations that we belong to (Presbyterian, Methodist, and Christian Reformed). Denominations provide much needed accountability, shared convictions, and kingdom partnerships. Each denomination may have a certain accent or much-needed emphasis. For example, we are thankful for

5. Todd, "Metro's 70,000 Ethnic Koreans."
6. McNutt, "Division is Not Always a Scandal."

charismatic churches such as the Pentecostal denomination, for they continue to teach and remind us of the power and work of the Holy Spirit. But while denominations are important, what we are discovering is that it is less important for Asian Christians in the Lower Mainland.

When Nicolas Lai, today an urban planner for the city of Surrey, first arrived in Canada landing in Calgary as a teenager from Hong Kong, he had to make a choice. Calgary only had two Chinese churches at the time, a Chinese United Church and the Chinese Pentecostal Church located in Chinatown. Despite many non-Asian churches in the city of Calgary to choose from, Nicolas made his home at Chinese Pentecostal. Upon graduation, Nicolas' work led him to Port McNeil on the northern tip of Vancouver Island where he attended the local Baptist church that was introduced to him by his boss from whom he rented the basement suite. Port McNeil was, and still is, a very small town (you may need to Google it!). But upon moving to a new job in Vancouver, Nicolas went immediately back to attending a Chinese church (Vancouver Chinese Alliance Church). When it was time to look for another church, Nicolas did not venture to find another church in a familiar denomination, but instead choose a church based on ethnic solidarity and identity. In many of our interviews, we have discovered that for Asian Christians who are looking for a church the ethnic name on the church sign on the building is far more important that the denominational one, whether due to familiarity, ease, or kinship.

Historically, we understand that many denominations have been closely identified with an ethnic group. For instance, Scottish Presbyterian, English Methodist, and Dutch Christian Reformed to name a few. Yet over time, these European denominations have largely lost their historical or ethnic origins and been replaced by other ethnic titles such as Taiwanese Presbyterian, Korean Methodist, and Chinese Christian Reformed. While Sylvia, Winnie, and Nicolas are quite comfortable jumping from one denomination to another, we wonder if that is true for non-Asian Canadians as well.

In the Bible, faith is passed down from one generation to another. We see that in the covenantal promises from Abraham, to Isaac, to Jacob, and so on eventually down to us. As God says to Abraham in Genesis 17:7: "I will establish my covenant as an everlasting covenant between me and you and your descendants after you for the generations to come, to be your God and the God of your descendants after you" (NIV). In the same way, one's membership in a certain church or denomination is often passed down from one generation to another. You hear things like, "I'm an eighth generation Presbyterian," as one of our authors (Ross) personally can attest to. This is certainly true in religious-cultural groups like the Mennonites, in which religion and ethnicity are closely intertwined. There are statements like, "Once an Anglican, always an Anglican." But when your Anglican church closes, for instance, will you move to another denomination, or do you stop attending church altogether?

The Anglican Church of Canada, once a large and important denomination in our country, may be only one generation away from extinction. A recent report in 2019 shows the Anglican church running out of members in little more than two decades if the church continues its current rate of decline. "We've got simple projections from our data that suggest that there will be no members, attenders, or givers in the Anglican Church of Canada by approximately 2040."[7] This is certainly disconcerting, and we wonder what will happen to those who identify as Anglican. Will they find another church?

Unlike those with a generational identification with a certain denomination, the faith of many Asian Christians is not wrapped up in any identification with a particular denomination. Many Asian Canadians are only first-generation or second-generation Christian, thus they do not have the long history of belonging in a certain denomination. Their denominational allegiance is much more fluid. In fact, it is estimated that over half of the Chinese Protestant churches have no denominational affiliation of any kind.

In Cascadia, in an ever-increasing post-Christian society where established denominations continue their downward trend, it would seem that Asian ethnic churches are trending another way. Clearly, Asian churches are not held so strictly to denominational

---

7. Folkins, "Wake-Up Call."

affiliation or by historical memory but are instead *on mission*. The mission includes welcoming their fellow ethnic brother and sister to Canada and to their growing church community.

Chapter 3

Vocation

When Jason's wife Jaylynn was hospitalized for more than three weeks with abdominal pain, they had trouble getting the right diagnosis. Canadian health care may be the envy of many Americans for its public funding, but it is not renowned for being efficient. This group of doctors said it wasn't their call, that group said the same. Jason was frustrated trying to advocate for her, wondering if he should complain to the media, when someone at their church at the time mentioned that Dr. Stephen Chung was head of one of the departments in question. Their friends had prayed with him, Jason had met with Dr. Chung's wife about a possible mission opportunity, and their kids had been in youth group together. Jason reached out, and the surgeon-extraordinaire promised to pray for them. That wasn't all he did. The next time another physician came in the room, she looked at them quizzically, and asked, "How do you know Dr. Chung?!" Suddenly they weren't just patients to be managed in the system. They had personal connections to her peers through their church. And wouldn't you know Jason's spouse got the care she needed much more expediently after that!

Both of Dr. Chung's parents were themselves physicians, one born in Victoria, British Columbia, the other in Shanghai, and in a typical pattern, both sides of his family arrived to stay in Canada after previous starts and stops, returns to China and back to North America. Immigration, for the Chungs, "was not a straight line, but more curves and bends." His parents were quite serious Christians, and so of course he rejected their example. But a Christian cousin in Seattle nudged him toward faith: "teenagers don't like to be forced to do anything," he says. But she helped him realize "there was a personal relationship to be had here, and after that everything flowed."

Dr. Chung is renowned as one of the top surgeons in his field. While he is a general surgeon technically, he describes 90 percent of his work as being in liver and pancreatic cancer and in transplantation. He also teaches at the University of British Columbia and trains medical school students to become surgeons. And, once in a while, he will hear a fellow church member's difficulty managing a foreign medical system and go to bat for them. He assured Jaylynn that her surgeon was hardly his subordinate, but rather his peer, one of the best in her field. Jaylynn got the care she needed. And when Jason tried to thank him, he demurred. Dr. Chung said, "God gave me these gifts. It became my responsibility to be a steward of them. I'm heading toward the end of my career now and know they can be removed at any moment. I'm ready for that. If it were to happen, I'd have no regrets, because they're not mine to begin with. They're on loan—that's the way I look at it."

And they wouldn't have been spotted, curated, encouraged, and deployed on behalf of other British Columbians without a Christian household, extended family, church, and framework to understand them. His parents were Christians and doctors and immigrants, so his career path may have seemed predestined. Yet medicine and faith can be uneasy compatriots. "You'd think that'd be one of the fields where spirituality would be in play, but through no fault of the profession, it's the opposite. . . . That's a basic concept in medicine: to be self-reliant, collect data, collect X-rays and bloodwork, examine them and make your own decision." Every good doctor knows that their input has to be rigorously evidential. There is no *deus ex machina* coming to the surgical ward. Let the preachers pray beforehand, sure, but hand the scalpel to the one in the white coat, please. "Our basic training as we advance in our field is to trust no one but yourself, find out yourself, do not rely on anyone else. It's good advice!"

VOCATION

This is staunch *immigrant* faith, borne to Dr. Chung by his parents and their experience of escaping a repressive regime in China. He said, "The fact that they went through such hardships and got through it by the grace of God lets me say to my kids, 'I didn't get to where I am on my own. I didn't escape, my house didn't burn down, I didn't swim across shark-infested waters, I didn't get here by self-willed determination, but someone's looking after you, and not just a grand puppeteer, but someone you can have a personal relationship with." Stephen goes farther, marvelling at his life: "I'm almost waiting for the other shoe to drop! My life has been so easy because of my parents." Contrary to some achievers, Stephen remembers he didn't get to where he is alone. Neither should anyone else expect to. Stories of hardship pre-immigration can make for harsh and oppressive parenting—*work harder, you must validate my life!* Or they can make for grace-filled, glad-to-be-here dependence on someone else. Stephen Chung's is immigrant *faith*.

All those years of implicit training for self-reliance as a physician are "a little at odds with having God at the center," Stephen said. But as a Christian and a surgeon he's often asked about their intertwining, and he's glad to answer: "Yes, I feel God's hand, not every day I admit, but there are times when it's very clear he's helping me along the way, when I'm in a difficult position, not knowing what to do, and I can feel a little nudge saying, 'This might be a good way, what do you think?' And it works.... In some situations, I hear 'I wouldn't do that if I were you.'" Stephen knows how to speak to someone facing catastrophic loss. "God's faithfulness and what he's done can prepare me for talking to someone in tragedy. I can give hope where there is none, so folks don't give up on life."

Another renowned healer in the Lower Mainland is Dr. Winnie Su, a family physician with a speciality in obstetrics who practices at BC Women's and Children's Hospital and teaches residents. She also describes herself as "a firm believer," naming faith as "a big part of my practice." She also exercises her faith as a board member at Tenth Church, a multi-site megachurch here in Vancouver. She didn't plan to be a physician, but rather found herself pushed more toward the mission field. She heard a speaker at a missions conference insist that believers are called to bring everyone we know, in

27

whatever field we're in, to Christ. "I was blown away by the fact that we can make a difference, but we have to be deliberate—life doesn't just *happen* to me." Having experienced God's love, she felt called to share it as broadly as she could. Medicine is a "tack-on" to that foundational experience. Because Dr. Su comes to medicine with her missional orientation, she provides the kind of interpersonal care that all patients prefer. "It's humbling," she says. "My work tells me every day that people are hurt, that we need God. I pray for people when I can, I cry with them." And she heals and delivers them, as, she thinks, Christ has healed and delivered humanity.

A tender manner is a good thing in any doctor, whatever its source. But its origin in Winnie's own life and character is of particular relevance to this study.

Winnie has never quite been sure where she belongs. She is not just the child of immigrants—she is the child of immigrants *from two different cultures*. Her father was a staunch Taiwanese ("so don't call him 'Chinese'!") and her mother was ethnically Chinese but grew up in Indonesia. They brought Winnie up in a Mandarin-speaking church in Vancouver, "so I can change my accent to whatever country you want!" she said. She also experienced one-on-one attention from her church growing up. Winnie and her sisters didn't love Sunday school—she, in particular, was too shy to engage the others. But one woman named Ellen spoke to her parents and offered to meet with the girls by themselves—a sort of designer Sunday school with a killer teacher-student ratio. "That was the first time someone cared enough to sit down and explain the gospel," Winnie said. "I thought there was truth to this." It is not hard to see the parallel to the way Dr. Su explains the marvels and perils of the body and of health to patients now.

Winnie has not only navigated between various cultures and languages on the way to her professional success now, but she has also negotiated a variety of church cultures. The congregation in which she came to her own faith as an adult saw the gospel as demanding. At times she was at church daily, sometimes for hours. Her parents worried she was in a cult at times. The congregation ran a faith program that was more like what some would call a seminary. The program was rigorous, with courses in things like hermeneutics and church history. Syllabi were extensive and one had to graduate from one course to move to the other. Winnie didn't realize this was unusual. She did notice it was pietistic. Women's clothes were a big topic. Dating was mostly frowned upon. And, unlike most white churches, grades were part of the piety! One speaker insisted a <u>Christian student had to make As and Bs</u>. That struck Winnie as strange: "Where is that in the Bible?!" The strictness leaves wreckage, of course. Winnie's husband Kenny insists he would never go back to a Chinese church. Winnie sees the problems with the strictness but found ways around them even then: "We'd go clubbing with fake IDs after Friday night youth group!" And she sees the gifts she received as well. She is still a learner, taking notes during sermons and retreats. Not everyone is drawn to weighty content in faith, but Winnie notices that she is not alone among Asian-Canadian Christians in wanting more wisdom, knowledge, and rigor in her faith.

[margin note: Xian ttd to]

It was a pastor at the church who first sat her down and said "Winnie, you've been experiencing emotional abuse from your parents." Kenny didn't need as much education for his profession as Winnie did—he worked in IT and so didn't need the university training of a physician. Winnie's stern, proud father kicked her out of the home for wanting to marry him. The Christianese rationale was that the two were not "evenly yoked," though of course a man having more education than a woman is not a problem. This was the culmination of years in which the father drank and intimidated his family, often throwing and breaking things. Several weeks before the wedding he tried to forbid, the father phoned to say he'd be attending. Winnie explains that she is not the only woman she knows who had to have security at her wedding in case a family feud got ugly. What broke out, instead, was grace. Winnie's father was overwhelmed by how many friends she and Kenny had. He didn't realize the fortitude of friendships born in a church. He, like many Asian parents, had valued status, money, and security more "than the quality of a person or their heart or their spiritual life." It's enough to make one wonder whether a strict church can actually be a tonic for a volatile home front.

Winnie Su knows what it's like to feel isolated, endangered, threatened. She also knows what it's like to feel supported, seen, named, and encouraged. And for all the faults of the conservative church she has left behind, it clearly helped make her the physician she is. She wanted to answer her father's surprise at her wedding by asking, "Do you love God? Do you love Jesus? Do you know who he is?" Often enough, Christianity is just a box on a survey. But then, once in a while, it profoundly changes persons and communities. Westerners may stereotype immigrants and their descendants from the east, but Dr. Su is having none of it: "Someone who doesn't know might look at me and say, 'that Asian girl who plays the piano and listens to her parents got into medical school like they wanted.' I hate that stereotype." Ask a few questions and you'll see that Dr. Su does more than hate the stereotype: she annihilates it.

Asian-Canadian Christians don't just serve their Vancouverite neighbors as doctors. Larry Yen describes Asian kids like him as being encouraged to practice medicine, since as a new immigrant work that requires command of English can be difficult. But he didn't get into medical school, and so he started wondering what else he ought to do. Law school triggered his competitive juices, he got to practicing law, and "before you know it, I've been doing this twenty-plus years!"

Yen actually became a Christian in Taipei before his family immigrated to the United States from Taiwan. Then his family started attending church in their new home in Houston, which Yen welcomed since that meant he didn't have to work in the family restaurant on a Sunday morning! He got to know folks from all over the Asian world—from Taiwan, the Mainland, Hong Kong, Cantonese-speakers, Mandarin-speakers. This has served him well as a lawyer. He suggests that law has actually allowed him a broader public impact than medicine would have done: "it enables you to get involved in so many different areas and to get to know so many different kinds of people." Folks are always asking for legal help—including pastors and churches!—and Yen gets to help start-up-minded kids with no money all the way "up" to billionaires.

Another attorney, Daniel Shih, works as a crown prosecutor. He learned from a Christian mentor how to handle difficult cases: the "most difficult files, the most complex ones, often involving exploitation of children." The mentor credited his survival in that field for a quarter century to God's grace. Even then, he retired early, but he advised Daniel to keep his relationship with God in good working order. With all these broken relationships one is surrounded by in court, "you have to fix your eyes on God and on the good." Daniel has seen plenty of the opposite. What spurred him into the law in the first place was a sexual assault on a friend in high school. Walking her through that court process helped him to see "what good you can do—that's what drove me there." The demands are high, with political pressure and 80-hour work weeks assumed. Yet he feels he's making an impact: "not for the wealthy or powerful, but for people who wouldn't be able to advocate for themselves."

Shih does think his experience as an immigrant helps him connect with some navigating the justice system, especially as they deal in public with issues not often broached in their communities, such as intimate partner violence. He estimates that he is one or two Asians out of a hundred or so prosecutors with whom he's worked in Canada. "As an immigrant a lot of times you gravitate to maths and sciences, not languages or literature, and if you go into law, it's the more corporate side of things, being an in-house counsel. That is a better paying job. Prosecution pays fine, but you're still a civil servant, where you don't get bonuses in the two or three millions. Asian prosecutors are not over-represented."

Shih's own experience as an immigrant affects how he works, not just where. He sees a major flaw in Western justice systems: our treatment of those *already harmed*. Someone whose loved-one has been injured or even killed might not ever hear anything about the legal process of meting out justice until they get a form letter telling them the matter has been resolved. They might have to rely on the press to tell them how. Shih's language and cultural skills allow him to bridge this gap with fellow immigrants: "I can engage folks who've been harmed. To phone and ask, 'What would *you* like to see done?' They feel empowered that way. To be personal and find out what they need can make all the difference." There is nothing in his job that requires Shih to make this phone call. But as an immigrant himself, Shih knows what it's like to confront a faceless bureaucracy in another language that determines one's future. The phone call is a profoundly Christian, and human, gesture.

Christianity

Alphil Guilaran works to help those ambitious but penniless starter-uppers to become successful, and even wealthy. His parents immigrated from the Philippines when he was a child, and he grew up with significant health challenges. That story of immigration and of overcoming illness gave him resilience in the face of other sorts of challenges. "My father always used to say he came here with 90 dollars." His parents started "from nothing, so seeing that motivated me—I can start from nothing too." Guilaran tells the story of his conversion to Christ and of his entry into the investment world in equally providential terms. He sees God's hand in both, and even in his side-step out of investment advising and into a start-up aimed at building financial literacy. "I realized, sitting down with clients, we weren't educating young people about money—and these are millionaires! They think they have enough, but their children are going to lose it all." So, he hung out his own shingle building financial acumen for ordinary people. His clients include ministers and physicians and others of all sorts. And he roots his work in an observation from Regent College's faith and work program: a "company" comes from two words that mean "shared bread"—it is no accident that one's company takes on one's personality, one's DNA, one's own character, it reflects who the founder is as a person. "Businesses can lift societies out of poverty when money is not their only purpose," Guilaran insists.

Several of our interviewees noted that it would be inappropriate in their line of work to evangelize openly. They try, rather, to set an example by how they do their work that will be a blessing to others. Nicholas Lai, for example, spent a career in city planning, another field where "there are not a lot of Asians or Chinese—because it is not science." Yet he found his way into a successful career, concluding with the city of Surrey, and he is still working now as a consultant. Yet leading a staff did give him an opportunity to support and encourage others. After 9/11 he invited the staff at his Christmas party to watch a video of a spouse of one of the doomed pilots bearing witness to hope. "I don't openly talk about the gospel, however I learned to show my care for them," especially as younger professionals face the same challenges Lai once did starting out in the profession. When team members would face illness

Vocation

or hospitalization it would get Lai a chance to visit their bedside, to pray for and with them if that seemed non-threatening. "I was concerned about their life, not just their work," he said.

Several of our interviewees hold remarkably high-profile public positions in British Columbia. For example, we talked to the Honourable Nelly Shin, then the member of parliament for Port Moody and Coquitlam, and the first Korean Canadian MP in Canadian history. She reports some of the tensions that immigrant children feel—compelled to succeed at all costs. She had a successful pop music career (look up her work online!) and then worked as a teacher, without quite finding her niche. She came to what she calls "a Solomon moment," a fork in the road that changes everything after: "Everything seemed so meaningless, I went through a depression, and prayed 'God, I'm ready to throw it all away if you'll show me what I have to do.'" She sold her Toronto condo and spent several precarious years in the United States as a Christian missionary, no agency support behind her, subsisting on prayer and working in faith-based counseling for the marginalized. "I spent the next several years learning how to share God's love with very broken people, especially those who'd gone through trauma, so that they would feel seen like Hagar, and know they are not invisible to God." During her most recent campaign, the MP personally knocked on the door of one of us authors (Jason), canvasing for votes to return to office. My neighbors may think Christianity irrelevant to their lives, but the woman representing them in Ottawa is willing to knock on strangers' doors in the rain to work on their behalf—and she does so because of her faith.

One of the most recognized faces in Canada belongs to Ms. Mi-Jung Lee (who kindly wrote the afterword for this book), a Korean immigrant to Canada and a news anchor for CTV in Vancouver. Her recognition comes not only because of her face being on the nightly news, but because of Hollywood North—for years Lee was often asked to play a newscaster in Marvel movies and other films before professional regulations changed and kept working journalists from being able to play themselves. When she was growing up in East Vancouver there were no newscasters on the air who looked like her. Now it is inconceivable that a television program in

33

this region would *not* have women or people of color at the news anchor's desk. She changed that culture partly by being a doggedly determined reporter herself, "fighting for the underdog, exposing injustice and abuse.... As both a journalist and a Christian I'm supposed to question and challenge things that have been hidden, and push and push." Lee does more than "afflict the comfortable"—she also "comforts the afflicted." She is a cancer survivor and has spoken of this struggle in public often. "That was seven or eight years ago, and I still get contacted by folks who know I've gone through the same thing. I'm open about saying I'll pray, and I've never encountered anyone who has not wanted prayer when they're sick."

Ms. Lee's conversion experience is not coincidental to her work. She didn't come from a Christian background. Her family lived in then much-more-affordable East Vancouver. And their neighbors were an older German couple who had no children of their own. The Mekelburgs took it upon themselves to "adopt" children around the neighborhood, including Mi-Jung and her sister. They invited them over regularly for dinner. They gave them books to read. They sent them to a Christian camp on Anvil Island. And every Sunday they went around the neighborhood and picked kids up for church. Ms. Lee calls the Mekelburgs "the M's," and describes them as an "amazing, holy couple." And suddenly their church, Pilgrim Baptist, founded by and for German immigrants, had immigrants of all kinds from all sorts of different parts of the world. The Lee girls found faith, eventually their parents followed and did too. One can't help but imagine that the skills of identifying with people both different (Germans?!) and the same (fellow immigrants!) has helped propel a local media career.

Some of our most prominent interviewees make an impact precisely by being *unknown*. Dr. Joe Tham is a clinical psychiatrist, and so, he claims, part of the most secular medical field in this most secular corner of North America: "most psychiatrists are afraid to talk about religion, because it intertwines with the concept of delusion. But for myself it comes with great power to be able to recognize what's normal and accepted, and to talk about it, especially with a Christian patient." After all, Tham notes, what's the definition of a delusion? "Whether a culture accepts it or not!" This acceptance of faith within a secular profession has almost a mirror parallel in Tham's acceptance of science as a conservative Christian. His church is explicitly anti-Darwinian in its teaching. He has taught Sunday school, brought his kids to youth group, prayed with them before bed, supported his congregation, and he speaks in the personal language of "hurt" that his fellow Christians are still so fearful about basic science. "The church needs to square with that because we're losing people, and if you don't engage in where society is going—all the good, and also speak to the bad—if you can't speak to the good and true and embrace that without fear, you can have no voice in society because it will dismiss you." Tham speaks of his admiration of Steven J. Gould's language of Non-Overlapping Magisteria (NOMA) to speak of theology and science—and it is little wonder. He holds both non-overlapping fields together in his person and prayers.

That would be a set of issues that any committed Christian and scientific practitioner would have to think through. But this would not be possible without the simple kindness of a believer in Joe's story. Joe was ten years old when his family moved from Malaysia. As one of two ethnically Chinese people in his Alberta school at the time, he experienced racism and panic attacks. He also experienced living next door to a Baptist church that helped house the family. They were one of only two or three non-white families. One of the church ladies in particular, a schoolteacher, used to come home after work and help Joe learn English. First the lessons were of a *See Spot Run* variety, then they gained complexity as she encouraged him to sing with her at church, then to sing solos. As Joe mentions her name in our interview, he begins to weep. "I'm not sure what drove her to that, but it was massive. God brings people into your life that add so much, you can never repay it. Dr. Tham still goes and visits Ms. Hazel Kaiser's widower when he's back in Calgary. He also stays in touch with the one other Asian boy from his school. Little wonder he identifies with outsiders and understands their mental health challenges, and why he works so intensively to integrate them into their communities.

Christians know that our calling to follow Jesus and our calling to work are intertwined. We also know that *how* we work is affected by our Christian life. As Eugene Peterson never tired of saying, Jesus is not only the "truth" and the "life," he is also the *way*, citing a beloved verse (John 14:6). One interviewee, who wished to remain nameless, speaks of the "unhealthy" work environment she was in as she worked in a large bureaucracy. Her manager was more enemy than advocate; another coworker took after her for her Christian beliefs out of a perception that she'd be anti-LGBTQ. "So, I went and started praying for my enemies, especially my manager, though she made me feel anxious, depressed, and angry." And she learned to stand up for herself: "that's a good and godly thing, because God is an advocate, and doesn't say 'be a doormat.'" Note she didn't just ask for the courage to withstand difficulty—she asked that God would transform the workplace for herself and others. And God did! The manager realized she couldn't "get away with things." She stopped bullying her, eventually leaving off bullying anyone else too. The colleague who had been "trying to sabotage" her took to confiding in her—about personal issues, mental health challenges, "all these personal things. He was my enemy, and yet now he respects me enough to disclose all this information. I earned people's respect by being strong and unwilling to compromise." We asked where she got the fortitude to assert herself, especially over against stereotypes of Asian women being retiring and quiet, and she said this:

> It's because I met Jesus. I've become someone who could fight. I grew up as a woman too, and so was meant to submit, not even just in Chinese culture, but within Christian circles. But then that didn't work for me, I went through a healing journey, and met the God *who loves my soul*.

Such healing, born of belovedness, coincided with "standing up for God's values and trampling the bad ones. I didn't just go to work or do the job—I made friends, I had enemies and won them."

One interviewee might be the most broadly influential in Canadian culture and beyond without being a household name. Jason was preparing a sermon for Vancouver Chinese Presbyterian Church where he pastored and saw the email signature of the kindly volunteer who was helping him with a PowerPoint for the

COVID-19 era of worship. It indicated that his correspondent was a member of the Order of Canada, the equivalent of a knighthood if Canada were still part of the British Empire. Jason found himself, almost involuntarily, asking Dr. Victor Ling, "Who *are* you?" He was at the time the head of the Terry Fox Foundation, raising tens of millions of dollars per year for cancer research, and specializing in seeing cancer discoveries actually make their way into cancer-fighting remedies. Most knowledge dies in the lab or the scientific paper, never making it to the pharmacy or into patients' treatment regimens, and the Terry Fox Foundation, with one of Canada's most beloved names, works to close that gap. Jason had previously known Ling as one of the elders who was present every time church took place, whether in person or on Zoom. Now he knew him as one of the most influential cancer researchers and fundraisers in the country. Somehow, he had previously managed to engage with Jason without sticking his chest out (metaphorically speaking!), indicating what a big deal he was. Were Jason to have the same temptation to noticeability, he confesses that he would not try to hide the prominence, and if he did, he would fail.

Ling speaks compellingly of the need for objectivity in scientific research. Since the scientific revolution, we have known that "objectivity is paramount—otherwise it's snake oil you're selling." Research is funded if it is found, under peer review, to be repeatable, whoever is doing the reviewing, from whatever culture, religion, nationality, or culture. "Everyone has to pass through that test," or else knowledge is not furthered, and no one will be cured. And yet, Ling notes, you can't ask a researcher to leave their own cultural particularity before they do their work. Ling tells a story of a conference in Calgary in which indigenous researchers shared their research on cancer. Speakers were not only from Canada, but also from Australia, New Zealand, and elsewhere. And Ling noted that nearly every scientific session opened with prayer! There was no stigma attached here to asking the Creator for guidance, in this most secular of disciplines, at least when it's First Nations leaders at the microphone. Now, the proof of the validity of their *work* comes in objective research that is repeatable by others. But it is long past time when "objective" white European male researchers can tell

First Nations peoples not to pray before presenting. And at least one, and likely many more, Asian scientist was quick to say "Amen."

We recognize that this study is subjective, made up of interviews that claim no representative status. We have not done the hard research to indicate that our interviewees represent x percent of their field in Vancouver. We have simply been impressed how often highly influential servants of their neighbors here in Vancouver are Asian Canadian immigrants or their children serving in the broader world *because of their Christian faith*. One might skeptically ask whether *their* children will serve from the same motivation. Time will tell. For now, we maintain that if you want to marshal evidence (or anecdote!) for secularity in the Lower Mainland of British Columbia, you do best to ask white people, preferably the privileged. They will express surprise—or even outrage—to learn that the person teaching their children, managing their portfolio, representing them in Parliament, reading them the news, curing their heart disease, and eventually caring for them as they age—is likely an Asian-Canadian Christian doing their work with excellence because of their faith in Jesus.

But let the nations rage (Psalm 2). Scripture says they will. Meanwhile, go on serving them.

Chapter 4

A New Family

There was a time in his youth, when one of the authors (Albert) did what many who grew up in the church do in their youth: challenge one's Christian upbringing and faith. He wasn't sure if Christianity, especially the church, was really something he believed in and he did his best to behave like the prodigal son in Jesus' parable. Despite his "wild living [and it wasn't *that* wild!],"[1] he never missed attending church. Not even once! Albert remembers a time when he arrived at church with a terrible hangover, but he nonetheless dragged himself out of bed to show up. Why? To "*save face.*" To *save face*[2] is part and parcel of Chinese and other East Asian cultures. It refers to a cultural understanding of respect, honor, and social standing. Actions or words that are disrespectful may cause embarrassment and shame, and so cause somebody to "lose face." Albert's father was one of the founding members and the acting senior pastor of his Chinese ethnic church. Thus, Albert *had* to show up every Sunday in order not to bring shame to the family or to his father. It was an unspoken expectation.

This notion of saving face is tied to the key virtue of filial piety. Found in Confucian, Chinese Buddhist, and Taoist ethics, filial piety is a virtue of respect for one's parents, elders, and ancestors.

---

1. Luke 15:13 (NIV).
2. 面子 or mianzi.

> The concept underlying the principle of filial piety is simple. Parents gave life to children, gave them food and clothes, an education etc. For all the things that children received from parents, children have an eternal obligation towards them. They have a debt towards their parents, a debt that can never be fully repaid. The only thing that children can do in order to repay at least a small part of this debt, is to take care of their parents in their old age, to make them proud and happy, to obey and serve them.[3]

The concept of filial piety continues to exist today and to play a role in both church attendance and stories of conversion. For many of those we interviewed, church attendance didn't feel like a choice. Instead, they felt compelled to attend church due to family obligation. It was seldom expressed verbally, but it was an unspoken duty. Yet, in hindsight, it was an obligation that eventually led to a faith commitment.

For Albert, it was in his early twenties that things started to shift. He was taking a sociology of religion graduate course that required him to read all the original religious texts (the Koran, Bhagavad Gita, The Tibetan Book of the Dead, etc.). Naturally, this compelled him to think of his own belief system and to ask what he truly believed. It was during that time that Albert began to realize that the stories and sermons he had dutifully heard every week at church made sense, not only in his head, but also intuitively in his heart. Christianity was no longer the faith of his parents, but also his own.

Daniel Shih tells a familiar story. Now a crown prosecutor, he and his family immigrated to Canada from Taiwan when he was five years old. Both his parents were committed Christians, and he went to church for as long as he remembers. There was certainly a "duty to attend church in part due to growing up in a Christian household, but also the fact that my mom was a pastor!" For Daniel, Christianity became more personal in high school when he took part in a mission trip to Mexico to help at local orphanages. It was during that trip "where I was able to see God in the work he's doing, and that's when it became personal for me and my own faith, that's something I carry today."

3. Teon, "Filian Piety in Chinese Culture."

A New Family

Charlotte Woo, a tax and immigration lawyer with the federal government, was born and raised in an ethnic Asian church in Canada. Before Charlotte's father immigrated to Canada from Hong Kong at the age of fifteen, he was the first in his family to become a Christian. Since then, he has encouraged the rest of his family to follow suit, not only in immigrating to Canada, but also in finding faith. When he sponsored his parents to come to Canada, he brought them to church to help in their transition to a new country and a new faith. He has continued to do this with other family members who have immigrated to Canada over the years. It was under this same influence that Charlotte dutifully attended church with her parents. She began to take her faith more seriously in high school and in university, "when you can make your own choices and go through your own problems by yourself for the first time in your life." Thankfully, she had pastors who provided mentorship, encouragement, and community, who "prioritized and cared for us; that made a difference in our lives."

For Albert, Daniel, Charlotte, and others we interviewed, the need to *save face* and dutifully attend the church of their parents eventually led to the turning and seeking of the *saving face* of Jesus.

Secularization has resulted in decreasing levels of involvement and attendance in organized religion in Canada. This includes many who have grown up in a church context and are choosing not only to leave their home church, but also their Christian faith. The fastest growing religion in Canada are the "religious nones." Religious nones are those who, when filling out their census form, mark "none" under religious affiliation. Religious nones make up 23.6 percent of the Canadian population, and in British Columbia, they make up nearly half of the population. In British Columbia, the least religious province in Canada, religious nones have steadily increased from 13 percent of the population in 1971 to a whopping 41 percent in 2016.[4] A segment of religious nones are those who grew up in the church, but have chosen to leave their church behind. Disaffiliation from church often happens in transitional

---

4. Thiessen and Wilkins-Laflamme, *None of the Above*, 17.

41

phases in life. Research has found that late adolescence and young adulthood are crucial times for becoming a religious none.[5]

This is also true in Asian ethnic churches. In the United States, this is what has been dubbed the "silent exodus,"[6] church-raised young people who make an exit from their Asian immigrant churches. However, is there a difference in the drop-out rate between those in Asian churches compared to non-Asian churches? When asked, many who we interviewed left their ethnic church for several reasons, finding their ethnic church to not be inclusive enough to bring non-Asian friends, an overemphasis on cultural identity, or conflict they witnessed among church leaders. However, they have not always left their Christian faith altogether, choosing to attend other churches in Vancouver. This was certainly the case for Albert, Daniel, and Charlotte, who have all left the ethnic churches of their youth and now attend multiethnic churches in the city. Unfortunately, the statistics are inconclusive, but we do wonder whether cultural virtues such as filial piety and duty encourage Asian Christians to remain committed to their Christian roots longer than non-Asian believers . . . long enough for their Christian faith to eventually become their own.

It can be argued that one of the major differences between Western cultures and Eastern cultures is that the virtue of individualism tends to be more pronounced in Western societies while collectivism tends to be more pronounced in Eastern societies. Westerners tend to value individualism, personality traits, and autonomy while those from Eastern cultures tend to value family duty, group cohesion, and cooperation.

In our interview with her, Charlotte stated that this "communal aspect of Asian culture nicely integrates into Christian faith and work as well. Lots has to do with when you achieve something or want to do something, you also have to think of how it affects other people." She goes on to say,

> In Asian culture, that's how you help each other. Go to Costco, buy a big chunk of meat and you can split it!

---

5. Thiessen and Wilkins-Laflamme, *None of the Above*, 30.
6. Lee and Olsen, "Silent Exodus."

A New Family

> You can help do each other's yard work, and in terms of faith too! Being able to have big barbeques for your fellowship, or physical distance means you have room to host someone who's coming. I really like that from Asian culture and Christianity. It almost goes against Canadian lifestyle and its individualism, where your pot of money and mine don't mix. We can go more toward living like the book of Acts and help each other.

In a culture that values individualism, one could argue that the ability to walk away from faith and church is *easier*. Secularity has set in motion the movement away from institutionalized religion, such as church participation, toward more privatized and subjective expressions of spirituality. In the last few decades, the language that seems to be prevalent among Christians, especially evangelical Christians, is one of an "individual and personal relationship with Jesus." If one's faith is only between you and Jesus, devoid of obligation and a shared faith lived out in community, it comes as no surprise that a secular North America is currently experiencing such a decline in church attendance. Yet, for Albert, Daniel, Charlotte, and others who grew up in an Asian immigrant culture, the ability to walk away from faith and church, which is tantamount to walking away from family, is a lot more difficult.

Interestingly, what we have discovered among many that we interviewed is that their Asian parents are now starting to attend church with them. It's happening in reverse! Family bonds are so valued that parents are leaving their Asian ethnic churches to attend the church that their children have chosen to attend for themselves. For example, Albert's mother shows up to the Tapestry Richmond campus each week, even when Albert isn't preaching! She helps on the hospitality team in the kitchen with other older Asian mothers that have also started coming to the Tapestry because of their children.

For those who grew up in the church, maintaining one's faith is a way of honoring one's family and community. However, for those that did not grow up in the church, coming to faith has resulted in conflict and even separation from their families.

Christianity

Andrew Tan, who currently works at an investment firm, was born in Canada soon after his parents immigrated from Guangzhou, China. His family were Buddhist and they expected him to go to the Buddhist Temple. However, at the age of twelve, stressed from parental pressure and school, Andrew began to ask "questions about the meaning of all this work. 'Am I going to be doing this for the rest of my life?' It was stressful, and I started to question things about life, and turned to Google and asked what the meaning to life is?" For Andrew, this turn to Google and YouTube began a two-year journey. He explored Islam, Judaism, witchcraft, new age, but "none of that was fulfilling until I came to Christianity. It truly fulfilled me, because salvation is a gift no one can ever reach on their own. This is different from all the other religions, with rules and traditions you need to follow to reach salvation. Christianity is different, it's a free gift that God sends His son."

Andrew's family, however, did not approve of this change in allegiance. They threatened to "kick me out of the family and called me names." They think that he is brainwashed and a member of a cult. Andrew states, "Maybe it's because of their experiences with cult religions in China where family friends gave everything away to follow. Maybe they are relating that to Christianity." Nevertheless, tension around faith continues to exist in the family. For instance, his Dad occasionally venerates his ancestors and burns incense in the house, but Andrew has chosen to abstain from participating in these activities. Andrew is not alone, as many Chinese Christians have chosen to avoid and refrain from any kind of ancestor-worship. However, other Chinese Christians do respectfully go to the cemetery, some choosing not to bow or burn incense. There does seem to be a wide spectrum of behavior among Chinese Christians when it comes to their interaction with Chinese folk religion. While he remains in relationship with his family, including his two siblings, Andrew admits, "I can't talk about faith with them. It is challenging. I *have* talked to them about faith, but it's just that they don't want to hear about it anymore. I'm trying to discern when the next best time to talk about faith would be. Maybe where I can find opportunities to share."

A New Family

Lucinda Tecson, a church administrator, tells a similar story. Born in Malaysia to a Catholic family, Lucinda came from a "very religious family. My uncle was a priest, and my parents made sure we went to church every Sunday; it was not an option for us." Aside from formal Catholicism, education was also important to the family, and it was the hope that all four children would attend university. With a brother already in Hawaii, the younger three siblings, including a sixteen-year-old Lucinda, were sent to Vancouver with the hopes for citizenship and the opportunity to seek higher education.

It was during Lucinda's first year at Columbia College that a woman instructor who taught English as a second language began to invest in her. Perhaps sensing the questions that Lucinda had about life, faith, and meaning, this instructor began to go through the Bible with her once a week on Friday afternoons. They also began to attend church together. One day, while riding the bus, Lucinda asked her instructor, "How do I become a Christian?" Immediately, the instructor rang the bell on the bus, exited the bus, went into the McDonald's on West Broadway, and led Lucinda through the "believer's prayer." As Lucinda expressed, "right after that, I was honeymooning with the Holy Spirit."

Lucinda's family, especially her mother, did not take her conversion well. Her mother was "freakishly upset with me, threatened to kick me out of the house, and for the whole year, I had to secretly read my Bible in the bathroom, because it was a betrayal of faith." To this day, Lucinda and her mother, who is still a staunch Roman Catholic, agree to disagree with it comes to particularities of Christian faith.

When someone comes to a vibrant expression of Christian faith, there is always risk. There is risk of losing one's family, community, and relationships. This is especially true for those who identify as Asian. Due to the gravity of filial piety, coming to any kind of faith different from one's parents can often feel like a betrayal of one's family. It can cause one to "lose face."

For Andrew, Lucinda, and others, becoming a Christian comes at a cost. For those who grew up in Christendom, their identity as a Christian did not cause any tension with family or loss of relationship. However, the same cannot be said to be true for many Asians who came to a Christian faith independently from their family. It has cost them, and because of that, the cost of living as a Christian in a secular society like Canada is anything but negligible. Amid the pressures of secularization, these new converts will steadfastly hold onto their newfound faith and family in the Body of Christ.

Coming to Christian faith can indeed be seen as a change of loyalty from one's family of origin to a new family of faith. Throughout the New Testament, the church is likened to a family. Even Jesus seems to elevate faith instead of genes when it came to describe one's true family. "Who is my mother, and who are my brothers?" Pointing to his disciples, he said, "Here are my mother and my brothers. For whoever does the will of my Father in heaven is my brother and sister and mother" (Matthew 12:48–50). This new identity as God's adopted children (John 1:12; Romans 8:15; Ephesians 1:5) and members of the household of God (Ephesians 2:19; Galatians 6:10; 1 Tim 3:15) is how these new Asian converts now find their primary identity.

Jotaro Kawabata, a supervisor with Shaw Communications, was born in Canada soon after his parents immigrated from Japan. His grandfather was imprisoned as a prisoner of war in Russia. Jotaro grew up agnostic, but his best friend from high school invited him to church. It was at North Richmond Alliance Church, a Chinese ethnic church, where Jotaro began to feel a degree of love and hospitality that he had never felt outside of his family. He shares:

> That church is where I not only experienced God, but God's people. I always thought there was this barrier between ethnic groups, between Chinese and Japanese people, obviously because of World War II, which caused a lot of pain. These brothers and sisters (*note the language Jotaro used!*) brought me to their homes, provided me with a meal, they just let me be me and part of their lives. Deep down, I realized how much they loved God. This was the first time I felt love outside my family. That was an amazing relationship, and I wanted to be in that kind of relationship with God. Nine months later, I got baptized.

A New Family

His parents were shocked and concerned about Jotaro's newfound faith, as they were opposed to Western religion of any kind. Yet over time, they began to accept Jotaro's decision. Eventually, Jotaro began to attend the Japanese Gospel Church in Vancouver with the sole intent to bring his mom to church and to faith. However, the Japanese church was located in Vancouver, and thus made it difficult to attend due to distance from his home in Richmond, so he now attends the Tapestry Church campus in Richmond. His reason for this change was: "70 percent for my own growth, and 30 percent for my mom."

As a part of God's new family, Jotaro hopes that his earthly Japanese family would one day join. Evidence suggests they will.

Chapter 5

New Hands for the Harvest

Dr. Victor Ling, whom we met earlier in this study, is the long-time head of the Terry Fox Foundation, raising tens of millions of dollars for cancer research. Fox is a Canadian icon for his grit, trying to run across Canada on his one good leg and one 1980s-era prosthetic, to raise awareness and support for cancer research before losing his own life to the disease. Statues of Fox are more plentiful than those of Her Majesty Queen Elizabeth II in Vancouver. Ling was recruited to Vancouver from his perch as a cancer researcher at the University of Toronto by David Lam, the first Asian-Canadian lieutenant governor in British Columbia's history. Ling gave up his own promising and renowned cancer research to find the funding to help others.

Ling tells a story of his family's slow departure from its rural village in China. His father went first, going to Australia, then eventually Canada, before coming back for his family. They left Shanghai's port in dramatic fashion as Communist bombs fell on the city. Later in life Victor's father took up seminary and ordained ministry, following a common pattern by which Chinese folks first make enough money to live on before braving a pastor's salary. Then, in his later years, Victor took care of his father, like any good Asian son would do. For the first time they became friends, of a sort. Victor thought to ask his father why he chose Australia as his first point of landing outside China. His father's answer was illuminating.

New Hands for the Harvest

"Choose?" His father laughed. "You don't understand how Chinese village life works, do you? I didn't choose anything. The elders of the village *came* to me, and told me I was to go to Australia, make good, and send money back." It's a near-perfect illustration of the difference between Western individualism and non-Western communitarianism. Victor, growing up in Canada, assumed individualism and choice to be natural. His forebears knew better. Villages choose if anyone does. Individual preference adjusts.

One wonders what it will take for statues of Asian-Canadians to proliferate in the Lower Mainland the way Terry Fox has. What often proliferates instead is stories of Chinese as *takers*. It is not uncommon for Chinese people to travel to Canada to birth their babies, who will then have Canadian citizenship. That passport is a ticket to affordable and excellent higher education, a relatively clean environment, and an escape route out of China should things get too politically difficult there (without boats or bombs involved). When a new high-rise tower goes up in Greater Vancouver it is not uncommon for jokes to ensue about how these are not actually apartments—they are Asian stocks. The 2008 real estate crash never affected Canada's real estate, so worldwide capital decided it was a safe investment, and it has grown in value apace ever since. Jason once asked a beat writer on Canadian real estate what it would take for Vancouver's housing market to make a major adjustment, and after a moment of thought, he said "I think it would take the big earthquake."[1] Perhaps the moment's pause was only to consider whether even that apocalypse would do the trick! When the Coronavirus outbreak began to be blamed on China, especially by a certain American president, it was no surprise that Vancouver became a site for anti-Asian hate and random race-based assaults. A city that saw anti-Asian riots in the past and a Chinese head tax well into the twentieth century, as profiled in chapter 1, drew international media attention for racist slurs and fists.

At the congregation where Jason served, these public incidents of shaming and aggression became a common topic of conversation. Folks worshipping at Chinese Presbyterian today knew folks who

---

1. Schulz, "Really Big One."

actually paid that head tax—designed to allow Chinese laborers to enter Canada but to bar their families. Parishioners remember their families being barred from buying property in certain parts of town, and heavy pressure to conform socially so as to be "model" Chinese citizens, representing an entire hemisphere of the globe to white, European Canadians. Some of their grandparents told first-person accounts of race riots and remembered those as watershed moments that prompted them to change their hairstyle and dress to Western ones. Canadians, who are often proud of their tolerance in contrast to their southern neighbors, may forget that anti-Japanese legislation lasted longer in Canada and affected more people per capita than the same World War II–era policies in California. Vancouver's Japantown was erased, its fishing businesses seized, and the property never returned, with Japanese Canadians not being released from internment in British Columbia's interior until 1949. That is still living memory.

It is hard to serve a people who don't want you. Yet Asian-Canadians have done precisely that. Some of that motivation is biblical. Jeremiah 29 is, perhaps, the "ur-text" for serving among an alien people. Israel is in exile, some hoping for immediate return to God's promised land, and the prophet Jeremiah counsels instead to settle down, build dwellings, plant vineyards, give your children in marriage, and, most famously, "to seek the peace of the city to which I have sent you" (Jeremiah 29:7). Evangelicals have long drawn on that passage in their return to a love for urban ministry, spearheaded by Tim Keller's Redeemer Presbyterian in Manhattan, New York, and before that by Cascadian born Ray Bakke's love for the city of Chicago. Yet it is not about cities or urban settings in general. It is about a city of a conquering people who have dragged your people against their will to live far from God's temple and promised land and blessings. Israel had to rethink itself entirely in this new situation, and did so with aplomb—inventing the new role of the synagogue, writing the Babylonian Talmud, recognizing that while many people's defeat would mean the demise of their gods, the God of Israel, YHWH, is actually the only God there is—whether his promises seem presently fulfilled or not. Asian-Canadians in Vancouver have also settled down, built dwellings, given their children in marriage, and sought the peace of their city, and through it, the peace of the world beyond.

For example, Dr. Santa Ono was, until recently, the president of the University of British Columbia, one of the top thirty universities on the globe. He actually grew up on the University of British Columbia's Point Grey campus when his father was a professor of mathematics. The world first heard of President Ono when he led the University of Cincinnati and was an early adopter of social media, becoming a sort of celebrity CEO among students and admirers. Long before that, he held academic and administrative stints at Oxford and Emory Universities, studying previously at McGill University, and becaming a concert-quality cello player in addition to a research scientist (feeling jealous yet?). The University of British Columbia faced a tumultuous few years under previous leadership before Ono righted the ship, expanding the school's campuses, breaking fundraising records, and all the while remembering the names of students he has met only once before. He is a marvel.

And, he is also an outspoken Christian, having served on the board of InterVarsity Christian Fellowship (IVCF) for years. He speaks openly and publicly of how friends in IVCF saved his life. He was a depressed freshman at the University of Chicago, drinking too much and reacting badly to his newfound freedom, and was determined to throw himself out of his dorm window. Two friends from IVCF stayed up with him all night and showed themselves just as determined not to let him destroy himself. Ono sobered up, came to his senses, sought out the reason for these two's determination, met Jesus, and committed his life to him. His mental health troubles did not immediately cease—Ono has won a prize from UCLA for his advocacy for the mental health of students, knowing the issues personally and in their depths. Yet a great Christian public service career was also launched. When an articulate evangelical was chosen as leader of the highly secular British Columbia's flagship university, some of us wondered whether the school was indeed so secular it forgot to check on the candidate's irreligiosity! Kidding aside, UBC recognized that a Japanese Canadian academic and artistic and mental health rock star was the perfect person for this highly contentious job. One quiet hallmark of his leadership has been his unofficial sponsorship of a site of Tenth Church on UBC's campus, where he and his wife Wendy Yip frequently worshipped.[2]

The Onos have moved on since the research for this book; he has become president of the University of Michigan. He looks forward to reconnecting with InterVarsity. It would be a safe bet that he has a hand in a church plant on campus, as he did previously at Cincinnati and UBC. But his eyes positively light up when he speaks of helping bring faith back to university administration and to STEM fields like his own (immunology). "Universities have become too secular. Folks are missing something, like I was. So, I want a safe place to explore faith in a non-threatening way." He is planning to work with the Veritas forum to push its work beyond scholars in the humanities, where it has had great impact, especially at Ivy League and similar schools, pushing that impact to more public institutions that shape a different kind of public. He also wants to see more Jewish and Muslim communities on campus: "If you don't create that space, then ironically you'll be more likely to have a flash point for misunderstanding and lack of civil discourse."

Neither Ono nor Ling draw attention to themselves ("Look, I'm an Asian, and I'm a *big deal*"). To do so would be not very Canadian, not very Asian, and not very tasteful. Yet they bear articulate witness with their lives that Christ is indeed renewing creation, here through an Asian religion in Greater Vancouver called Christianity.

Laurence Ho is trained as a lawyer and works in philanthropy here in Vancouver. He is also a close relative of Victor Ling's, as it happens. Ho advises clients in how to think about their wealth holistically—what to give away and how. And he speaks warmly of beloved former Lieutenant Governor David Lam's mentorship in showing the entire Asian-Canadian community how "to be visible with their charity." Chinese Canadians have been here as long as or longer than European ones, they are no Johnny-come-lately, and yet they face challenges in showing this with their philanthropy. Often the countries from which they come are not places that encourage public giving. "Asian Christians haven't been dominant at home, so when they migrate, they continue to be non-dominant *and do great*

2. Todd, "Santa Ono."

things because they're non-dominant." The unnoticed margin is a powerful place from which to influence others. Asian Canadians often give profligately to their churches, which indeed bless and benefit the wider world, but which giving is necessarily unnoticed outside church walls. Vancouver's culture of philanthropy is not nearly as well developed generally as that in eastern Canada. Money has always been made here in extractive industries like timber and gold and fish and transport, so its beneficiaries need not live here or show themselves good neighbors. As a younger city, Vancouver came of age at a time when Canadians expected the welfare state to do all the good that needs doing and was willing (in most cases!) to pay for it with higher taxes. And despite many Asian names on public buildings in this city (Lee, Lam, and more), Chinese Canadian Christians could stand to let their light shine, not to hide it under a bushel (Matthew 5:14-15). Or so Ho argues.

Ho describes his work in terms borrowed from Keller, the Gandalf-like guru to urban church planters everywhere. For Keller, the church does well not to be in the mainstream, but just outside it, so we can speak into the culture from a position without dominance. If the church is perceived as more culturally dominant, like, perhaps, in Texas or parts of Alberta, "cultural Christianity seeps in and you can't tell who is a cultural Christian as opposed to a real Jesus follower." Ho and his physician spouse themselves tend not to be part of majority-Asian churches—as a lawyer-philanthropist and doctor they would immediately be on a pedestal in many Asian Christian settings, so they tend to worship in majority-white spaces. He works within those spaces to nudge Asian-attendance upward from single digits to a more Vancouver-reflective percentage. When he hears fellow Christians complain about their perceived loss of cultural prestige in more Christendom-nostalgic places, he suggests "maybe this is God's plan, to make you real and authentic." Europe is a good example of how Christendom concludes—one minute you're in kings' ears, and the next your churches are empty. Asian-Canadian Christians, Ho says, can be more "faithful?" He pauses to consider the generalization, then rewords, "Spiritually attuned?" Perhaps never having been anything other than marginalized, Asian-Canadian Christians are perfectly situated to influence

Canada more broadly. If the typical Canadian secularist's presumption is of a white Christianity oppressing Indigenous peoples and others, an Asian evangelist may find their approach draws much less defensiveness.

Ho's own experience is like many of our interviewees. He grew up entirely in Canada, Ontario in his case. His weekends saw him as part of a homogenous group among Asian Christians in Asian churches. Then weekdays at school saw him as a tiny minority in majority-white culture. He later taught in China and then relocated to more multiethnic Vancouver. He observes, "It's a unique blessing being bicultural," especially since Canadian culture often regards itself as simply a binary opponent of American. He suggests it is too parochial and limited and limiting to value "tolerance," as liberal Canadians tend to do. "Tolerance is not love," he said. "I can tolerate you, but I don't have to love or accept you." By contrast, he suggests with Tim Keller that Christians be "city soluble," loving the city with friendships far beyond one's own most natural connections, being salt and light in places unaccustomed to them. And remember this is no individualistic commitment for Ho—he means giving wealth away in publicly noticeable ways that encourage others to do the same, while making clear that it's being done for Jesus.

We heard of another adage of former Lieutenant Governor Lam from Andy Yan, head of the Urban Studies Program at Simon Fraser University in Vancouver. Yan is the media's go-to person on the housing crisis in Vancouver, and like Ho has been inspired by Lam in his position of public leadership. When Lam met with certain groups, his first question would be whether they went to church (there are urban legends of Santa Ono asking his faculty the same question). This is not commonly asked of strangers in British Columbia—it'd be akin to asking for medical history or an ATM password. Why did he do it? Because networks of trust are important in business and philanthropy. Before you do business with someone, you need to know whether you can trust them, and church is one of the avenues in which such difficult-to-quantify information is passed on. Yan hopes it will become so again in broader Vancouverite culture. Pointing to the crisis of loneliness, and also more global crises like climate change, he asks where the motivation to change for the sake of others comes from.[3] Rising housing prices benefit individual homeowners in a way. In another way they corrode civic life and make things harder for neighbors who will never own a home in this market. But how does one learn to be his "brother's keeper" or "sister's keeper" without a religious community? In Yan's own prophetic words:

> The big issue is systematic and financial and monetary policy, which is guided at one level by religion—ideas around Christianity, for better or worse.... Actually, going down the secularism path is problematic, because all these things we do as part of the church cannot be taken care of by the state. I don't think we're doing a great job these days in terms of lots of social ills. The roads and sewers are just fine.

As if the epidemic of loneliness in Vancouver can be cured by a trip to the Insurance Corporation of British Columbia (ICBC)—that's the Canadian equivalent of the Department of Motor Vehicles, for you myopic American readers. Yan points to figures showing that church-sponsored refugees in Canada do much better long-term than government sponsored ones. He is not surprised. Churches are relational; governments, transactional. Which would you guess works better?

Yan also knows his history and is not afraid to grab the nettle. He points to a long history of anti-Asian zoning laws ("it's as bad as you think") but then also points to the city council meeting in which those were rejected for the final time. The mayor at the time asked a question almost unthinkable in public discourse today: "If we can't coexist with the Chinese here in Vancouver, how can we coexist with them in heaven?" Religion has been guilty of plenty of horrors no doubt, Yan is quick to point out. Yet there is "also another side that brings out this universalism in terms of seeing everybody as a human being." Where do we get that once faith is gone and the only identifiers left are those of financial accumulation?

---

3. On loneliness as a public health crisis in Vancouver see The Vancouver Foundation, "Connect and Engage."

CHRISTIANITY

Yan knows this history personally, having grown up going to the Nanaimo Road Sunday School class in a small gospel hall that is actually Korean. "'Asian' is a description of half the globe, so false and lazy generalizations are rife. Yet we have to say something." Yan notes the rolls of Korean and Filipino and Vietnamese communities being "re-anchored" by these churches once they arrive from Asia. Those populations, like all others, move on for economic reasons, leaving those churches' missions confused and confusing (any minister or church *not* felt that?! It's capitalism, not just race . . .).[4] All the same, churches do good that would be irretrievably lost without them: "people who subscribe to a faith tend to be happier, less alone, living in a network of support." That's not just his sentiment. The statistics are widely available and fairly unequivocal. And the government can't organize that for you.

The great Scottish missiologist Andrew Walls used to tell a story about the four great downtown cathedral churches in his hometown of Glasgow.[5] As he aged, he realized that three of those buildings had become nightclubs (who knew that neo-gothic architecture could make for such cool nightclub space?!). The fourth, he said, was occupied by an African immigrant church that was bursting at the seams, and asking itself questions like, "Wow, how do we reach out to all these lonely old white people in our community?" Those with an eye for such things know that's how the Holy Spirit works. We look in this direction, and she sneaks up behind you and taps you on the shoulder. Christianity may not be gone from the Lower Mainland. It may just be an Asian faith for all people. Stranger things have happened.

---

4. See here Jonathan Tran's brilliant new book *Asian Americans and the Spirit of Racial Capitalism*.

5. See "Andrew Walls."

CHAPTER 6
"Jook-sing"

"Banana," is a slang term for an Asian person who is "white on the inside and yellow on the outside."[1] This was a common term that one of the authors (obviously Albert!) was often called growing up in Canada. Although he looks Chinese, the perception was that he had been fully acculturated into mainstream North American culture. Not surprisingly, many understand this term to be pejorative.

More recently, another slang term (also understood to be pejorative), that is used among Cantonese-speakers is the term "Jook-sing." Jook-sing is a Cantonese term for an overseas born Chinese person. The origin of the word relates to the bamboo rod. If you were to take a careful look at the stem of a bamboo plant, you would notice that the stem of the bamboo plant is hollow and compartmentalized. Thus, water poured in one end does not flow out of the other end. The metaphor then is that Jook-sings are not part of either culture; not truly Asian, nor truly Canadian. Even more disparagingly, because they are neither truly Asian or Canadian, some would say that Jook-sings are hollow and ungrounded.

What then if you were to add someone who also identifies as a Christian into the discussion? Is a "Jook-sing" Christian even further compartmentalized? Not truly Asian, not truly Canadian,

---

1. "Twinkie" is another slang often used similar to Banana, while "Coconut" is used to refer to those from South Asia or the Philippines.

57

nor truly Christian either? Or is the foundational claim of Galatians 3:28 actually *true*, and baptism gives us an identity that gathers up our lesser ones in Christ?

Jotaro Kawabata, when asked about his identity as a Japanese Canadian Christian, argues against this notion. Instead, he comes with another helpful description. Jotaro sees his identity more like a Venn diagram. He sees these three core identities not as competition, but instead simply as descriptors of who he is. As Jotaro states: "I'm Christian, I'm Canadian. I'm Japanese. It's all mixed up. It's not one over the other. It's not mutually exclusive." Much like how someone may have a hyphenated name, Jotaro and many other Asian Canadian Christians have come to fully accept their hyphenated identity.

This does not suggest that there is no tension. The typical Asian Canadian Christian must negotiate between not two, but three worlds, hoping to find a balance between family, church, and Canadian society. For Jotaro, it is the struggle between his Japanese heritage and Canadian culture that causes the most tension and stress. Interestingly, it is his identity in Christ that helps reconcile this tension. As Jotaro states,

> This is why Vancouver is so unique. I needed a grounded identity, which I found in Jesus. I was so lost in my identity as a Japanese Canadian. Even to this day, I struggle with it. The Japanese culture is to give to others, to work hard for others, but in the Canadian culture, that may not be highest priority. Even to this day, I still struggle with it, but time and time again, I realize that Jesus is the one who wants to center me to make sure I have balance between the other two.

Although Jotaro didn't use the words, he is pointing to something that is found throughout Scripture, a recurring emphasis for the people of God to place their ultimate allegiance and primary identity upon Christ.

Lesley Chung has taught math and French at Terry Fox Secondary High School in the Vancouver suburb of Port Coquitlam for the past twenty years. Born and raised in a Buddhist family, she had numerous good Christian friends in elementary school who persistently invited her to church. Lesley would say "No, I'm Buddhist, why would I?" These friends were so persistent that Lesley, while in grade six, even went with them to a Billy Graham crusade, but "nothing came of it except they kept pushing me to the front. No, I don't want to go up!" Nevertheless, her friends would not give up, and continued to be persistent. From time to time, Lesley would get picked up in the church van, filled to the brim with kids, to attend Vancouver Chinese Evangelical Free Church. One Saturday, Lesley remembers quite vividly, in her room as a thirteen-year-old with the sun streaming through the window, she decided to pick up the Gideon Bible that she received a few years earlier. While reading the Bible, and in particular the biography of Gideon founder John Nicolson, she was "overcome with deep emotion, really profound emotion, started crying, and for whatever reason, got on my knees and prayed, 'Lord if you would bless me, I promise I will read the Bible every day,' which I did."

As a teacher who has worked with immigrant students over the course of twenty years, she has seen how "immigrants have one foot in different places all the time." For instance, she has talked and walked with numerous Iranian and Iraqi Muslim female students, who have struggled with the wearing of the traditional veil or hijab. Hijab wearing is certainly a very visible outward expression of one's ethnic and religious identity, and one that causes not only an internal struggle of whether to wear one or not, but an external tension with society. In Quebec, Bill 21, which prohibits provincial employees from wearing religious symbols, has certainly been a topic of much debate in Canadian society in recent years.

As Lesley reflects on this in relation to her own life, growing up in a place in which parents and family expected her to be a certain way, the church another way, and Canadian society a third way, she admits that this "tri-influence has been difficult." However, she states,

> I care for my freedom, but it's hard when I'm being tugged in different places. Canadian culture has its beauty, but I'm glad things keep me grounded. Christian faith has been so instrumental to form me into who I am. I'm so thankful. . . . If anything, the church has instilled

in me the sense of awe and wonder at God, of fear in this almighty God, that also influences how we are, how we ought to live, that reflects awe and glory of God. It helps me not to go towards Canadian culture that pushes and pulls in so many directions.

It's interesting that Jotaro and Lesley both use the words grounded when it comes to the role of their Christian faith in forming their identity. It is out of "being rooted and established in love" (Ephesians 3:17), that these two Jook-Sings are finding their true identity.

Under secularity, the church no longer finds itself in a position of privilege, and thus Christians find it increasingly difficult to maintain a distinct identity. In response, some Christians advocate for a withdrawal from the world. Other Christians advocate for a different response, accidentally capitulating to the values and norms of the society in which they are located. Instead, we ask, what does faithful engagement with a secular society, specifically from a minority position, look like?

As authors, we wonder if Asian Canadian Christians have an advantage to this endeavor, as Asians in Canada have always found themselves in a minority position. Immigrants and newcomers to Canada are constantly needing to find ways to maintain their culture and ethnicity. Even Jook-sings are constantly needing to both affirm and challenge certain parts of their ethnic culture. What values should one keep and from which culture? Could it be that this daily negotiation of what it means to live as an ethnic minority provides Asian Christians the tools and skills to better sustain a distinctive Christian identity in a secular setting?

John Suan admits that he is not your "typical Asian." Born and raised in Sri Lanka, John's father fled China at the outbreak of Japanese occupation, and while en route to India, accidentally wound up in Colombo! It was there in Sri Lanka that he came to faith through a ministry that grew out of the work of Watchman Nee. John's mother also fled from China during the same time, ending up instead in Malaysia. Growing up in a Christian family, she was sent to Colombo as a missionary. It was in Colombo that John's parents met.

"Jook-sing"

Influenced by his parents, John came to faith at the age of ten. Driven by a desire to grow in his faith, and wanting to go to a Christian school, John grew up in the Brethren Church of South India, was educated in an Anglican school, and attended university overseas in the United States at Oral Roberts University. Upon graduation, John found himself in Singapore, where he worked in various areas of health care such as the Ministry of Health and became the CEO of Services of the Anglican dioceses in Singapore, which included a wide range of services from rehabilitation homes for the elderly to support for autistic children. It was through this experience that John came to the understanding that one's "belief system should not be in a silo but intertwined and integrated with a service arm as well." As John observed,

> Singapore is a very secular society. Politically they look upon faith as good to have, but preferably that they don't have to deal with it politically. So, [the government] encourages faith partners to be more social work oriented and less belief oriented. The distinction is very strong there. In Singapore, it's against the law to share faith with someone of a different religion without their permission. One can be arrested for that!

How does the church flourish as a minority presence to be an authentic witness in such a context? For John, and for his fellow Christians in Singapore, they had to "find ways of being able to integrate our faith and values so people will find an example." In terms of health services, for example, it is to do things in such a way that it is exemplary and adds value not only to patients, but to the entire health system. John continues, "There's a description we use there in order to ensure we don't forget what we have to do, it is 'we as faith-service providers need to be a *viable alternative* the state cannot do without.' Thus, service must be excellent, and folks so grateful that if they also hear of faith they don't complain!" John pauses and then continues, "That's allowed me to balance 'secular' issues and faith issues: instead of fighting the system we've learned to work with it."

In Scripture, Daniel and his friends lived not only in exile, but in a secular Babylon. With Nebuchadnezzar's strategy of deporting the elite of all their conquered nations to Babylon, people with strange customs, different languages, distinct cultures, and different religious beliefs were mixed together. The Babylonian adage was, "You can believe in whatever you want to believe—privately, as long as it doesn't get in the way of the public or secular rule of the Empire!" Daniel was thus under tremendous pressure to conform. That is, his religion was tolerated, as long as he did not allow it to intrude into public life.

Sound familiar?

Yet Daniel does not give us a template on how we are to act. On one hand, he refers to himself as Daniel, but on the other hand, he also takes on a new Babylonian name. On one hand, he willingly seeks a Babylonian education, but refuses to eat of the king's food. On one hand, he quietly talks to a chief official about not eating the king's food (perhaps the king might not have known), but in the next chapter, his friends will boldly stand and refuse to bow before the giant statue of Nebuchadnezzar. On one hand, he lives as a citizen in the city of Babylon, but on the other hand, he stays a citizen of the city of God first. Daniel thus imparts the liberating, and potentially frightening news, that there are multiple ways to respond as a minority presence in our culture.

As scholar Tremper Longman summarizes in his commentary: "What can the book of Daniel contribute to our own struggle and sense of identity in a modern secular world? Not only does it reflect a similar tension between God's people and the 'world' it gives us insight into how we should interact with the world—and it does this in a surprising way, in part by undermining many of our current attitudes and practices." Longman concludes, "As we will see, the book does not simply give us a pattern of behavior as much as opens our eyes to multiple strategies for cultural engagement."[2]

We need to admit to the stark realization that being a minority presence as the church in North America is the new norm and will be increasingly so. While the church in North America faces this

---

2. Longman, *Daniel*, 64.

new reality, we need to remember that the church has always been a minority presence in many places in the world (in places such as those we have listed out in our chapter: Japan, Sri Lanka, Malaysia, Singapore, and yes, even Babylon). The church in these countries has always been a minority presence, sometimes badly treated for it, and yet the church has learned not only to survive but thrive in such contexts.

Perhaps this is a unique opportunity for Vancouver. As more immigrant Christians come to Vancouver, they bring with them their experience as Christians living in a minority and unprivileged place in society. Many even come from places of persecution and suffering. The Western church has lots it can learn from them.

Moreover, as Jook-sings continue to grapple with the complexity of their ethnic identity and Canadian culture, perhaps they can help the Western church discover what it means to provide a faithful witness from a minority culture perspective. Christians of all backgrounds in Vancouver would do well to heed the advice and wisdom of the Jook-sing Christians in their midst as they seek to engage a secular culture with a vibrant Christian witness.

Chapter 7

The Church God Is Bringing

One of the great missionary pioneers in the Lower Mainland of British Columbia is a Chinese man named Augustus Chao (1912–2006). He did not originally study to be a minister, but rather trained and worked as a banker in China before the Cultural Revolution. He made his way first to Hong Kong, and then, upon hearing of Chinese people in Canada and guided by the Holy Spirit's prompting, he immigrated to Winnipeg. He planted some of the Christian and Missionary Alliance's first churches there on the Canadian Prairies, of which one of our authors (Ross) claims to be the true "Holy Land of Manitoba." Like St. Paul, Chao didn't stay in one congregation long, but quickly moved on after organizing a new church, eventually planting more churches in Newfoundland, Australia, and in Greater Vancouver. One pastor said that every Chinese church in this city was either founded by Augustus Chao, or in opposition to Augustus Chao! He was a force. And like St. Paul, he made devoted friends and passionate enemies.

The final congregation he planted in his long and momentous career was Fraserlands Church in 1991, still going strong on the southeast side of Vancouver all these years later. From the beginning, Pastor Chao's vision for Fraserlands was that it would be a church not just by and for Chinese people, but one that reaches the nations. In the "Our Story" section of their church website, Chao is quoted as saying: "Anyone can preach the gospel and any people can be reached." While it was planted by Vancouver Chinese Alliance, it never featured an ethnic or cultural or denominational name. And Fraserlands has worked hard to reach out to non-Chinese people. Flags of many nations ring the attractive sanctuary. Its music and hymnody and preaching are as broad and welcoming as any place in the city. And it does its work with excellence. The church is building a new ministry building and growth has continued even amid the COVID-19 pandemic.

Vitaly Kan, a sales manager at an education technology company, has come to call Fraserlands home. Vitaly is not ethnically Chinese. Born on the Russian island of Sakhalin, Vitaly is Russian-speaking, but ethnically Korean. The history of his family is quite interesting. His grandparents moved originally from Korea to Russia yet were forced by the Japanese in World War II to relocate to the island of Sakhalin. After the War, Sakhalin eventually became part of the Soviet Union, and his family decided to stay.

Over time, as the doors to the USSR began to slowly open, Presbyterian Korean missionaries came to the island and began to plant churches. It was at the age of fourteen when Vitaly first began to get involved in the Presbyterian Church, and it is there where "I enjoyed the messages by the pastors, and the community. I felt like I was getting the answers I was looking for regarding life, death, and heaven. Eventually, I learned about Jesus and God, and that's where my journey of faith began." Upon graduation, at the age of seventeen, with a lot of hope and ambition, Vitaly moved to Canada. So where does a Russian-speaking, ethnically Korean Presbyterian go to church in Vancouver? Why not Fraserlands?

A friend who was getting baptized at Fraserlands invited Vitaly to church one day, and "immediately, I felt a sense of community and closeness and intimacy. I felt drawn there." Vitaly recognizes that some of the attraction to Fraserlands was the shared Asian culture he had with other members, but more than that, the church seems like a microcosm of Canadian culture, a blend of different things.

Jabin In, a child protection social worker with the Ministry of Children and Family Development, also calls Fraserlands home. Jabin's father had visited North America several times in his youth, fell in love with Vancouver Island, and decided to immigrate to Canada with his family. His father wanted his children to fully integrate into Canadian culture and learn English, so he intentionally avoided other Korean immigrants who would often congregate together in Korean communities. Thus, Jabin and her family grew up in Chilliwack, a small town in the Fraser Valley, eventually moving to Victoria.

It was there in Victoria that Jabin came to faith, attending a tiny Baptist church just down the street. "I was the only Asian in that church in Victoria. They had sixty to seventy attendees on a good day, and most elderly. I was so immersed in Canadian white majority culture by then. I knew I looked different and all, sure, but never felt out of place by then." Yet upon moving from the island, and after ten years at Cobble Hill Baptist, she has felt very much at home at Fraserlands. And she thoughtfully states, "After moving to Vancouver, I was looking for a home church here. We went to the closest Baptist church right around the corner. It's also white majority, so I thought I would feel more at home, more connected because of where I grew up, but the way they worshipped was not what I was used to. I was so sad, so homesick, missing family and church." Pausing, Jabin continues, "We then started going to Fraserlands because my husband's extended family goes there. Even though the church is Asian majority, the style of worship is exactly what I was used to. It's still a bit of a culture shock being in an Asian majority congregation and a much bigger church! But it wasn't so significant, I felt so much more at home."

As both Vitaly and Jabin exemplify, Fraserlands has seen success among pan-Asian populations. However, it has struggled more to reach its white neighbors. There seems to be something in white people that, when they enter a non-white space, they intuitively recoil: "this isn't for me." No amount of flags or friendliness or familiar hymns seems able to change that. Yet.

Another great congregation in this city, Tenth Church, also speaks of reaching people "from all different backgrounds," as their worship leaders intone from the microphone. Tenth is also Christian and Missionary Alliance, and some of that denomination's first Chinese ministry took place under Tenth's umbrella. It is

The Church God Is Bringing

now a multi-site church, with its central hub led by the legendary Ken Shigematsu. Ken speaks often of his splicing (in his person) both Eastern and Western identities, and whatever he's doing, it works—Tenth is full on Sundays (including its multiple campuses), and the city's best seminary grads line up to work for him. Yet one can notice without too much difficulty that Tenth's sites where Ken preaches are noticeably more Asian than the sites where white preachers pastor in East Van, Westside, and in Tenth's evening service at the hub. There is something about Ken's own identity that signals welcome to Asians and about his Canadian-ness that offers welcome to others.

When asked about the growing attendance of Asians at Tenth, Ken reflects, "I feel that for many people of European ancestry, Christianity feels like a relic in the rear-view mirror, I've been there and done that. Asians represent the potential future face of the church in Vancouver. Many of them come from nominally Buddhist backgrounds, have achieved a measure of success in their education or professional lives, but still feel something essential is missing. This unmet longing can create a hunger for Christ."

Privately, over drinks, pastors at Tenth will admit they don't have to do very much to grow. All they have to do is to wait for children of Vancouver's ethnic churches to grow tired of their parents' immigrant congregations. The myopia, the confusion of ethnic and Christian identity, and above all, the high demands for nights and weekends to be spent at the church, burn people out, especially the more Canadian and the less Chinese (or Korean or Filipino) they feel. So, they come to Tenth. Ken is Asian enough for their conservative parents (who often come along to "keep the family together," whether they understand the English service at Tenth or not). And they often sit down at Tenth, exhale, and say "this is great! I don't have to do anything!" Tenth's pastors find themselves having to suggest "well, you don't have to burn out here, but you should do *something*," and encourage mission there too. Tenth is one of the most engaged churches in the city in social justice ministries.

It is this emphasis on mission and social justice that has led many that we interviewed, including Winnie Su, the family physician we met in the earlier chapter on vocation, to Tenth Church.

67

Christianity

Upon their arrival to Canada, Winnie's family began to attend a Mandarin-speaking Chinese church. According to Winnie, it was one of the only Chinese ethnic churches in the Lower Mainland at the time. It was in high school that Winnie, through invitations by her Chinese Christian friends, began to attend another Chinese ethnic church. It was at this church that her faith grew and where she was baptized. However, over time, Winnie and her family began to feel a need for a change, especially when it came to the church's social engagement. "Tenth was a breath of fresh air. Ken and the pastoral team were refreshing, messages that went outward and to a missional place, looking out for the world beyond itself. I'm not saying the other church didn't, they tried, but it was often met with opposition. With words such as 'No, we don't want homeless persons here!' or 'No, we don't want to give shelter to drug users, they'll steal from us!' Tenth tries to live out what God wants." Inspired by the outlook on missions, Winnie has gone from just being a member, to a leader at Tenth, serving in an array of ministries at the church.

One of the book's authors (Albert) often jokes that Tenth is one of the Tapestry's biggest "feeder" churches. "When Tenth families move away from Vancouver into the suburbs like Richmond or Coquitlam where our campuses are located, they often find a church home here at the Tap. Thanks Ken!" Whether it's worship style, or being a multi-site church, or even its senior leader also being Asian, many Tenth members, especially second-generation Asians, are finding the Tap home.

As already mentioned, Albert grew up in a Chinese ethnic church, yet like Augustus Chao, felt compelled for the Chinese church to be not only for the Chinese, but instead for everyone. Thus, when he planted the Tapestry in 2004, diversity was one of the church's very first values. Even through the name on the sign, the church sought to intentionally become a multiethnic congregation, weaving diverse people into the fabric of a Christ-centered community. Moreover, the church was intentional in the ethnic representation of its leadership, and the events and programs offered.

Albert, whose wife is non-Asian (a Mennonite if you are keeping score of the many denominations mentioned in this book)

The Church God Is Bringing

has noted that a good number of biracial couples have found their home at the Tap. In one relationship, the husband had grown up in a Chinese ethnic church and the wife, a German Lutheran church. As the husband said, "there are bi-racial couples like us here . . . this feels like home!" After getting married, neither of the couple felt comfortable attending the church of their partner. Now, in some ways, they get a bit of both!

This is certainly a growing trend in the Lower Mainland. In fact, Vancouver has more couples in mixed unions per capita than any other Canadian city. According to the 2011 census, nearly 10 percent of Vancouver's couples are made up of partners from different ethnic backgrounds.[1] Often there can be tension in interracial marriages, not to mention if the marriages also happen to be interfaith! There are lots of layers to culture and identity to navigate (see our Jook-sing chapter), but perhaps churches like Tenth and the Tapestry, and their posture of being multiethnic, have a place in the new expression of Christianity in the Lower Mainland.

It was only a few months into his journey of creating a multiethnic church in 2004 (it didn't take long!), that Albert began to realize that when one aims to be a diverse community, you cannot only aim for ethnic diversity. When one talks about diversity, one must talk about diversity across the board. Diversity is also about being intergenerational, as the Tapestry learned in managing the affordable seniors' housing complex next door. Diversity is about being accessible to people with physical disabilities, so the Tapestry renovated their building to remove barriers and make it accessible. It was important that individuals from Bethesda (an organization with three care homes in Richmond with individuals with severe disabilities) are eager to come each Sunday, because the church is a place that welcomes them.

When one talks about diversity, one must talk about diversity across the board. Of course, that includes people across different social economic strata. Albert admits that "this has been the hardest for us. What does it mean to be a church not only for the comfortably middle class of Vancouver, but also for those who are

1. Todd, "Vancouver Has Highest Ratio."

marginalized?" This is certainly a similar question that Tenth has asked for decades, seen in their ministries for people who struggle with homelessness and poverty, and their advocacy on behalf of women and children vulnerable to the sex trade in Vancouver.

This commitment to diversity and mission is also something that Fraserlands Church has exemplified in their recent response to the devastating 2021 forest fires in British Columbia and in particular, to the city of Lytton. Notably, not only did Fraserlands take monetary donations for the evacuees (like many other churches), but they also took physical donations (such as food, clothes, and other basic necessities such as toilet paper) and delivered the donations themselves through countless trips (including a twenty-foot U-Haul truck, loaded up SUVs, trucks, planes, and yes . . . even helicopters!). On one of their trips, volunteers from Fraserlands not only conducted a technology clinic to help people with their computers and smartphones, but they also brought along a hairdresser to do haircuts! During the Queen Victoria May long weekend, Fraserlands was invited to participate in the town of Lytton's May Day gathering named "Lytton Strong." Forty members of their church traveled up to run games, make crafts, and serve dim sum.

When asked to reflect on this, Joshua Koh, the English Ministry Pastor at Fraserlands, comments,

> As a pastor in a majority Cantonese immigrant church, I've always wondered if our kind of churches would ever turn our attention from overseas to our local Canadian context. We have been praying and preaching God's desire for us to be a loving presence in our neighborhood. In the summer of 2021 God presented us an opportunity. With the devastating fires that swept through Lytton, BC, there was a sudden need for relief supplies for mainly indigenous families displaced by the fire. One family in our church who has been quietly nurturing relationships with Indigenous neighbors for years received a personal email asking for help. I watched as our church leadership green-lighted overnight funds and efforts to gather supplies for these neighbors they didn't know. Word got out of our efforts and before we realized it our lobby filled with donations and calls came in from many other

immigrant churches offering funds and help.... All this hasn't been about us. The Spirit of God has blown us in the direction of Lytton, and I am excited to see that our leaders have not only been available but obedient to His call. God teach us to love our neighbors as we love ourselves.

Without a doubt, this was (and continues to be) a Kingdom-orientated response that goes much beyond their own ethnic group.

As a preacher in a Chinese church in Vancouver, Jason has noticed that Fraserlands, Tenth, and the Tapestry churches are the places to which his church's adult children gravitate. Their parents wish they were still with them, but they understand, and console themselves by saying their kids are at least in church somewhere. Tenth Church, under Ken's leadership, has seen itself as an evangelistic outreach in Vancouver for decades. Fraserlands would like to be that as well, though its success has been slightly less ethnically expansive. Yet these two places show us something of the future of Christianity here in this region, and perhaps far beyond. Augustus Chao used to say that white missionaries brought the gospel to China, and now China was returning the favor. Today, a former Christendom place like British Columbia is either bored with or hostile toward Christianity. Mainline (read: white) churches are disintegrating. Who will bear witness in this space? The daughters and sons of Chao's church plants, or their disaffected opponents? Now thoroughly Canadianized, appreciative of their ethnic heritage yet not limited to it, they will have to find ways to witness to their post- and non-Christian neighbors. Not only is Fraserlands going to be a Chinese church for non-Chinese people. Every church in Vancouver is going to have to be something like that.

Conclusion

Where Is God Moving Next?

Local municipal governments in the Greater Vancouver area are working together to get a better sense of what the future of this West Coast city might look like over the next three decades. The latest demographic prophecy suggests that Metro Vancouver's population will increase by around a million people to 3,600,000 by the year 2050.[1] The report notes that immigration will be the primary variable affecting future population growth and the corresponding impact upon housing, employment, and land use considerations in Vancouver.

Given the significant impact of Asian immigration on Vancouver over the last several decades, we are left to ask how these dynamics will further impact the changing face of Christianity as an Asian religion in this West Coast city. If Metro Vancouver is to grow by a million people over the next three decades, and with the expectation that a majority of those immigrants will come from Asia, what does that mean for Christian witness and practice in Canada's third-largest city? How will Vancouver churches welcome, evangelize, and integrate these newcomers who will be both new to the city and, in many cases, new to the Christian faith as well?

---

1. "Metro Vancouver Growth Projections."

Conclusion

Scholars such as Elaine Graham caution that organized religion in the West faces perhaps its deepest challenge from within, in the form of "declining membership and increasing detachment from public sympathy."[2] One of the authors (Ross) recalls visiting a local Reformed congregation in a south Vancouver neighborhood formerly filled with Scottish working-class immigrant families in the 1950s. In conversation with the few octogenarian members left in the congregation, stories were enthusiastically shared of when the church was full decades earlier. They took particular pride in sharing memories of when people used their cars parked on the nearby streets during Sunday school classes, due to a lack of ecclesiastical space and an abundance of young children. Today, the neighborhood is overwhelmingly made up of Asian immigrants. "Who knows," said one gentleman after the service, "maybe we'll get a new round of Scottish immigrants one day." Oh my. The response was heartbreaking on two accounts. First, even if immigrants arrived from Scotland today in Vancouver, they would be coming from a context with church attendance at record lows in the "land of Mother Kirk." Few would be interested in church here in Vancouver, arriving as affable agnostics representing new forms of Western (ir)religious expression that are "more heterodox and personalized, such as the growing number of those who identify as 'spiritual but not religious.'"[3] Second, this gentleman appeared to be blind to the mission field right before this fading congregation. The neighborhood around the church teemed with families and streets full of newcomers from Asia *who could be* engaged in evangelistic outreach—if only one had eyes to see what God was doing in their neighborhood.

In many ways that's the question that remains as we near the end of this project. "Where is God moving next and will we have eyes to see what God is up to in our midst?" If municipal governments are working together to ask what Vancouver will look like in 2050, surely the Christian churches should be pulling together to ask similar questions. Indeed, that work has begun, including a significant study of Chinese churches in Canada, including

2. Graham, *Apologetics without Apology*, 4.
3. Graham, *Apologetics without Apology*, 3.

Vancouver, entitled "Listening to Their Voices: An Exploration of Faith Journeys of Canadian-Born Chinese Christians." In the report Rev. Francis Tam asks, "What will happen in 2050? What will the Chinese Church in Canada look like by then? To be honest no one really knows ... but we must embrace genuine and innovative change for Christ."[4] The report does, however, make eight "directional action recommendations" that propose normative guidelines for Chinese churches in Canada looking towards 2050 and seeking to integrate both Canadian born and newcomers from Asia.[5] Scholars such as Li Yu have noted the changing nature of the Chinese Christian community in Vancouver from initial nineteenth-century immigrant churches to today's place of welcome for wealthy immigrants from Asia. Yu writes, "Chinese churches in British Columbia play an important role in strengthening their members' Chinese identity, but they strengthen it in such a way that all the Chinese traditions they are going to keep have to be re-evaluated or

---

4. Wong et al., "Listening to Their Voices."

5. These eight directional action recommendations include: *1. From "Jiaozi" (dumpling) to Jesus*—Strengthening the gospel-centric preaching and teachings that holistically engage faith, vocation, identity, community, culture, and values. *2. From belonging to being discipled*—Developing and implementing a set of radical yet biblical-based discipling principles and practices that accept risk-taking and shape a life-long devotion. *3. From textbook instruction to journeying*—Creating a set of mentoring practices that are not necessarily formal but organic, championing a space for reverse mentoring and mutual support. *4. From protecting to preparing*—Putting in place a concrete transition plan for high-schoolers to move into university, and for college students from university to career. *5. From "a museum of the saints" to "a hospital for the wounded"*—Fostering an environment that is safe and respectful, allowing doubt, questions, and failures to be expressed without condemnation. *6. From rigidity to fluidity*—Reimaging and redeploying rituals and symbols in a way that is both biblically centric and culturally adaptive (e.g., worship, ambiance, ministry orientation, and practices). *7. From hierarchy to lower power distance*—Rethinking and resetting leadership practices such that: (a) power distance is narrowed; (b) a structure and culture is espoused that is local-born friendly, with open communication, distributed decision-making responsibility and trust; (c) leadership apprentice is encouraged. *8. From being "stuck in the middle" to "reigniting the vision"*—Reigniting the CCIC's vision to (1) incorporate the input of the local born; and (2) to increase the share of ownership of the local-born through practices of inter-generational ministry for the sake of God's kingdom and a holistic world mission.

Conclusion

reinterpreted so that they will not be incompatible with Christian doctrine."[6]

Throughout this project we have noted that for too long a simplistic secularization thesis has been applied to Vancouver that pays attention primarily to the decline of white, Euro-tribal denominations that moved via colonization from Western Europe, through eastern Canada and across the Prairies in the development of Canada as a nation in the nineteenth century. It is more accurate, however, to describe the current reality as "post-secular" characterized by "contradictory and unprecedented currents of religious pluralism and diversification, coupled with institutional decline and strong resistance to expressions of religion in public."[7] Therefore, we have invited the reader throughout this conversation to reorientate their gaze in order to see the significant impact on the Christian church in Vancouver through an Asia lens, moving *east towards* the West Coast of Canada and beyond. Throughout the pages of this book, we have encountered the testimony and witness of ordinary (and in so many ways extraordinary) Asian Christians who have made Vancouver their home and by doing so have helped improve the lives of all in the city.

But what comes next is difficult to discern, and many in the church today are longing for certainty and clarity about the future where there appears to be little. Like King Saul seeking after the Witch of Endor, churches employ costly consultants to help them try to survive in a quickly changing cultural landscape. Many churches seek a word of counsel from the past, like elders on the lookout for more Christendom-era Scottish immigrants who will simply not appear despite sincere but misguided wishes. Instead, our encouragement is for all the churches of Vancouver to attend to what God is actually doing in our midst, with a particular focus on the life, ministry, and practice of Asian Christian believers. Wherever possible, churches in Vancouver should be building friendships and partnerships with Asian Christian churches, to learn how best to engage their new

---

6. Yu, "Christianity as a Chinese Belief," 242.
7. Graham, *Apologetics without Apology*, 28.

neighbors with the gospel, and thus help seek the welfare of the city together while attending carefully to the church God is bringing.

To be clear, we do not assert that somehow Asian Christian churches hold a secret formula for Christian witness in Vancouver. Far from it. Indeed, there are ongoing questions to be addressed in the next three decades regarding the role of 1.5 and 2.0 generation Asian Christian believers and whether they retain a Christian identity or, like others in immigrant communities, move toward a more secular orientation.[8] In addition, the question of the future of so-called "pan-Asian" churches, including those with multi-site expressions as profiled in this study like Tenth or Tapestry, is an important area of research. For example, this study includes the stories of many Asian Christians who grew up in an ethnic specific church (Chinese Baptist or Korean Presbyterian, etc.) and then in their adult lives sought out a pan-Asian congregation (such as Tenth or Tapestry) where there was a familiar sense of community, but without the distinctive cultural expectations and traditions of their family of origin. What will happen to these pan-Asian churches in the years to come in Vancouver? Will the children of these couples who moved from an ethnic-specific congregation to a pan-Asian one remain in that space, or will they, like their parents before them, feel the need to move again to a new form of Christian community to have a sense of belonging of their own? Or perhaps this is where we will see the 2.0 generation begin to fade into the broader, more secular expression of Vancouver culture?

Therefore, rather than seek normative outcomes at the end of this project, the research leads us to further curiosities and wonderings about the future church that God is bringing here on the West Coast of North America.

First, this project has further stoked our curiosity about how those inside the church and in the broader community tell the story

---

8. This includes an outstanding curiosity of the researchers regarding the impact of the ongoing LGBTQI inclusion within Christian communities, and how that will impact Vancouver churches with a majority Asian constituency. Our research did not produce enough data on this question to comment, but we suspect it will be an important cross-cultural challenge for Christian witness in these communities moving forward.

Conclusion

about Christianity in Vancouver. There is ample evidence in this study that the default story of Christianity's decline is faulty. As described earlier in this chapter, a simplistic secularization thesis fails to capture the thick description of the evolving and diverse nature of Christian witness in Vancouver. While observers of religion in Vancouver have been looking at the numeric decline of mainline Euro-tribal denominations in a place where Christendom was never fully established,[9] this project has attempted to turn our gaze toward a different narrative of the growth and impact of Asian Christian believers. Others will need to continue investigating and articulating this shift in the demographic of Christian faith in Vancouver over the years to come.

Second, as the face of Christianity changes in Vancouver, reflecting a greater impact of Asian believers, those both inside the church and in the broader community will need to revisit and re-evaluate what they assume to constitute "the church." This project has gone to considerable length to bring the story of Asian Christian laypeople to the forefront as a reminder that those who are teaching our children, curing our diseases, and managing our retirement investments are also gathering to worship Jesus as Lord on Sundays in communities of Christian faith. The extent to which Asian believers integrate their Christian faith in the workplace and wider community has the potential for a significant impact on Christian witness in Vancouver for decades to come. Justin Tse notes the importance of this impact by Asian Christian believers in the city, raising questions about the "ideological, theological . . . ecclesiastical . . . [and] multicultural integration . . . in Vancouver as it is situated as a gateway to the Pacific Rim and . . . Chinese Christians make of its metropolitan area . . . a home for themselves."[10]

Third, this changing face of Christianity in Vancouver will make it an Asian religion rather than a Western one. This does not appear to be a passing fade, nor a reversible action. The (formerly) mainline European-Canadian missionaries who established

---

9. While many scholars have advanced this claim, it is most clearly articulated by Lynn Marks, historian at The University of Victoria, in her book *Infidels and the Damn Churches: Religion and Irreligion in Settler British Columbia*.

10. Tse, "'Fraught' Chineseness," 188.

missions for working-class Asian immigrants in Vancouver in the nineteenth century could not have imagined either the fruit of their evangelistic labor, nor the reversal of their own powerful position in Canadian society. As you have read in the pages of this book, the future of Asian Christian witness in Vancouver is yoked to a humble past, where gain in society was measured with simple but clear steps. As Vancouver poet Jim Wong-Chu reflects in "Inspection of a house paid in full," a former restaurant employee proudly announces he has saved enough to buy his own home. Having arrived "young and penniless," the man has pursued "wild hopeful impossibilities." Wong-Chu describes the man "looking me squarely in the eye you tell me you have arrived" perhaps most importantly with "your family at your side."[11]

---

11. Wong-Chu, *Chinatown Ghosts*, 43.

Afterword

Mi-Jung Lee

My sister and I were nine and seven when we started attending Sunday school at Pilgrim Baptist Church in south Vancouver. We were the only Asian faces in a tight-knit German congregation full of families that had known each other for years. The cultural differences were stark, and I felt like an outlier. We were the only kids who didn't come with our parents. We came because of our neighbors, Elisabeth and Kurt Mekelburg, who brought us every Sunday.

Soon, other children from the neighborhood from diverse backgrounds (mostly Asian) started attending, thanks to the Mekelburgs. The monocultural church was becoming multicultural. The church felt more like Vancouver. All it took was one faithful couple who were filled with the love of God for their neighbors. They knew in their hearts what Christian researchers also confirm—most people who remain active Christians were introduced to Christ when they were young.

Social and family ties to a church aren't enough to keep adults engaged in a Christian life. My parents, when they first immigrated to Canada, attended the Korean United Church at Burrard and 16th Street. It was a way to connect with the then-much-smaller Korean community in Vancouver. Being part of a community wasn't enough to keep them as regular attendees. They drifted away from the Korean church. Years later, after their daughters had been attending Pilgrim, they also came to know the Lord and joined as members of Pilgrim Baptist.

When they saw the love of God in their dear friends, the Mekelburgs, they knew there was something real about Christianity. It resonated with them in a way it hadn't years before in a Korean church.

Now I attend Tenth Church and I see mostly Asian faces in the pews. I don't feel like an outlier anymore. But am I too comfortable surrounded by people who are like me—Asian heritage, similar socioeconomic class? As a journalist, I know that being too comfortable in my upper middle-class life can blind me to injustice, need, and stories on the fringes of society.

The same goes for the church.

Is there more I could be doing to make sure that our church reaches people living on the edge? Asian immigrants know about discrimination. It hasn't completely disappeared, but many are much more comfortable now, including ones who attend churches throughout Metro Vancouver. I hope the adaptability and resiliency Asians have relied on to navigate new lives will also apply to our churches. The tremendous growth of Asian-dominated churches is exciting, but I hope they don't forget what it's like to be the underdog.

Bibliography

Anderson, Kay J. *Vancouver's Chinatown: Racial Discourse in Canada, 1875–1980.* Montreal: McGill/Queen's University Press, 1991.
"Andrew Walls: An Exciting Period in Christian History." *Faith & Leadership*, June 5, 2011. https://faithandleadership.com/andrew-walls-exciting-period-christian-history.
Atkin, John. *The Changing City: Architecture and History in Central Vancouver.* Vancouver: Stellar, 2010.
Blennerhaassett, Patrick. "Asian Community Blamed for Vancouver's Affordability Crisis." *South China Morning Post*, September 18, 2018.
Byassee, Jason, and Ross Lockhart. *Better than Brunch: Missional Churches in Cascadia.* Eugene, OR: Cascade, 2020.
Chow, Alexander, and Eastern Law, ed. *Ecclesiastical Diversity in Chinese Christianity.* London: Palgrave Macmillan, 2021.
Clarke, Brian, and Stuart Macdonald. *Leaving Christianity: Changing Allegiances in Canada since 1945.* Montreal: McGill/Queen's University Press, 2017.
Coupland, Douglas. *City of Glass: Douglas Coupland's Vancouver.* Vancouver: Douglas & McIntyre, 2009.
DeVries, Larry, Don Baker, and Dan Overmyer, ed. *Asian Religions in British Columbia.* Vancouver: UBC Press, 2010.
Dives, Jackie. "'Astronaut' Families Stressed by Straddling 2 Worlds: China and Canada." *New York Times*, March 21, 2020. https://www.nytimes.com/2020/03/21/world/canada/vancouver-chinese-immigrants.html.
Donaldson, Jesse. *Land of Destiny: A History of Vancouver Real Estate.* Vancouver: Anvil, 2019.
Folkins, Tali. "'Wake-Up Call': CoGS Hears Statistics Report on Church Membership Decline." Anglican Journal, November 9, 2019. https://anglicanjournal.com/wake-up-call-cogs-hears-statistics-report-on-church-membership-decline/.
Geddes, Gary, ed. *Vancouver: Soul of a City.* Vancouver: Douglas & McIntyre, 1986.

Bibliography

Graham, Elaine. *Apologetics without Apology: Speaking of God in a World Troubled by Religion: Didsbury Lecture Series.* Eugene, OR: Cascade, 2017.

"Immigrant Demographics, Vancouver, BC." NewToBC, 2018. https://newtobc.ca/wp-content/uploads/2013/07/Vancouver-Immigrant-Demographic-Profile-2018.pdf.

Lee, Helen, and Ted Olsen. "Silent Exodus: Can the East Asian Church in America Reverse the Flight of its Next Generation?" *Christianity Today*, August 12, 1996. https://www.christianitytoday.com/ct/1996/august12/6t9050.html.

Ley, David. "Christian Faith and the Social Sciences in a Postmodern Age." In *Alive to God: Studies in Spirituality*, edited by Packer, J. I., and Loren Wilkinson, 273–85. Grand Rapids: Eerdmans, 1992.

———. *Millionaire Migrants: Trans-Pacific Life Lines.* Oxford: Wiley-Blackwell, 2010.

Lin, Julia, Allan Cho, Jim Wong-Chu, ed. *AlliterAsian: Twenty Years of Ricepaper Magazine.* Vancouver: Arsenal Pulp, 2015.

Longman, Tremper. *Daniel.* Grand Rapids: Zondervan Academic, 2011.

Marks, Lynn. *Infidels and the Damn Churches: Religion and Irreligion in Settler British Columbia.* Vancouver: UBC Press, 2017.

McElroy, Justin. "Majority of Metro Vancouver Residents Now Identify as Visible Minority, Census Data Shows." *CBC News*, October 26, 2022. https://www.cbc.ca/news/canada/british-columbia/2021-census-minority-demographics-metro-vancouver-bc-1.6630164.

McNutt, Jennifer Power. "Division Is Not Always a Scandal." *Christianity Today*, December 30, 2016. www.christianitytoday.com/ct/2017/january-february/division-is-not-always-scandal.html.

"Metro Vancouver Growth Projections—A Backgrounder." Metro Vancouver, December 2018. http://www.metrovancouver.org/services/regional-planning/PlanningPublications/OverviewofMetroVancouversMethodsinProjectingRegionalGrowth.pdf.

Noll, Mark. *What Happened to Christian Canada?* Vancouver: Regent College, 2007.

Northam, Jackie. "Vancouver Has Been Transformed by Chinese Immigrants." *NPR, All Things Considered*, June 5, 2019. https://www.npr.org/2019/06/05/726531803/vancouver-has-been-transformed-by-chinese-immigrants.

Paas, Stefan. *Church Planting in the Secular West: Learning from the European Experience.* Grand Rapids: Eerdmans, 2016.

Packer, J. I., and Loren Wilkinson, ed. *Alive to God: Studies in Spirituality.* Grand Rapids: Eerdmans, 1992.

Schulz, Kathryn. "The Really Big One: An Earthquake Will Destroy a Sizable Portion of the Coastal Northwest. The Question Is When." *The New Yorker*, July 13, 2015. https://www.newyorker.com/magazine/2015/07/20/the-really-big-one

Soerens, Tim. *Everywhere You Look: Discovering the Church Right Where You Are.* Downers Grove, IL: IVP, 2020.

Bibliography

Statistics Canada. "Visible Minority and Population Group Reference Guide." National Household Survey, 2011. https://www12.statcan.gc.ca/nhs-enm/2011/ref/guides/99-010-x/99-010-x2011009-eng.cfm.

Stewart, Ashleigh. "'Gone by 2040': Why Some Religions Are Declining in Canada Faster than Ever." *Global News*, January 17, 2022. https://globalnews.ca/news/8471086/religion-decline-canada/.

"Strengthening Our Relations: Canada 150+." City of Vancouver, People and Programs. https://vancouver.ca/people-programs/vancouver-commemorates-canada-150.aspx.

Taylor, Charles. *A Secular Age*. Cambridge: Belnap, 2007.

Teon, Aris. "Filian Piety in Chinese Culture." *The Greater China Journal*, March 14, 2016. https://china-journal.org/2016/03/14/filial-piety-in-chinese-culture/.

Thiessen, Joel, and Sarah Wilkins-Laflamme. *None of the Above: Nonreligious Identity in the US and Canada*. New York: New York University Press, 2020.

Todd, Douglas. "Metro's 70,000 Ethnic Koreans: Most Turn to Fervent, Conservative Christianity." *Vancouver Sun*, March 2, 2014. https://vancouversun.com/news/staff-blogs/metros-70000-ethnic-koreans-most-drawn-to-enthusiastic-conservative-christianitys.

———. "Santa Ono Helps 'Plant' Church Congregation at UBC." *Vancouver Sun*, October 29, 2019. https://vancouversun.com/news/staff-blogs/santa-ono-helps-plant-church-congregation-at-ubc.

———. "Vancouver Has Highest Ratio of Mixed Couples. But Victoria, Kelowna Real Surprises." *Vancouver Sun*, June 17, 2014. https://vancouversun.com/news/staff-blogs/metro-van-has-most-mixed-couples-in-canada.

———. "Vancouver Is the Most 'Asian' City Outside of Asia." *Vancouver Sun*, March 28, 2014.

———. "Vancouver's Chinese Flock to Christianity More than Buddhism." *Vancouver Sun*, February 5, 2011. https://vancouversun.com/news/staff-blogs/vancouvers-chinese-flock-to-christianity-more-than-buddhism.

Tran, Jonathan. *Asian Americans and the Spirit of Racial Capitalism*. New York: Oxford University Press, 2021.

Tse, Justin K. H. "'Fraught' Chineseness: 'Chinese Christians' in the *Vancouver Sun*." In *Ecclesiastical Diversity in Chinese Christianity*, edited by Alexander Chow and Eastern Law, 183–208. London: Palgrave Macmillan, 2021.

The Vancouver Foundation. "Connect and Engage: A Survey of Metro Vancouver." 2017. https://www.vancouverfoundation.ca/wp-content/uploads/2022/08/VF-Connect-Engage-report.pdf.pdf.

"West Vancouver Makes Racist Land Covenants History." *Canadian Broadcasting Company*, January 28, 2020. https://www.cbc.ca/news/canada/british-columbia/land-covenants-1.5442686.

Wong, Enoch, et al. "Listening to Their Voices: An Exploration of Faith Journeys of Canadian-Born Chinese Christians." CCCOWE, August 31, 2019. https://cccowe.ca/drive/ebook/LTTV-full-final2020.pdf.

Wong-Chu, Jim. *Chinatown Ghosts*. Vancouver: Pulp Press, 1986.

Bibliography

Yee, Paul. *Saltwater City: A History of the Chinese in Vancouver.* Vancouver: Douglas & McIntyre, 2006.

Yu, Li. "Christianity as a Chinese Belief." In *Asian Religions in British Columbia*, edited by Larry DeVries, Don Baker, and Dan Overmyer, 233–48. Vancouver: UBC Press, 2010.

TO JI[...]

ENJOY CREATING
YOUR
DESTINY

Wade Norman

7/28/25

Creating Destiny

Wade Nomura

Creating Destiny, Wade Nomura
Copyright © 2020. Wade Nomura Incorporated. All rights reserved.

All rights reserved. No part of this publication may be reproduced, distributed, or transmitted in any form or by any means, including photocopying, recording, or other electronic or mechanical methods, without the prior written permission of the publisher, except in the case of brief quotations embodied in critical reviews and certain other noncommercial uses permitted by copyright law.

Front cover design – Michael VanStry, Coastal View News.
Back cover image – Fran Collin.

Published in the United States of America

ISBN: 978-0-578-83686-7

Wade Nomura Incorporated
PO Box 95
Carpinteria California 93014
USA

Web Site: www.wadenomura.com/book/

email: creatingdestiny@wadenomura.com

Contents	Page
Foreword by Barry Rassin - Rotary International President 2018-2019	7

GROWING

1.	The Power of History	12
2.	Be Good	17
3.	Family	23
4.	The Fat Kid	29
5.	Open Your Eyes	32
6.	Sprouting	36
7.	Ancient Principles	44
8.	Roxanne	52
9.	Paradise	55

LIVING

10.	Natural Athletes	60
11.	Flying on Air	72
12.	An Unlikely Career	78
13.	Nomura Racing	86
14.	The Pro	90
15.	Behind the Lens	97
16.	Small Town Charm	104
17.	Into Darkness	114
18.	A Second Chance	118

GIVING

19.	My House is your House	132
20.	What's Rotary?	136
21.	Groundwork	141
22.	Water Works	145
23.	Playground of Dreams	148

24.	The Motivator	156
25.	Joy of Service	161
26.	India	165
27.	The Wadenator	171
28.	Camp KEEP	181
29.	Connecting the Dots	185
30.	Showtime	190
31.	Community	194
32.	Fighting Fires	202
33.	Tournament of Roses	212
34.	Clean and Safe	219
35.	Transformation	225
36.	The Accidental Speaker	231

AFTERWORD   239

Foreword

Wade Nomura provides an incredible example of not allowing adversity to rule life by overcoming it in a positive manner. We should all listen, learn and relate his experiences to our own lives. He has had to deal with the prejudice of being Japanese in a tough time of the century for the American Japanese. He has had to deal with being overweight and short at a young age. He has had to deal with having Polio, fortunately with no residual effects. He has had to deal with the loss of loved ones.

Being part of a family that has had to face extreme prejudice he could have reacted, as many have, in a negative way. But no, not Wade. Sure, he didn't like the prejudice and occasionally reacted, especially if aimed at others, but he never let it take away from the positive direction in which he wanted his life to go.

At every step of the way he has reached out to others, especially the youth, to provide guidance and mentoring. He has been driven by helping others to improve their lives, whether it was with his motorcycle, BMX prowess, golf, or with his Volunteerism.

You can see his incredible competitive nature in all that he has done in his life. Whatever he has taken on he had to be the best, in a good way. Never showing an ego but focused on the hard work it would take, the time he would have to put into practice and the sacrifices he would have to make. He has always stayed focused on excellence, whether it be judo or BMX racing or landscaping design.

He constantly maintains an exemplary character with respect for others, no matter who they are or what they do. In return all who know him respect him and want him to be a part of whatever they do. You can see his love for mentoring the youth. His desire to teach and to train comes from a clear love of people and an internal knowledge that he might be able to help others to accomplish their dreams. This was especially true as he worked with the disadvantaged youth to help them go in a direction in their lives that did not include drugs and gangs. He has saved many and given them a direction they didn't even know they had available to them.

He is a humble man who is never driven by personal gain but by bringing creativity, compassion and excellence to every role he takes on. To win at BMX racing he designed and built a new kind of bike. He realized he could train young golfers to be their best and he did. He created Nomura Racing and was recognized "as one of the most successful racers in the history of the sport". So, of course, he started training youngsters how to be the best riders with amazing success. Even when he went to a Rotary Leadership program for the first time, he helped redesign it and train based on the new program.

His journey in Rotary has been exceptional in his rise to various positions because in each one he has given it all he has with innovation and enthusiasm. He has moved up the ranks faster than most and maintained his humility as he honestly expresses surprise that he would get elected to some positions because he is Japanese. He learned that in Rotary diversity is welcomed and embraced. His personal approach to all the Presidents of the Rotary Clubs when he was District Governor brought him success. From District Governor he continues taking on assignments and, as usual, excels in each one causing frequent requests to take on greater leadership roles, such as with the Cadre for which he is now a Coordinator for one of the seven regions around the world. He is a worthy recipient of The Rotary Foundation's Distinguished Service Award, the highest recognition given to a small number of Rotarians globally for their outstanding service. He is clearly the role model that Rotary needs and wants.

Of course, the same happened with his rise within his beloved city of Carpinteria. It wasn't his goal to be in charge but a drive to help his community. He did an outstanding job as a member of the Architectural Review Board and so after many years was asked to move onto the City Council and then to be Mayor. Not something he longed to do but something he realized he could bring a new perspective to and make a difference to his community. Clearly, he has done that in many ways, from the COVID-19 pandemic to addressing racial equity.

He weaves throughout his story his love of family. His deep respect for his grandparents and his parents, from whom he has learned so many life lessons. And then his wonderful obsession with Roxanne and his love for his children, Ryan and Lisa. You can feel his broken heart and his deep sense of loss when his precious Roxanne passed away. For him it was another tragedy, perhaps he has had to face more than his fair share. And then along came Debbie and gave him back his engaging smile and renewed his love of life.

Wade Nomura has endured many hardships and tragedies during his life and yet he always emerged with a positive response and a desire to help others with whatever knowledge he has gained. He is leaving his legacy by helping others better themselves and by making our communities and world a better place. All of us who have known him have benefitted from his friendship.

Barry Rassin
Rotary International President 2018 – 2019

Growing

1. THE POWER OF HISTORY

At 7:48 a.m. on December 7, 1941, Japanese military forces launched a surprise attack on Pearl Harbor causing mass casualties and driving the United States into World War II. Though I was not yet born, this dark moment in history was to impact the rest of my life.

Three months later, Franklin D. Roosevelt signed Presidential Executive Order 9066. This led to over 100,000 men, women and children of Japanese ancestry being forcibly incarcerated in concentration camps across the country and another 20,000 being displaced.

My family were among those people who had their lives upended. They were only able to take what they could physically carry during the evacuation, leaving behind their homes, friends, pets and every other part of the life they had known. Their possessions, they were told, would be moved to warehouses and given back to them when they returned. Of course, this never happened, except for a few cases where family friends took it upon themselves to hold belongings personally.

My mother remembers being taken to the train station, where she was put on a cattle car, since there were not enough passenger cars for everyone. When she arrived at the camp in Poston, Arizona, she found the accommodations were not much better than facilities for livestock.

The wooden barracks she was assigned to were just four walls, with cracks you could see through, a raised floor, and a roof. These single, small rooms would sometimes house as many as two or three whole families. She recalls stuffing gunny sacks with hay to be used as her mattress, and the blankets she was supposed to use as bedding she hung up as makeshift walls for some privacy.

My grandmother was given a job outside the camp as a maid and my mother assigned to be a Taster, meaning she had to sample food if there was concern it had spoiled. She hated doing this and would always cry. In the end, no matter what she tried she would get sick.

My father talked about the constant hunger. He and his friends would sneak out at night and break into the commissary to steal food. They thought they were being clever, until one day the chef came up to them, telling them take only what they needed since others were going hungry, too. After that, they stopped.

For my grandfather, sheer boredom was a struggle. He was used to working, not sitting idle in a baking desert. He took up woodcarving – a hobby he kept up for the rest of his life. I remember seeing him many years later sitting outside, carving little figurines with his pocketknife he gave to me and his other grandchildren to play with.

He left me two carved horse bookends made from burlwood he created in the camp I proudly have on display in my living room. I still don't know how he was able to acquire a knife in camp, since they weren't permitted for internees. My father later took up carving too, and I also have his pride and joy, an eagle he crafted from a piece of redwood. They are reminders to me of injustice, but also the indomitable spirit.

Though the pain and struggles created by internment were never forgotten by those who had experienced it, many were unaware it had even taken place. When I was an 11-year-old student sitting in 7th grade American History, my teacher asked if any of us knew someone interned in a concentration camp during World War II. I raised my hand.

When she asked where, I replied, "Poston, Arizona."

She gave me detention for lying, saying no such thing had ever happened – if it had, it would be in the history books, surely?

She was right about one thing. The internment of Japanese Americans was mentioned in hardly any histories of the time, and certainly not the ones read by students or the general populace.

When I was sitting in detention, the School Principal came in and said there had been a mistake and sent me home, without further explanation. Word of my 'misbehavior' had clearly been in discussion in the staff room, where someone must have known what I had spoken of was true.

Even I had my doubts after my experience at school. When home, I asked my father if the internments really happened, why wasn't it covered in my class? Why did no one seem to know anything about it? His answer was, "It wasn't important enough to be included."

In the following decades, as further details came to light, the internment has almost universally been condemned as the result of racial prejudice and war hysteria. It turned out the two government reports commissioned at the time on the potential threat Japanese Americans might pose to national security both determined they were harmless, and in fact argued against incarceration.

Japanese were not the only group to be relocated to internment camps, with approximately 11,000 people of German ancestry and 3,000 people of Italian ancestry targeted. However, this number was a fraction of the people of Japanese heritage taken, for the simple reason Europeans 'blended in' better. There were other inexplicable decisions. For example, Japanese internees almost entirely came from West Coast states. The Japanese Americans who formed nearly half of the Hawaiian population were largely left alone.

No Japanese national or Japanese American living in the United States was ever found guilty of any sabotage or espionage throughout the war. In 1988, President Reagan signed bill HR 442 granting restitution of $20,000 to every living survivor after much work by the redress group chaired by my brother-in-law John Tateishi.

My father had died only a week prior to the signing, meaning my mother was the only one of my family eligible to receive compensation. When I told her the bill had passed, I was surprised to find she was far from pleased. She didn't want the money and feared the announcement would draw negative attention back to the Japanese community.

Eventually, she agreed to accept, on the principle she would otherwise be excusing the internment. However, she split the money between myself and my siblings rather than keep what she saw as tainted money for herself. Some wounds no amount of money can wash away.

There is now a permanent display on the internment camps at the Japanese American Museum in downtown Los Angeles, including an actual barrack. The museum buses in thousands of the local students from the public schools annually to help educate them on this dark part of American history. A few of the sites of the camps themselves have also been turned into educational displays, such as the Manzanar National Historic site in Independence, California.

I have personally been invited to speak on the internment on a number of occasions, including three Rotary International Presidential Peace Conferences. I discuss the topic not in the spirit of resentment and condemnation, but to educate how fear and ignorance can bring out the worst of humanity, and in the hope, history will not repeat itself.

2. BE GOOD

My family ended up in Santa Barbara after the war, following friends they made at the camp. Japanese Americans needed to stick together to begin their new lives, since most of them returned to society without any belongings. They were stripped when they were interned.

My grandfather was fortunate to be recruited by a kind man named Avery Brundage. Brundage had served as President of the Olympics and lacked the prejudices of many people of the time. He had an estate in Montecito right next to the famous Lotusland and employed my grandfather as a gardener. Though he had never actually worked maintaining gardens before, being the innovative and determined man he was, he was quick to adapt.

My parents moved there also, living in the gardener's cottage that was provided on the grounds. When I was born, Mr. Brundage gave me a Japanese model of a Samurai helmet I prize to this day, and a lifetime honorary membership to the Boys Club of America.

I remember walking with my grandfather as a very young boy, in awe of how well kept the Brundage estate was. The hedges were all tightly trimmed and perfectly symmetrical. There were no weeds or leaves on the walkways, the plants were green and lush. Even the soil was meticulously groomed. We walked to the mansion entrance and around the pond and fountain, to do a walkthrough inspection before Brundage came home.

My grandfather was a quiet man, who would only say things that were important. During our time together, he shared stories of his experiences, and lessons he had learned. For example, the best way to get respect was by giving it first. Instead of disciplining me, he would explain to me what would have been a better action and why.

Young Wade Nomura sitting on his uncle's car.

He introduced me to the joys of art, showing me woodcarvings and charcoal sketches, he did in his spare time. He considered it a form of enjoyment, but also a way to build discipline and patience, because you couldn't do it well, if you did it fast. Additionally, there was always room for improvement. Even the best could be better. He instilled in me to take pride in my work and seek continuous self-improvement.

I remember going to my grandfather's house and sitting in his car, a 1936 Chevrolet coupe, and wondering what it would be like to drive it someday. One day when my grandfather was out working, my brother, sister and I got inside, to pretend we were going on a trip. I remembered seeing my grandfather push a button when he started the car, so I pushed it too. The car suddenly surged forward, before jerking to a halt. I was terrified for a moment, but I had to try it again, with the same result.

Getting bolder, the next time I held the button down to see how far the car would go. I drove it out of the carport into the backyard to the end of the garden. Of course, I had no idea how to get it back into the place.

When my grandfather came home, I was afraid he was going to yell at me. Instead, he sat me down and said I must never do such a thing again. Tears pooled in my eyes, and I asked for forgiveness for letting him down.

He nodded, then much to my surprise, he said, "I will teach you how to drive properly." Then he took me out to the car, putting me on his lap and we drove down the driveway and back. I learned more than about driving that day – how taking responsibility led to being trusted with new opportunities.

He also imparted to me the importance of my role in the family. As the first son of the first son, according to Japanese tradition, I would someday lead the Nomura family when he was gone. He educated me on our history, and the many different personalities within our family. He explained how these different types of people interact, and how to help them to work together in harmony. His great wisdom has become ever clearer to me over the years.

Stories of his early life have filtered down to me, showing his tremendous grit in the face of adversity. His mother, my great-grandmother, passed away when he was only a boy. When his father remarried, it was to a woman with young children of her own. She looked upon my grandfather, the only child of the first marriage still at home, with scorn.

One winter, a plague spread through Japan. The entire household fell ill with fevers. With her own children to worry about, his stepmother decided to throw my sick grandfather out of the house. It was freezing cold, and snowing. He had no choice but to shiver through the night on his own.

When morning broke, he somehow managed to survive. His fever had broken, so his stepmother decided to let him back into the house, to help her take care of the others.

To escape this life, my grandfather dreamed of going America. He had an older half-brother, who went by the name of Charlie, who had established a fruit orchard in California.

The problem was, he didn't have any money to pay for the trip over. He decided to try to get work on a ship he knew was going to the United States. The captain asked if he knew how to navigate, to which my grandfather replied yes, sure he did, he had learned from years of experience working on fishing boats. This was of course complete fiction – I'm not sure he had even been on a boat in his life.

The captain gave him the job. When the ship was out in open water, he asked my grandfather to take over and point them towards America. My grandfather had no choice but the confess he had made everything up.

The captain told him he suspected he was telling tall tales all along, and he was lucky he wasn't going over the side. His punishment was to work for free for the span of the trip.

When they landed, he joined his brother in Arcadia and worked on his farm. Later, he settled in the Imperial Valley of California, near El Centro, where he established a melon farm. I heard a story about him bringing in a Clydesdale horse to the Valley to pull his plow, knowing the power and size of the breed. He paid top dollar, believing it would pay for itself in output. The first time he used the horse, it was able to double what the other horses could do, and he became the envy of his peers. He was always looking for new and better ways to achieve his ends.

My grandmother came to America through an arranged marriage. I have been told she came from Samurai lineage, the only member of our family that came from the upper class. Why exactly a lady of her bloodline would leave her homeland to marry someone from a lesser class in a strange land remains a mystery. They had three children, two daughters and one son: my father.

My grandmother was a very good-looking woman, with elegant mannerisms. She was soft-spoken, yet able to be very direct when she had a point to make. She always dressed impeccably, never having a hair out of place, even around the house and garden. She often told me how much my grandfather appreciated me, and how he counted on me to care for the family.

She hardly ever showed emotion, which made me think she did come from a Samurai background as it was said. She was full of mystery. I remember one afternoon at her house my siblings and I were watching the Ed Sullivan Show, and a juggler came out to perform. We watched in awe, exclaiming how cool it was.

When we went into the kitchen for a snack, my grandmother asked if we would like some oranges. She asked me to toss her one from the bowl, then another. With three in her hands, all of a sudden they were circling in the air, my grandmother juggling like the person on television. When she was finished, she cut them up for us to eat and walked out of the room, never saying a word or breaking a smile.

In the last few days of my grandfather's life, he became bedridden. We children were not allowed to spend a lot of time with him and I couldn't talk to him like before. The last thing I remember him saying to me was, "I'm not doing well...be good".

His passing was the greatest loss of my young life. I only hope I have been able to live up to the faith he put in me.

3. FAMILY

In 1950, my father was drafted into the army to fight in the Korean conflict. It seems ironic only six years before he was behind barbed wire in the Arizona desert and considered a threat to the nation. Yet his generation had a lot of patriotism, and he went into the army willingly to serve his country.

He was assigned to be a driver of munitions, otherwise known as a 'suicide jockey'. The convoys would travel under the cover of darkness, oftentimes without headlights. My father volunteered to drive the lead convoy as he felt it was the safest position to be in, since the middle driver could get trapped in during an attack and the back driver could get left behind.

He lost three trucks. Once, it was when he got too close to a rice paddy, and his truck slipped in. Another time was when he fried a clutch trying to climb a steep hill – after this they used a tank to winch up the rest.

The third was blown up by a landmine the sweepers had missed. My father was thrown through the canvas roof by the explosion and landed about 150 feet away. He came to with his Japanese American buddies dragging him away from the scene, terrified the ammunition the truck had been transporting was going to blow.

My father was later taken to the hospital to be treated by medics. They asked him to sign a document stating he had been injured in battle, which he refused, in fear he would be sent back home for rehabilitation, only to be redeployed for another tour of duty when he only had a few more months to go.

He did receive a few awards, and when he passed away, we were given a flag honoring him as a veteran. Yet the tour did take its toll on him. My father would have nightmares on a regular basis, yelling, screaming and thrashing in his sleep. My poor mother would try to wake him up, doing her best to avoid being struck. It wasn't until recently I realized he was almost certainly suffering from Post-Traumatic Stress Disorder.

I was born in 1953. I was by all accounts a cheerful and healthy little boy, until I was four years old, and fell suddenly ill. My mother thought I had a bad case of the flu, yet when our family doctor came to the house, he instantly said I needed to go to hospital.

When we arrived, I was put in an isolation room. The door had a small vertical viewing window, and I could see my mother looking in at me with tears in her eyes. I remember crying and calling out to her, not understanding why she would not come to me. I had been diagnosed with polio; the highly infectious disease able to cause lifetime paralysis or death.

The nurses and doctors wore masks, making them seem strange and unknowable. Two male attendants would come and hold me down, and another would insert a needle into my spine, to draw out fluids.

I always knew the needle was coming, and there was nothing I could do to stop it. It is the most terrifying and helpless feeling I can remember. I wasn't allowed to touch anyone, not my mother, or my friends and family. They would just come to peer at me, through the glass, like I was a goldfish in a tank. This went on for a week, which to a four-year-old little boy felt like a lifetime. To this day I can feel the pain of the needle. Fortunately, I recovered with none of polio's horrible residual effects. Others were not so lucky.

My mother and I have always been close. She always would take me on her errands from when I was very little, even though I was constantly getting into trouble. I found out later it was because she had a terrible sense of direction and would often get lost by herself. I had a knack for remembering everywhere I'd been, so took charge as her tiny navigator. But there were some places I couldn't help her out. One time when we were visiting Las Vegas I remember waiting for half an hour for her to come out of the lady's restroom. Finally, she emerged, and I asked what had happened. She couldn't find a way out and only managed by following another woman outside.

She came from a family of five children. Her brother Bob was the oldest and a famous runner, record holder and orthopedic surgeon who helped develop the orthoscope. Yoshi is the second oldest and was always the leader of the sisters. My mother's twin sister, Toshi, was more petite and ladylike. My mother pointed out you can also tell them apart in photos by the fact her own shoes were always dirty. Aunt Pauline was the youngest and moved to Hawaii after her marriage. She loved dogs, and after she passed away, I inherited her fluffy Maltese Toru who was used to being carried everywhere and experienced a culture shock coming to my place when he was expected to eat out of a bowl rather than being hand fed at the dinner table.

My mother always liked to stay under the radar, in part because of her natural shyness, but also because for much of her lifetime attracting attention usually led to unpleasantness. She has always valued simplicity over flash. The only piece of jewelry she ever really took to, was a small plumeria pendant from Hawaii. Flowers are a passion of hers, and at one point she grew begonias and orchids for sale commercially. Later on, she carried out specialty care of potted plants and flowerbeds on my landscaping jobsites. However, she spent most of her time taking care of our family, which was no easy task. After me came a brother and two sisters. Together, we were more than a handful.

My little brother Weldon has always been sharp-witted. Though I was much larger and stronger, he always knew how to get the better of me growing up. On one occasion, he told me to quit bothering him as he could beat me up whenever he wanted. I was indignant and told him it was in fact the other way around.

"Hit me as hard as you can, and I'll show you," challenged Weldon, so I did. Tears swelled in his eyes, and I knew I'd gotten him good.

Suddenly, he smiled and cried out, "Dad! Wade hit me – for no reason!" My dad came charging into the room, yelled at me to never pick on my little brother again and gave me a good smack.

When he left, Weldon started smiling again. "See, I told you."

After Weldon came Wendy. She was big for her age and an exceptional athlete. I remember at school my friends would watch the younger kids playing sports, and would come over and tell me, "Your sister is tearing them up again." She was my sidekick on adventures with my BB gun, helping to set up targets and pellets. She even dared to hold targets with her hands.

When I began shooting competitively, she was there to help. When I started motorcycle racing, she was my pit crew. When I opened my bike shop, she did orders, the books, all for peanuts. She has always believed in me, no matter what.

Wynne is the youngest, which meant she had no choice but to follow the rest of us and do what we were doing. She developed a passion for motorcycles, earning her the family nickname 'Jammer' after a professional motorcycle racer that she bears to this day. She also has a passion for dogs – the bigger the better. At first glance, she's an unassuming, small-statured Japanese woman, but she has no trouble bossing around a massive Akita and knows her way around an engine.

I have many wonderful memories of weekend family adventures, including sightseeing drives, fishing, hiking, playing sports, picnics and camping. My father had a real appreciation of the outdoors he shared with us. I still enjoy traveling and seeing nature's beauty, and I'm sure my passion for photography has its origins in those early days. I learned to stop and really look at the world around me, to take in the sights others just walk on by, never knowing what they have missed.

My mother has always loved to travel to new places, which I suppose I've inherited from her in part. Now she's in her nineties, her health has limited the places she can go, so I make a point to bring back keepsakes for her from all my trips around the world. I have breakfast with her most Sunday mornings and lunches at her favorite Japanese restaurant.

My mother still lives in the house we grew up in on Santa Barbara's Mesa with Wynne as her caregiver. Due to her mobility issues, we tend to host holidays and special events there so she can attend. Modest, mild-mannered and somewhat frail, she is still the glue holding our family together. When she has something to say, her words carry weight, and we all listen.

My father passed away years ago, but his memory lives on. When I was sixteen, like most teenage boys, I was set on getting a car of my own. My dad gave me a job on his landscaping crew, and I saved every penny. I had $600 by the end of summer and I scoured the newspaper classifieds looking for a hotrod I could afford. Most were pretty beat up, but a Chevrolet Impala looked like it would work. When I told my father about it, he scoffed it wasn't worth it – he'd give me his old Ford pickup instead. I had driven it for work and it bounced around everywhere, though I did discover it did great burnouts. When I told him I didn't want it, he got strangely upset.

Nearly thirty years later, he told me how he bought the truck after he got out of the Army to start his gardening route. It was also the 1953 model, the year of my birth, and a special limited edition 50th anniversary Ford. He kept it for the rest of his life and gave it to me before he died. I've spent nearly twenty years restoring it, scouring for parts to match, patching it up piece by piece, in honor of my father's memory.

4. THE FAT KID

As a child, I was a chubby kid. I loved playing football and baseball, but as a heavy, slow runner lacking coordination and balance, I wasn't particularly good at either.

When I visited my cousins' house, we would go and play in a nearby schoolyard. I remember them jumping over the fence and running off to play while I struggled to follow. I used to look for holes in the fence, or a gap for me to crawl under or through, since climbing was such a struggle. I vowed someday I would be the first over every time, jumping with two bounds.

I used to dread when my other, older cousins would come up from Los Angeles. They would tease me and beat me up with my younger brother and sisters watching. I decided to work as hard as I could to beat them. I would run, shadow box, hit boards to build up calluses on my knuckles – only to have them beat me up again.

Then one day, all that changed. When I was 11 years old, I had a huge growth spurt, growing nearly five inches in one summer. I went from the fat, little kid, to one of the tallest in my class. I gained strength and speed literally overnight.

Suddenly, my legs moved faster than I ever imagined. I could pick up a ball and throw it as far as I could spot a target. Pitching, I remember hearing the whistle of the ball as it left my hand. My bat also started making that whooshing sound, and the ball would sail through the air off into the distance. Overnight, I had gone from below average to a real athlete. It seemed a minor miracle.

But it wasn't all great news. When I had the physical needed for entering junior high school, the glucose tolerance test revealed I had a kidney malfunction and I was diagnosed as a renal diabetic. The doctor said I had two options: start on daily insulin injections or try to control it with diet and exercise. Insulin would mean probably staying on it for life, though I would be allowed to have desserts.

I went with the second option and have been able to control my diabetes through diet and exercise since then. To this day I do not eat refined sugars.

When I was around ten years old, my father insisted I take up a self-defense sport stressing discipline. I ended up taking on judo, a decision probably influenced by family friend Toru Kitamura who my parents met in the internment camp. He was short and slightly overweight, with high-pitched voice – definitely not the type you'd expect to be a Judo master. Yet he transformed on the mats into a fighter of incredible strength and skill, smooth, fast, and extremely well balanced.

I started taking judo classes at the Goleta Cultural Center during the summer under Ken Ota with my brother Weldon. I rode there on my bike after my baseball games. Ken trained us in the fundamentals of the sport, including Aikido.

I earned the nickname 'Speedy'. My *sensei* put me up against the upper belts to really push me. Many times, I was told they thought they had thrown me, only to find I was really dodging and countering. I had a real instinct for predicting my opponent's next move.

Toru would also give me private lessons, teaching me the importance of mental focus rather than physical strength. He taught me to never underestimate an opponent and analyze his traits and abilities, only using as much force as he was going to exert. I began to be able to intuit where they were vulnerable and notice small signs like the lowering of the body, indicating they were prepared to attack. It allowed me to catch them off guard, or plan a counterattack before they knew what hit them.

As part of my discipline, he asked me to promise to stay away from alcohol and drugs, so I could maintain full awareness of my mind and body. He said that since I could inflict serious injury, it was dangerous for my judgment to be impeded by substances, in a similar way it would be to drive under the influence. To this day, I do not drink nor have I experimented with other substances of any kind.

I found ways to cross apply my skills, though not necessarily in the way other people approved. I loved playing football but did not get a lot of playtime. I was thrilled when one day my football coach put me on the field, charging me with getting in the way of the other team's star running back. He was fast and strong, weighing about two hundred pounds. From the sidelines I watched him charge through many of my team; he seemed to be unstoppable.

I went out on the field, and suddenly the star was charging towards me like a bull, raising his hand to stiff arm me. As he came towards me, I grabbed his arm and tossed him with a judo throw. He flew into the air and landed about ten feet away, headfirst.

Soon enough a flag was flying next to my head and I was tossed out of the game for unsportsmanlike conduct. My coach yelled at me to never do that again, but as he was walking away a big smile lit up his face.

5. Open Your Eyes

From my earliest years, I have had to deal with being viewed with mistrust. When I started school, the other students were predominately white with only a few other minorities, mixed in. When we went out to play or had to pair up, we were usually the last to be picked. I was never invited to other kid's parties. "Why don't you have a nose?" they taunted. "Why don't you open your eyes?" "Can we touch your hair? It's so stiff!"

In those days, Japanese food was considered 'gross'. Raw fish and the smell of vinegar, pickled vegetables, and seaweed were not normally consumed by others. Teachers asked our parents not to include these eccentric items in our school lunches, because of the distraction it created amongst the other children, and the fact that they themselves were not accustomed to these strange sights and smells.

Japanese festivals were treated by some as a 'cult gathering' rather than a cultural event. Wearing a *kimono*, or *hapi* coat was mocked as like wearing a woman's dress.

We tended to frequent businesses owned by other Japanese Americans, to avoid the mistrustful stares of resentment lingering after the war. Sticking together was a survival strategy, and part of why we were so tightknit as a community.

There were no other Japanese Americans in my year in school, so I played with children from all ethnicities. The white friends I had would sometimes come over to my place to play, but I wasn't allowed in their house. I had to hurry and leave if their parents were due home, because they were forbidden from hanging out with a Japanese boy.

There was a time when I cursed being different and just wanted to be like everyone else. I would look in the mirror and wonder how I could change myself to better fit in. Sunglasses and hats helped mask some of our differences.

A number of Japanese Americans went further, denouncing our heritage, and rejecting our food and cultural gatherings in favor of those of white America. They would even avoid families like mine, who kept with our traditions, to create a distinction between 'us and them'.

I don't blame them for it. Those days were hard, dealing with discrimination at every turn. They were trying to cope in the best way they knew how. It never really worked though – the people who feared and hated us would still do so, whether we ate hamburgers or teriyaki.

Gradually things did begin to change. Asian culture started to be seen as 'cool', with martial arts rising in prominence thanks to the likes of Bruce Lee and Jackie Chan and series like *Kung Fu* and *The Karate Kid*. Asian cuisine was suddenly 'discovered' and made its way to dining tables everywhere. Asian culture and the arts began to be exhibited and studied not as exotic oddities, but as worthy equals of Western creativity.

Not everyone left old attitudes behind, or the shift was slow, but it made getting by a lot easier for all of us.

There was a memorable occasion when my children were little, we visited a fast-food restaurant in Santa Barbara. My five-year-old daughter went up to the counter to look at the menu. A big man suddenly went over to her, and shoved her away from the counter, saying under his voice "Stupid little Jap."

It was the one time in my life I truly lost it. I raced over and shoved him with my full force, then grabbed him and planted him headfirst into a trash can – where I felt he belonged.

He remained stuck, flailing his arms and legs comically, for some time until he finally got out with the help of a few other men.

I apologized for my behavior to the other patrons and disturbing their meal. But the men who pulled the man out of the trash told me, "He deserved it," and told him he was not welcome at the restaurant any longer. Some of the other patrons clapped.

I'm not saying my reaction was model behavior – but it sure was nice to be sided with by the room against someone bullying us for no reason other than our ancestors were born somewhere else to his.

As society learned to accept people like me, I learned to accept myself. My heritage is a big part of who I am and has intrinsically shaped the man I am today. In some ways being part of an ostracized minority has driven me to achieve, through instilling in me the determination to triumph and prove wrong those who thought no one who looked like me could ever be good enough. Things have gotten a lot better, yet there is still a lot of discrimination in the world. I consider it my duty to continue to fight against prejudice in all its forms, in favor of a truly inclusive society where all are treated as equal.

A part of this is preserving and celebrating cultural roots. My generation of Japanese Americans made major inroads towards integrating with the larger community, at the cost of losing a lot of the traditions of our forefathers. In my youth, I remembered big barbeques held every summer at the Dos Pueblos Ranch where many Japanese Americans worked in the orchid greenhouses. Hundreds of Japanese Americans would gather together, like one big extended family. It was a space where our successes, however small, were celebrated as if we were champions. There was a sense of pride, and facing the hardships of the world united.

Eventually, these barbeques stopped. Since I had such fond memories, I ended up setting out to find out what happened to them, knowing their importance for keeping our community and its support network intact. Mike Hide, the president of the Japanese Americans Community League, told me he was simply too old to organize them anymore. He had served for 28 years and was the only one left from the days of hosting the barbeques. I offered to help out, with the result of Mike handing me the reins of the league. Since 1994 I have been the president of the group and among other duties, have run the barbeques including spending most of the day behind the barbeque cooking around a hundred pounds of chicken and tri-tip roasts.

It's rewarding to see the many families I have known from childhood come together, growing and developing in the world. Together with the league, we initiated a scholarship program for the children of our members to support their journey through life. Recipients end up coming to all our events in gratitude, a part of maintaining our group and heritage for the future.

6. Sprouting

Just as a plant or tree, I grew up in gardens. My father, both grandfathers, and uncles were gardeners. So too were most of our family friends. Many Japanese were professionals such as doctors and lawyers before the war and the internment. On returning to the community, distrust of the Japanese meant few could return to their former advisory roles, forced to take on jobs like gardening where they serviced clients at a distance.

I spent a good amount of my childhood tagging along to projects, and playing amongst the greenery. When I was about 10 years old, I started doing odd jobs in the family business myself. I would work after school occasionally, on Saturdays, and during the holidays. One summer I went to work with a crew of my father's workers, under the supervision of the foreman, Adan Perez Salazar. He was a big guy who looked a lot like the singer Tom Jones. My father told me Adan would teach me about 'real work'. I wasn't sure what that meant, but I was about to find out.

Adan told me straight up he was not going to treat me like the boss's son, but just like any other worker. Since all the other members of the crew were from Mexico, he said I needed to learn to speak Spanish. While working, I wasn't to speak any English. If I wanted anything, including asking to go to the bathroom, all I had to do was ask – in Spanish. I hated learning at the time, yet becoming bilingual ended up being a major asset in my life. Adan had been a radio DJ in Mexico and was very well educated. He made sure I used proper Spanish and knew the difference between conversational and written forms.

Adan worked me hard. By the end of the summer, even though

I was 11 years old, I was giving orders to the other workers. It might have helped that I used my Judo techniques to take them all down when we were wrestling around.

Fast forward to high school, and I began a program allowing me to do my studies at my own pace. It was a reading class, and all I had to do was read a book a week – so I read forty books in four weeks so I could focus on my future.

I began working in my Uncle Joe Mori's retail nursery in Goleta, doing physical labor and deliveries. I would sometimes pick up plants from a wholesaler in Carpinteria. The owner, Lew Abe, would spend time with me and talk about the things in my life. He had children my age and taught me a lot about life, the importance of setting my goals high and always looking to the future. He ended up offering me a job and I spent three years being mentored on the importance of working hard physically and mentally.

Abe was a genius at mathematics. He showed me shortcuts how to calculate things by looking at numbers and how they related to each other in groups, and individually. He did his own books using an abacus. One day, a guy laughed at him for using such an old-fashioned tool. Abe challenged him to a contest, saying he could beat him even if he used a calculator. Abe literally finished in half of the time of his challenger, who wasn't laughing anymore. I discovered years after he had passed away, he had scored the highest marks in a test of all Los Angeles in mathematics.

While working with Abe, I was offered two career-type jobs, which started me on the course of thinking about my future. Soon after being married, my father-in-law who ran a large flower nursery in Goleta, said he would give me the position of running the entire operation. I knew how lucrative the business was; he was living very comfortably. However, I didn't want to be obligated to him my entire life, or be handed a position just because of family ties.

Another offer was to be a foreman to run a landscape crew and projects at a starting rate of $1000 a month – and this was back in 1970. I seriously thought about it, but Abe told me to consider after graduation I could be in a position to offer someone else a job as a business owner. So I decided to get a degree and start a company of my own, though doing what I wasn't sure. When I started at Santa Barbara City College I had no idea what major I wanted to do. I thought about going into the medical field, or psychology, and took general education classes in order to give myself more time to decide. At first, I told myself I never wanted to do landscaping as a career, because it was such hard work. Yet in the end I decided it was the path forward – I knew I had the talent and know-how from my childhood 'apprenticeship' to create award winning gardens and build a successful business to support myself and my wife.

We relocated to Cal Poly Pomona, where I began studying Landscape Architecture. However, we quickly found Pomona was not the place for us, so after the first quarter I transferred to Cal Poly San Luis Obispo even though I would have to enter Ornamental Horticulture. I found that the class material came easy especially since I knew much of the subject material already based on field experience with my family. I ended up with the Joseph Shinoda Scholarship in Floriculture that helped pay my way. Funny enough Joseph was my wife Roxanne's late uncle. I later received a call from the President of the foundation, whom I happened to know, and was assured he never mentioned to the selection committee my relationship to the Shinodas.

Upon graduating from Cal Poly SLO, I took my test for my C-27 State Landscape Contractors License. I was the first one done of 200, completing the four-hour exam in 20 minutes.

I also took my pesticides certification class, required for gardeners to complete their work. Again, I finished the exam in 20 minutes. The Federation Chair from Los Angeles was suspicious of my speed, accusing me of cheating as I began to leave. The president of the local chapter stepped in, telling him I had in fact graduated college with honors and had helped teach coursework to other students.

I immediately started working after completing college, as I wanted to buy a house. I went door-to-door introducing myself to all the local architects and had no luck until one day I walked into the office of Jim Zimmerman. He also graduated from Cal Poly San Luis Obispo and showed me some plans for a famous restaurant in downtown Santa Barbara called J. K. Frimple's. We ended up working together on this design. We received a Santa Barbara Beautiful Award for this project, as well as many others over the years.

My father also helped me out by referring me landscape jobs from his garden maintenance business he had established, which I later took over when he passed away. This included Casa Dorinda, a historic mansion and estate recently converted into an exclusive retirement community. I was tasked to do all the landscaping upgrades, creating spaces such as a Tranquility Gardens. This features a waterfall and pond under mature oaks, with meandering paths and observation deck designed for quiet self-reflection. I also designed gardens specifically for residents, such as world-renowned chef Julia Childs. She requested a private English style garden, complete with fruit tree orchards and cut flower and vegetable gardens.

In the early years of my business, I would do most of the work myself or with one or two crew members. As my business grew, I found myself busier and busier. I was the salesperson, designer, accountant, estimator, manager, responsible for layouts, installer, maintenance organizer, principle troubleshooter and crew chief for the business.

In my spare time I spent a lot of time at the local bowling alley where I got to know many regulars and staff. A guy named John Yamasaki, who was in his senior year of high school, heard I was looking for some extra help. I hired him as a summer laborer and John continued to work for me throughout his college years studying business administration. In his final year, I asked him if he was interested in continuing on with me since I could hardly keep up with all the demands upon me. John said yes, and a partnership was formed. I did not have a lot to offer in the way of salary at the time, so I offered him a portion of the business, a down payment to buy a condo and a work truck. We've been together thirty years now, have a great relationship and have received numerous beautification awards in Santa Barbara, Goleta and Carpinteria for our work. John handles the finances, billing, payroll, and oversees the maintenance team at Casa Dorinda plus some others. Thanks to John I can focus on the artistic side of the business, doing design and project management, and some maintenance work.

I don't think I will ever retire. I love landscaping and have established myself to be able to more or less pick and choose my projects. Garden design is living art – it's creative, artistic, rewarding and it brings me immense joy. Each landscape is a new challenge, as every design requires negotiation with an existing architecture, owner personal preferences, the topography and location, and more, all of which combine to make each project a unique puzzle to be solved.

Some of Wade's landscape creations:

Torii Gate at Shoreline Park, Santa Barbara (public park), honoring sister city Toba, Japan – designed, built and installed by Wade and Teddy Muneno.

ShinKanAn Teahouse and Garden, Santa Barbara Botanic Gardens – Fence by Wade.

Various private garden designs by Wade:

43

7. Ancient Principles

My Uncle Frank was a master gardener. He learned his trade under the mentorship of his father, Kinzuchi Fujii, who trained in Japan.

The famous Storrier-Stearns Teahouse Garden in Pasadena is a lasting testament to Kinzuchi's mastery of ancient principles of design. The feature elements are two ponds, and a teahouse, from which the name of the design derives: 'Niko An' literally translating to 'Teahouse and Two Ponds'. Kinzuchi actually had the teahouse constructed in Japan to his specifications to ensure authentic construction, then shipped over to California where it was reassembled on location.

Depressingly, in 1981 the beautiful teahouse was destroyed in a fire. It was not lost forever however, thanks to Uncle Frank cherishing his father's work and safekeeping all his working papers. He discovered the detailed plans Kinzuchi had drawn for the original teahouse, which were used to replace it with a replica.

Uncle Frank would take me to work with him on occasion, teaching me the principles of Japanese gardening I still use to this day. The theory of Japanese landscape is fairly complex though some general points can be applied to almost any type of design. Foundational elements are earth, water and life. Earth is represented with stone; Water is represented either by water itself, or pebbles, gravel or sand; and life is represented by plants in their many varieties. Time and age are another component which acknowledge a garden as living, growing, and ever-changing thing.

The stones are placed usually to represent the mountains

that are formed by nature. Some are in the shape of mountain peaks, while others represent symbolic objects such as boats, bridges, piers, animals or human forms. Every stone has a grain to it, which can be used to create horizontal, vertical or diagonal lines within the garden.

In order to create a naturalistic effect, Japanese design also prominently uses odd numbers, especially clusters of three. Gardens are made up of multiple layers of triangle forms, none of them the same size or angle. Triangulation is used in everything from stone and plant groupings to planning focal points.

Lotusland in Montecito was one of Uncle Frank's major gardens, owned by the famous Polish Opera Singer Madam Ganna Walska. She married six times, her husbands including a Russian baron, multimillionaire yachtsman and an English inventor of a death ray, and was said to be inspiration for aspects of the screenplay of *Citizen Kane*. After her divorce from her sixth and last husband, a scholar of hatha yoga and Tibetan Buddhism, she devoted the rest of her life to designing, expanding, and maintaining her estate's celebrated, distinctive gardens.

In my Uncle, Madam Walska found someone who mirrored her passion for gardens and creative excellence. I recall watching him take hours to set a single stone. He would consider the grain, the stone's dominant features, the background from all angles, the depth the stone would rest at and the triangulations each stone would create. He made adjustments inch by inch, until he was finally satisfied.

He trimmed plants in the same way, continually considering the balance between all elements, making continual cuts until everything was just right.

The time and energy he expended to attain perfection was immaterial to him. This discipline is a major component in the art of a true master and inspired me to take on his attitude as a way of life, with perpetual dedication to attaining excellence in everything I do.

When I was young, the Santa Barbara Gardener's Federation hosted a stall at the Orchid Show held at the Earl Warren Showground. Uncle Frank would always be in charge of the design, for which they often won an award. They would work long hours the entire week, sometimes until three in the morning, and my uncle was always the last to leave. One night he fell asleep on the freeway driving home and crashed. A metal irrigation pipe pierced the car, and grazed his leg, missing his torso by inches. Shortly afterwards, Uncle Frank declined to help at the stall any longer, since he knew he would push himself until breaking point on any project he did.

Later in life, I had the opportunity to work with him on a garden display at Japanese themed event *Nihonmachi* Celebration at the El Presidio De Santa Barbara. Frank did the design and I was in charge of construction. Since the flooring was tile, we built a box so we could raise the display surface and set the centerpiece stone. The one stone took us nearly four hours to set as my Uncle had to have it perfect. This meant viewing the stone from every possible angle to see how it worked best. This small project is one of those I treasure the most, since I was able to work side by side so closely with my uncle. As he slowed down in his career and approached retirement, Uncle Frank began to refer me work to do. This was the greatest compliment I could have received. It marked his approval of what I had learned of his techniques and style, and his confidence I would follow in his footsteps creating gardens up to his exacting standards.

Entry in Nihonmachi Celebration at the El Presidio De Santa Barbara. From Left Roxanne, Wade, Eric Kawaguchi, Frank Fujii, Dorothy Fujii, Naomi Muneno, Weldon Nomura, Robert Abe and Dino Corral.

I apply Japanese principles to all projects I undertake, regardless of the ultimate style. Yet by a stroke of luck I was recently able to create what I call my signature project, a Japanese garden amalgamating the knowledge of Uncle Frank with a lifetime of garden design.

The opportunity came about by pure chance; the owners of the property were looking for someone to create a Japanese garden when they saw a branded Nomura/Yamasaki truck drive by and wrote down the phone number. When they contacted us, I went over to convey my vision for the space. I immediately saw an opportunity to implement what my Uncle Frank had taught me on a large scale.

The design itself took nearly four months to complete, and construction another two years. Every inch of the landscape was incorporated into the master plan, with each item hand selected and placed. The clients were confident in my vision and allowed me a free hand in implementing my design – a dream come true.

Because of the owners' request for a garden with multiple functions, I decided to create sub-gardens within the space. I spent a lot of time developing the entry to the main garden.

Gates create sense of curiosity, like wrapping paper for a gift, and are important to get just right. I approached my friend Ted Muneno, who was trained by a woodcraftsman in the Japanese techniques of old, to create a traditional Torii gate. We borrowed from some of the elements used inside the house – it turned out Ted had earlier made their shoji screens.

This leads to a staggered walkway, forcing visitors to slow down to a stroll. A plank bridge arches over a hardscape dry pond, my solution to creating an interesting environment without heavy planting in what is a drought hit area with water restrictions.

In fact, over half of the entire landscape footprint uses rocks, sand and other such materials to substantially reduce the need for irrigation. Two paths circle the pond, and a small bamboo grove conceals the garage door. An existing storage shed was similarly disguised with bamboo fencing and a thatched roof.

The final element is a reading space, requested by the owners. Here is a halo light and a softly trickling water feature.

In the next area, I had to fit in a large swimming pool, which could be an eyesore if installed without careful consideration. I dug out a stream to create a natural visual barrier between the house and the pool, as well as suggested an intentional water theme. A traditional Japanese style bridge stretches over the stream, to an open space surrounded by bonsai pines, stones, water features and bamboo fencing. The pool was created using natural materials in shades of gray to blend into the landscape while also allowing reflections of the sky and background to soften the water.

The Zen Garden, or meditation garden, is a small, pocket garden, fully enclosed to create the feel of a private space. It has a Kyoto-style design, with lush, dark leaf plants that contrast with white-colored raked sand scattered with granite rocks and stepping stones. A *tsukubai* water feature drowns out external noise with the sound of water trickling over rock. The garden is designed to have multiple viewing points, including from a window in a room the owner routinely looks out and does her painting.

Off the kitchen, is another garden, this time with practicality in mind. It features raised planters and flowers perfect for cutting and displaying inside. There are also fruit trees, a surface for doing chores and storage facilities.

After years of hard work by a large team, we finally completed what I today call my signature project. I was honored it was featured in an Architectural Tour, with many visitors from across the county and beyond coming to see the work and speak to me about its creation. Even more importantly the owners have told me many times how much they enjoy their garden, when I visit to assist with continued maintenance and pruning, applying bonsai techniques.

When I walk through the space, I am still in awe of being granted the opportunity to translate so much of my history, skills and signature design elements into a singular, breathing work of art.

A selection of photos from Wade's Signature Garden:

The entry to the Zen Garden.

Dry pond with wooden walkway. Also serves as rain collection and percolating pond.

Maple with meandering pathways through garden.

Entry gate to Japanese garden.

8. ROXANNE

When I started high school, I got caught up in a battle for top dog in the tough guy pecking order. I was constantly off to detention, for fighting as well as causing distractions in class.

My parents reached out to their friends and family for advice about what to do with me. I've heard stories how my father would go to the local Japanese guy hangout at a gas station owned by a man named Toki with tears in his eyes, wondering where he went wrong.

My aunt suggested she take me to church with my cousins, in the hopes I would find religion, or at least some moral values. The Bethany Congregational Church had a mostly Japanese membership. My family would go once or twice a year, during special holidays. I remember the first time I went, at around four years old. It was in the Japanese quarter of town, in an old wooden building. I had insisted on wearing a cowboy outfit, including spurs that clanked over the wooden plank walkways.

Forced to go weekly as a high schooler, I hated it. The Japanese Reverend called me 'Wadie', which my cousins loved to tease me about. I was signed up to the youth group, hosted by a young couple who organized events for us. It was during one of these outings I first met The New Girl. Her name was Roxanne. She came from a family that was very well to do and had just settled in Santa Barbara to establish a new nursery operation.

The Japanese Santa Barbara community was small and my friends and I already knew all the girls eligible to date. None of them really impressed me, and at the time it was very unusual to date a non-Japanese.

Roxanne stood out. She had a warm smile and was outgoing and athletic. Also, she was a year older than me, which was a plus for a high school guy. One of our youth group trips was to see the Pasadena Rose Parade on New Year's Day. I made plans to ask out Roxanne then, which my cousins quickly figured out. They said if she said yes, they'd tag along, just to mess with me, until I threatened to beat them up.

At the parade, I worked up my nerve and asked Roxanne if she would like to see Butch Cassidy and the Sundance Kid with me. She said yes, and I was thrilled, until she turned around and asked the rest of the gang if they wanted to come too. My cousins smiled at me and considered, like they were going to say yes. I glared and they declined. I think it was the looks they all gave each other that made Roxanne realize she'd agreed to a date.

We started dating regularly after that, but since we were teenagers it was hard to be serious about a relationship. After graduating, Roxanne decided to go to Cal Poly San Luis Obispo, leaving me behind in high school. While there, she met a guy on the football team and decided to start dating him.

I remember going all the way up to Cal Poly, finding the guy and telling him I'd knock his lights out if he didn't leave her alone. He decided to move on. Mission accomplished! I never did tell Roxanne what I'd done…

She moved back to Santa Barbara after her first quarter and we started dating again. She enrolled in a two year degree in medical assisting at Santa Barbara City College. Within six months we decided to marry. Roxanne insisted I ask her father's permission to marry her in the old-fashioned way. All I could think was it wasn't going to go well, since I was only 16 years old and my family was far poorer than hers.

Wade with Roxanne on his first Motorcycle – a 1972 Honda SL 125 stripped for racing.

When I finally worked up the nerve to ask, he gave me a hard, disapproving look. "Where are you going to live? How are you going to afford it?"

Knowing there was no chance he was going to say yes, I replied, "Well I figure I could qualify for a Sears credit card, then I can buy a tent to live on the beach." I said I could use my fishing poles to catch us meals. I walked out, leaving him speechless.

After Roxanne did a bit of work on him, he later invited me over for dinner, and gave me permission. We married in June 1973. Given my age, I actually had to have my parents sign a consent form to allow us to take vows.

9. Paradise

Roxanne and I decided to move back to the Santa Barbara area because most of our family was still there. We initially stayed with Roxanne's parents in Santa Barbara, so we could save some money and search for a place of our own. My daughter Lisa was born a few months later, and the extra help from my in-laws was much appreciated by a young couple new to parenthood.

We were so proud of our little Lisa and took her everywhere. We saw creating such a perfect little new life as the greatest accomplishment of our lives so far, documenting everything she did, from her first bath to her first solid food.

We ended up finding a condo under construction in nearby Carpinteria and pieced together a deposit. Even back then Santa Barbara was an expensive place for a young couple to get their start and it was only about 15 miles away, so I was still close to my family.

It turned out to be one of the best decisions we ever made. It was and still is a fantastic place to raise a family and it has managed to retain its small-town beach charm even though we are only 100 miles from Los Angeles. It's a beautiful place, with a stunning beach and majestic purple mountains looming behind the safe and friendly town. Soon after moving here we could hardly walk down a street without many locals stopping to say hello.

There is strong sense of community spirit, with volunteering a way of life. Many people are involved in local charities such as Lions, Rotary, youth groups and other good causes. Whether it is a fundraiser, sporting event, or festival Carpinterians always show up in force, offering their support in every way they can.

We started going to Friday night football games at the local high school, the stands filled with families and local fans of the Carpinteria Warriors team. Whether the team was winning or losing, the chant rang out, "Warrior Sprit never dies".

Lisa's daycare entered in the annual holiday parade, and Roxanne and I volunteered to take part. Everyone in town came out to watch and all of the parade participants walked the route twice, just to make sure nobody would miss seeing any part.

We soon got caught up community volunteering and enjoyed seeing our efforts making a difference. Roxanne became a member of the Carpinteria Education Foundation, American Cancer Society, local Real Estate Board, and the Boys and Girls Club of Carpinteria. She was further invited onto the American Heart Association Board and UCSB Intercollegiate Policy Board. She could hardly ever say no when asked to help out.

Roxanne became famous for her cookies. Every week she was baking chocolate chip cookies for celebrations and events. She used to bake as many as 10,000 cookies during the holiday season to give away as gifts. One holiday, she literally wore the door hinges off the oven, meaning I had to hold the door shut while one tray of cookies was baking, and she prepared the next batch.

Around two years after we moved to Carpinteria, our second child Ryan was born. Unlike Lisa, Ryan was a very quiet and mellow. Roxanne's father told us to take him to a doctor to have him checked out, he moved so little and didn't start talking until he was nearly two. We realized it was because he completely relied on Lisa, who got him whatever he wanted; Ryan was happy to sit there and be pampered like a little prince.

As our children started preschool, we put them into local sports programs and soon I was a volunteer coach for many sports.

A few years later, my brother Weldon and his wife Ann also decided Carpinteria was a great place to raise their family, allowing us all to remain close, with my sisters and mother remaining in Santa Barbara.

Living

10. Natural Athletes

My children Lisa and Ryan were both natural born athletes. A lot of my fathering involved rough-and-ready coaching and being their personal taxi to training and events.

Lisa started walking and talking at a very early age. She loved to climb things and was utterly fearless. Once, when we were out shopping at a department store as a family, I saw a salesgirl started screaming and pointing. I looked up to see two-year-old Lisa running back and forward on top of the ten-foot shelving. In a flash, she had climbed up a ladder used by employees to stack shelves.

We bought her a big wheel plastic tricycle to power around the yard on. Soon enough she wanted a proper bike to match my racing bikes. She was riding BMX tracks by age three. She was tiny but had coordination, balance and incredible determination to succeed. She spent three years with me on BMX tours, logging over 100,000 miles a year travelling to and from events.

As a five-year-old, she earned a national title in the under seven girls' class. The only trouble was, her competitors quickly started becoming much bigger and stronger, until they were literally twice her size. She began getting disappointed not placing like she used to, so we let her try a new sport. She caught on quickly to gymnastics, where her slight build was an advantage. She already had great balance from bike riding and a natural fearlessness.

Lisa accelerated quickly through the ranks in gymnastics, passing her older and more experienced teammates. She trained four to six hours a day, six days a week. She would easily win school physical educational challenges, often beating the boys doing hundreds of pushups, pulls ups and sit ups with ease. When she was around eleven years old, her coach became pregnant meaning she could no longer spot, the gymnastics name for catching the girls as they were learning to leap through the air. Since without this training they would fall behind in their training, I volunteered to help, leading to me becoming the tumbling and vault coach.

It was a new experience catching bodies hurtling towards me at speed, over and over again, especially when some of the senior members of the team were my size. Eventually, the girls were skilled enough to do flips without me to catch them. It was wonderful seeing the excitement in their eyes when they finally landed by themselves. Lisa won a huge number of medals and trophies over the years. I was proud of her commitment, knowing behind every performance of grace and strength was thousands of hours of practice and willpower. She continued gymnastics into college, receiving a scholarship from Cal State Sacramento where she competed as a beam and vault specialist.

Lisa with Wade at Preschool Show and Tell – Lisa then 5-year old National BMX Champion. Father and daughter National BMX Champions in same year.

1983 track – Lisa on right hand side with Wade as the coach.

Lisa, first place, Beam and Vault, 1983.

Lisa – Balance Beam champion – on her way to a College Scholarship, 1986.

Ryan played as many sports as he could, including track, soccer, football, baseball and karate. I would go with him to many of his games and we would practice skills at home to help him develop further.

At the age of ten, Ryan tested for his first black belt, the youngest ever to do so in Tang Soo Do. A Master came in from Korea to watch Ryan test out. He did well in forms and was paired up with an adult also testing for his black belt for sparring. When they began, I could see Ryan's opponent holding back and Ryan getting frustrated because the action was so slow.

The Master came over and told the man to treat Ryan as if he were another adult, not to hold back. When the action started again, the man gave it his all – yet Ryan scored with a spinning back kick, then a front combination kick and finally a backhand to blank out his opponent, finishing with a 3-0 score and Ryan a black belt.

When Ryan was twelve years old, my old buddy Teddy took our family to the local driving range and golf course to have a go. We soon became addicted, taking lessons with professionals and going to the golf range to hit balls in the afternoon until the sun went down and we couldn't see any more in the dark.

We all picked up the game quickly, but Ryan was especially skillful. Within six months of starting he was able to shoot under par.

Lisa and Ryan joined the Santa Barbara Junior Golf Association, started in 1975 by PGA Buddy Allin, with the vision to allow juniors to play in a golf series including every golf course in the greater Santa Barbara area. With some coaxing, he was able to get every public and private golf course to participate, and at no cost to the players. By exposing the game to the next generation, the hope was to create a new contingent of lifelong golfers.

As he got older, Ryan started to play at higher levels, first locally then in the Southern California PGA sectionals. By this time, we were members of the Montecito Country Club with membership to the United States Golf Association for handicapping. It was a requirement of the Junior Golf World Championships to have a handicap of four or less. The head golf pro at the club refused to attest to this, saying there was no way Ryan could be that good after only taking up the sport a few years ago. Ryan straight up challenged the pro to a game to prove himself, with a side bet to make it "interesting".

The pro laughed at him, however said if he could beat his first assistant, who had a number of victories on the local tour, he might change his mind. He clearly thought it would never happen. Off to the first tee they went, the pro and I watching from afar.

At the end of the round the assistant came back looking embarrassed. He reported Ryan had shot a 68, and sulked off without another word to Ryan. The pro signed his form and told me, "Your son is the best player I have ever seen."

As Ryan approached the age where he needed a high ranking in Golf nationally for colleges to consider him for their teams, I started taking him around the country to compete. Two to three times a month we went to places like Denver, Oregon, Arizona, Washington, Nevada, Utah, and to Texas for the Rolex Boys National Championships. Ryan ended up making it into the top twenty Nationally Ranked high school golfers, even though we could only afford to take him to about half the events.

He ended up being recruited by Oregon State University to play golf, then transferred back to the UCSB to finish out his college golf career. After college, Ryan decided to turn professional. He joined the Canadian Tour where he competed for four years before injuries from a car accident sidelined him. Ryan still works in the industry as a PGA instructor, occasionally competing in events.

Out of Ryan and Lisa's participation in the Santa Barbara Junior Golf Association, came my own long-term involvement. In 1993, then President of the Association Jim Folks, asked if I would be interested in helping him out with the tournaments. Soon I was running them. The following year, when Jim decided to retire, he asked if I would be willing to take over as president. Since I enjoyed watching the kids mature into young adults and got along with them all so well, I was happy to accept.

Ryan shot putting at track event, 1983.

Wade with Ryan at Little League event – Ryan was the batting champion with .975 average and 27 home runs, 1990.

California Interscholastic Federation – Golf Championship Team. Ryan was League Champion, 1996.

Ryan in Monterey Open, California. First place playoff 2004.

The usual four-year term extended into twenty-six years and counting watching 3,000 young people go through the program. We are now seeing second and third generation participants.

Every summer, as many as one hundred and fifty players take part in fifteen events. The full program is just over a hundred dollars, including green fees, an association golf shirt, golf balls, sanctioning by official golf bodies, and an awards dinner at the end. There is also a scholarship program in place to cover those who would not be able to easily participate otherwise due to financial hardship or someone involved in a troubled youth program.

After running the program for about ten years, I decided to incorporate it, transforming it into a charitable foundation named the Santa Barbara Junior Golf Tour. We also joined the Southern California Golf Association as an associate member to be included in sanctioning, handicapping and invitations for players to championship series events they sponsored.

It requires about two thousand hours to run the tour each year, with an all-volunteer staff including myself donating their time to keep costs down. Toni Gentry is my current right hand, who is an immense help, and there have been many others over the years.

The golf program teaches a lot of important skills and lessons, regardless of whether participants become long-term players. It is a game where respect and integrity are integral. Golf is the only game I have ever played where participants must make rulings to penalize or disqualify themselves. They also must independently figure out how to best navigate the course, acting as their own coaches. It is a very individual game, requiring discipline and maturity – especially for ten-year olds, which is the age we start players.

There is a tendency for kids to come in with great expectations of their ability to win, not realizing how many great players there are out there and how much skill building is required to become such an athlete. For example, at first, many focus on hitting the 'long ball', hitting the ball as far as possible to impressive effect. Through the program they learn the short game, near the green and on the green itself, is just as important, since it is the only way to be consistent in scoring. Mental readiness plays just as big a part as physical skills. The best golfers are relaxed and patient, thinking clearly about each challenge in front of them rather than trophies at the end.

We do our best to instill in the players the value of good sportsmanship, integrity and honesty. The kids themselves help hold up these values, reprimanding anyone who doesn't play fair. Usually if I have to step in, it's because I'm asked to by the other players. Since the golf courses donate their green fees for the players, we arrange for our players to thank the course management for the opportunity to play there.

Occasionally the temptation to impress can lead to cheating on scorecards. We keep parents away from events to avoid interference and unnecessary pressure as best as possible. The other way we deal with it is to place them where the questionable score ranks them in the next tournament, playing with others who achieved the same results. Not only can players in these foursomes easily follow the scores of the others in the group, it is clear if one player isn't keeping up with the others. If a player shoots a similar score this time around, they can remain in higher ranked group. If they don't, they go back to where they were until they are truly ready to progress.

Through our program, I've seen troubled youth with a bad attitude turn around to become inspirational leaders focused on helping others who were like them when they started out. To me, this is the greatest part of the game and why I continue running the tour.

I wanted to find a way to officially acknowledge players in the program exhibiting excellent sportsmanship and setting the example for others. The opportunity came through my home golf course, the Montecito Country Club and its Men's Golf Club. This group approached with the offer to contribute to the program in acknowledgement of my decades of commitment towards youth golf. They suggested the purchase and sponsorship of a trophy, named after me. The Nomura Cup was born, recognizing the most inspirational player on the tour, as voted on by the players themselves at the end of year awards banquet. It isn't about who is the best player, but who is the most considerate, supportive and respected.

I remember one player, Sean Yamasaki, who started out as a ten-year-old in the program and participated through to his graduation in high school. Sean was never the top player, even though he was a champion wrestler, and started out struggling to score well. Yet he always had a positive attitude and was full of encouragement for others, including his competitors. As he moved up into the older age group, he mentored the younger players especially with reining in frustration and showing respect for the course and others. He always participated with a sense of good humor, even if he didn't take home the wins. In his final year in the program, he was shocked to be handed the big gold Nomura Cup, with a standing ovation from his peers.

The program has had great success in turning out high achieving athletes. Golf Digest rated our program as one of the best junior tours in the country, based on the opportunities offered at such a low cost, and the many successful players it has produced. Approximately sixty players have become Professional Golf Association members, either working in the industry or as players on tour. We have also helped approximately ten players a year onto college teams and every year, around three players from our program are granted golf scholarships to top universities.

These are great accomplishments, but I am most proud of seeing almost every student come away with new maturity and personal growth. Many players have gone on to become great adults and leaders of their communities.

Recently one former junior golfer sent me a note, after seeing me on television in my mayoral role and wrote, "I can't wait to come out with my girls and introduce them to you. My experience with the Santa Barbara Junior Golf Association and you made me the good person and great father I am."

Words like that make all the work involved with the program worthwhile.

11. FLYING ON AIR

Motorcycling is in my blood. My father always had a fascination for machinery. I remember vividly from my childhood an old photo of him before he was married, sitting on an old Indian Scout motorcycle he owned before leaving for the military service and Korea.

I had my first taste of motorcycling when my brother let me ride his new minibike up in the mountains. I was instantly hooked.

I saved up and bought my own bike, a 1972 Honda SL 125, one of the first dual sport bikes. It was designed to handle all kinds of terrain, back when most bikes were made for roads and owners would have to make modifications themselves to make them ready for dirt riding.

Soon my sisters Wynne and Wendy wanted bikes too, and we started riding every weekend in the desert and mountains. During every family vacation Weldon and I would explore all kinds of country roads. Weldon had the edge on me to start with. He would go faster, with ease I envied. One day we were out in the desert and we made up our own loop to race. When we were in a river wash, I decided to blast through a line of sage brush to make the pass. Before I knew it, I went flying over the bars, my wheel hitting a large rock hidden within the vegetation. I landed safely in some soft sand, but the next moment I saw my motorcycle was coming at me. It was flipping end over end, and landed perfectly upside down, pinning me to the ground. I couldn't push it off for fear the exhaust pipe or engine would fall on me and burn me.

After about ten minutes I saw Weldon coming around on the next lap, fear all over his face. "I thought you were dead!" he exclaimed, before bursting into laughter.

When my mother heard about it, she just shook her head. "When are you going to learn? You shouldn't ride so fast."

Roxanne loved motorcycles too and joined in with my family's adventures. When we got married, we didn't have a lot of money, so we decided to go camping in the Western Sierras as our honeymoon and take the bikes to explore. We chose a place in the Kings Canyon area below Yosemite, with beautiful mountain views.

At the time I only had two motorcycles, the only one Roxanne could ride being my Honda SL 125, I had converted into a flat track bike. I had removed the front brakes and kick starter to reduce engine drag, meaning Roxanne had real trouble on turns since she had no way to slow down. I had no choice but to ride my bike up the trail, then walk back to get Roxanne and ride the Honda up to the same spot with her on the back. As the trail got worse, I had to do it ten times, meaning I walked nearly the entire four miles of the trail. Since riding up the mountains had lost its appeal we headed back home, exhausted and tempers frayed.

We didn't stop riding together though. Her favorite bike was my 2003 Harley Davidson V-Rod, their centennial limited-edition model with the new Revolution water-cooled motor, installed with custom seats I designed and had made by Corbin. Roxanne said the back seat was as comfortable as a sofa – we would go riding on it for hours to destinations like Monterey, California or Mammoth Lakes.

We were riding nearly every weekend before my kids were born, and after that we started including them in our adventures at a young age. I took Lisa out on my bike even before she could walk in a child backpack, with her talking and singing as we rode around.

I also used to ride with friends who were into flat track dirt racing which I got a real taste for. It was a time when motocross was becoming more and more popular, so I bought my first real race bike, a Czechoslovakian CZ 250cc which was having success on the world scene. I started riding every chance I could get. I loved testing my limits and the way it felt to go fast. I dreamed of the day of becoming pro. My first race was in Santa Barbara, on the land the airport is now based. I was so nervous I was shaking uncontrollably, every muscle in my body tense. When the gate fell, despite how fast we were going, it seemed almost like we were all on a normal road, since we all kept pace with one another.

The faster I tried to go, the more mistakes I would make, and someone else would pass me. When I came to the jump section, I hit the throttle and flew into the air. I landed with the throttle still on, the bike standing up in a wheelie. I kept the gas on and flew by two riders in front still up on my back wheel. I was feeling pretty hot until I saw the corner coming up. I was going too fast, and off the track I went at full speed, eventually stopping a hundred feet away from the track. I continued racing, slowly improving and moving up the results. I spent hours with my sister Wendy working on my motorcycles. I would tear the engines down to see what was going on inside. I started to experiment with making improvements of my own. I could take a motorcycle apart down to the transmission in less than an hour and have it back together again in about the same time. I was once asked to be a mechanic for Japanese National Champion Koji Masuda, sponsored by Suzuki, who came to California for a time to work on his prototype racing bike.

I took a break from motorcycle racing when I started racing bicycles, though I still rode for fun in my spare time. Near the end of my BMX career, I decided to race a four-stroke national on my father's new Honda 100 in the mini class. The track had a good size double jump that large bikes were having trouble clearing.

The jump was difficult because there was no run, with a short straight that was all sand, but I decided to go for it and sailed over it on the first try. On the next round, I jumped it again. I was in fourth place, and the three riders ahead had chosen not to jump it. Mid-air I realized I was going to land on top of one of the lead riders coming out from between the jumps. I did my best to land softly and somehow we both avoided serious injury.

On that same lap I went through a sweeping left hander and I slid my bike under the three other riders to pass them, only to have my rear tire hook a groove. Down I went.

I jumped back up and kicked the bike to start, but no matter how many times I did so, it just wouldn't start. I ended up pushing the bike back to the pits.

In 1986, I once again entered a four-stroke national and decided to race in the open class, with full size bikes, and the mini stock bike classes. In the qualifying round for the open class I placed second. As I was resting for the main race, a wind came up and took off part of the tent above me. A pole crashed down striking me on the bridge of my nose, breaking it. I missed the open class race I had been waiting for, but by the time the main event came around, I was determined to race and win.

By then my nose had swelled up so much I could not wear goggles and as the gate dropped, my bike stalled. I could see all the other riders speeding off as I tried to figure out what was wrong. My petcock was switched off by my well-meaning friend. I adjusted it, then my bike started on the first kick. The other racers were already into their second and third turn. I rode like I never have before, never shutting off the throttle. I was riding like a man possessed and on the very last lap passed the leader in midair. After racing motorcycles off and on for fifteen years, that first place earned me my one and only motorcycle trophy.

Motorcycles continue to mean a lot to me, even if I don't get out on the road as often as I'd like. A couple of years ago, on a trip to Birmingham, Alabama for Rotary, I was hosted by Rotarians Bill and Mary Lou Petty, who took me to see some of the local sights. This included the Barber Vintage Motorsports Museum and Speedway, the largest motorcycle museum in the world with over a thousand vintage and modern motorcycles in its collection. I saw many of the bikes I have owned throughout the decades, summoning memories of my experiences with each of them – the exhilaration of the rides, the many places I had seen riding them on the open road. It was an emotional encounter I will be forever grateful to Bill and Mary Lou for giving me the opportunity to experience.

I now have a collection of vintage, dirt, naked, street legal enduro, and large Harley cruiser bikes. Motorcycle riding remains one of my greatest diversions from life's pressures. Riding brings freedom – the feeling as if I am flying on air. Wind, sights, sounds and scents are all heightened with adrenalin. The vibration of the bike on the road and the roar of the engine evoke memories of past adventures. There is always the promise of a new unique journey around every bend of the road.

Motorcycle riding is a family passion:

Wade and Weldon riding at Mammoth Lakes, California cc1975 (Weldon taking photo).

Left: Roxanne in foreground, Wynne Nomura in back Guadalupe, California 2008 (Wade taking photo).
Right: Wade and Weldon going for a ride, Carpinteria, California 2020.

12. AN UNLIKELY CAREER

My BMX career started in the most unlikely way. One of my early landscaping jobs was in a low-income project housing development. As I worked, five kids ranging from ten to thirteen years would come around and hang out. They were curious about everything, asking me all kinds of questions.

I began to see they were waiting for me each day when I arrived. I realized they had a tough road ahead in life, with little chance to step beyond their disadvantaged neighborhood and its social problems, so I gave them all the time I could.

Soon I found out a gang member from the projects did not like them hanging out with me. He claimed he was a Golden Gloves boxing champion and if they kept talking with me, he was going beat me up. I could see him lurking in the background as they told me this, so I laughed loudly, "A boxer is no match for Judo champion. He can try and take me down any time he wants. Since he's a friend of yours I won't hurt him too bad." That was the last I saw or heard of the guy.

I could see clearly if the kids had nothing to do, they would easily be absorbed into these gangs. At that time, I was racing motorcycles and competing in events. I offered to take them out to some dirt tracks, and let them have turns riding on the back of my bike. They jumped at the chance and the six of us set out for the day. As they started getting braver, I started going faster and flying farther on the jumps.

They loved it and we started going regularly each week. I also took them to watch me practice on some of the tracks I would race on and let them ride my children's small motorcycles. They told me they wanted to someday race too – but since I knew they were never going to be able to afford to race motorcycles, I thought about BMX. It was a growing sport at the time, they could start experimenting with their own bicycles.

They got a real taste for it and started getting pretty good. The problem was their bikes were pieced together from scrap parts they had found. To have any chance racing they needed real BMX bikes.

Since I had at the time only a small landscape operation with four employees and the kids were always there, I offered to pay them to do some small jobs for me and told them I'd match whatever they saved towards buying BMX bikes.

They embraced the opportunity; whenever I turned up, they were ready to help. They weeded garden beds, raked leaves and helped clean up and put the equipment away each day. I also had them start collecting aluminum cans and other recyclable items we could redeem for cash.

About this time, my sister Wendy and I were considering starting a new business since she needed a job. We decided to open up a retail BMX bicycle shop, so we could get the bikes for the kids and motorcycle parts for me at wholesale prices. Nomura Racing was born.

Wendy ran the shop while I landscaped, and I would come and work on bikes in the afternoons. The kids and I got enough to buy two brand new BMX bikes along with helmets and other equipment, and set off for the BMX track in Goleta. They all raced that first day, but did not do well against the other racers who had been at it for years.

A lot of the experienced racers were keen to talk to me, since we had opened a specialty shop. Even though I did my best to retain the friendship of the project kids, we slowly started seeing each other less and less.

It still pains me greatly we gradually fell out of touch. I heard decades later one had committed suicide and another was in jail. The experience left me with a sharp picture how difficult it is to escape the trap of disadvantage; I wish I could have done more.

Yet I also found out many of the racer kids hanging around the shop were having family troubles. They were looking for a way to get away from this on weekends and didn't necessarily have anyone to take them to tracks further away. My brother Weldon and I started taking them to Los Angeles nearly every weekend to race, hooking up a trailer crammed with bikes to the back of my truck. We figured not only was it good to help out, it was also a good way to promote our business and meet potential new customers.

At one of the events in Monrovia, which happened to be on Father's Day, they were running a special Father's race. My team ended up talking me into it. I had built a bike since starting up the bike shop just to ride around for fun and happened to have it with me. I ended up winning by a significant margin. I was surprised there were so many other fathers that had their own bikes, with some of them even racing regularly.

The kids told me I should start racing since, "I was pretty fast for an old guy." I signed up for the Cruiser class – the larger of the two BMX bike classes. Cruisers were named after the bikes that gained popularity amongst beachgoers of Southern California. The smaller, traditional models were instead based on the more agile Schwinn Stingray bikes.

I ended up doing well, each week moving up more in the results.

Weldon also decided to give it a try, and we built a bike for him too, with him coming along on our racing trips.

That winter, the National Bicycle Association held their national championship in Las Vegas. The only place we could find to stay was a room at a terrible hotel. Eleven of us crammed into one room with a leaky roof, a fact we became well acquainted with because it rained all night. We left for the track before the sun came up.

At the race, they announced a special exhibition race for anyone twenty-six years or older, since the promoter and owner of the sanctioning body had like me, just turned twenty-seven. I was first off the starting line and well in the lead of the ten others by the first turn. I was never challenged during the race and crossed the finish line in first place. It was my first national race and first national win. Since it was the finals, I was immediately recognized as a national champion.

The new class of racing opened up the following year, the twenty-seven and over Cruiser class. I entered every race and won over three quarters of them, earning my next national title in that class.

Wade Nomura leading the pack.

For the next four years, we travelled to events across the country. During the summer when the kids were out of school, our trips ramped up to every weekend. Since I could not afford to fly myself and a team to all the events, I bought a motorhome and hitched a trailer we filled with bikes. We would easily cover twelve thousand miles in a ten-week period, experiencing adventures across all different states. I started sponsoring some racers who were in contention for national championships. Many came from households working hard to just get by, with parents happy for them to come with me on the road.

Our crew had a collection of colorful nicknames. There was 'Insane' Wayne Croasdale, Billy 'Gumby' Harrison, Turnell 'Tuni' Henry and Billy 'Yoda' Light. Lisa and Ryan were 'Little' and 'Kato' respectively, and I was the 'Old Kook'.

I remember one time we were driving through Texas at the height of summer when the air conditioning went out. The heat and humidity were unbearable and I drove with as few breaks as possible to get back to the Pacific Coast. As we travelled through one small town, the only traffic light for miles turned red. As I came to a stop, the kids all jumped out. I was concerned for a moment someone had fallen out somehow, only to hear laughter. I spun around to see them all running towards a motel with a fenced pool on the roadside. Within a minute, they had all climbed over the fence and plunged in.

I was furious and as I pulled over, I saw the motel manager emerging from his office. His face slackened in shock at the sight of this wild tribe of youths that sprung out of nowhere splashing about. He rushed back into his office and I ran over to the kids trying to get them out, thinking he has probably calling the police.

Then I noticed the manager had reappeared, with a camera. Instead of yelling, he took a snapshot of the scene. "You guys must be from California," he said to me, smiling, "I needed to get a picture because no one would believe me." He then invited us to stay awhile and cool off before starting back on our way home. One of the ways we paid for our travels was by giving racing seminars along the way, as well as one on one instruction sessions for the super enthusiastic. People were hungry for our knowledge of the increasingly popular BMX sport, wanting to learn our techniques and strategies. We would also do autograph and photo signing at restaurants in exchange for meal and gas money.

One of the places we were invited was in the extreme north corner of Wisconsin. It was organized for us to run a clinic for locals in a remote area about three hours in the middle of nowhere. We passed by a Native American reservation and an Amish community, though most of the roadside was just forest. When we eventually made it to the track, we were greeted by a crowd of about a hundred people. Our racing clinics usually attracted a maximum of forty people in much more populated areas, so this was pretty surprising in a town of about five hundred.

The group was made up of much more than racers, with many family groups ranging from infants to elderly grandparents. The entire group was engaged with our lessons, walking with us to each of the areas of the track we were working on. We discussed racing tactics, techniques for starts, straights, turns and jumps. It actually helped that family members were present, since they were following everything we said and made sure to tell the racers if they were missing a point of instruction.

Once we were finished, I asked some of the older attendees why they and all the others had come. They said, "To meet you! We have never had someone famous come to our town. Also, we've never seen an oriental in person before."

I was pretty shocked to say the least. Firstly, I'd never really thought of myself as someone with celebrity status. I also found it quite strange to be a spectacle, like an elephant in a traveling circus. However, it was kindly meant – such an isolated area really did have very little contact with minorities, so they had little idea of 'protocol'. When I asked if anyone would be interested in an autograph, a big line formed. It was probably spoken of for years and years afterwards, the time that a Japanese racer came to town.

Another time, we were invited to a racetrack on Navajo land near Albuquerque, New Mexico. I was told by a racer from a nearby town the locals would not take well to being beaten on their own track. To avoid any trouble, I told my racers to play it safe and leave the top spot for someone else. However, at the start of racing their lead rider crashed, putting my four racers in the four top spots. I decided we may as well go all in and told them to forget about what I had said, and go as hard as they could because it was too late now. We ended up with a clean sweep that day, winning a total of sixteen races.

At the end of the day, we were packing up our bikes when a crowd of around twenty locals approached, making us pretty nervous. We weren't sure what the consequences could be of showing them up on their home turf. Their leader came to the front of the crowd, facing us down. "You had a very good race," he said.

"We got lucky," I replied, cautiously.

He scoffed. "Luck had nothing to do with it. You are the fastest team we've ever seen. Never before has anyone come onto our land and won."

He apparently had no idea others were advising visitors to make sure they didn't win. He invited us all out to a big community barbeque and we had a great night enjoying their hospitality. One of the local racers was talented enough for a spot on our national team. If all our spots weren't already filled, we would have taken him on. He was soon picked up by another team however, so all ended well.

Touring felt a bit like being a Wild West cowboy, roaming the wilderness for months at a time. After one ten-week tour, I was to meet Roxanne and Ryan at Bakersfield. As I approached, Roxanne frowned. She later confessed she quite literally did not recognize me.

It had been so hot I'd spent most of the time in board shorts and Vans tennis shoes, so my skin was tanned and dark. My hair had gotten shaggy, and I'd lost twenty pounds from all the exercise and irregular meals. Around me were a bunch of kids she didn't recognize. I started the tour with four racers and finished with nine. We had picked up along the way the two Bauer boys in Michigan, John McHenry from Colorado, Bernstein from Minnesota and Eric O'Connell from New Mexico. They'd all decided to tag along for the rest of the summer, visiting the famous racetracks of Southern California.

I made a lot of great memories on those trips and I'm happy to have given a lot of young people opportunities they would never have experienced otherwise.

13. Nomura Racing

I always look for ways to improve whenever possible and BMX bike riding was no exception. I began researching bikes to give me a mechanical edge over competitors, however was met with limited options. I set out to develop a frame of my own.

I started by charting the exact details and dimensions of as many of the popular bike frames I could find. Since this was long before easily accessible computer design programs, I graphed this data on paper to make comparisons. I also started asking riders which bikes were fastest off the gate, in sprint, over jumps and through turns.

Comparing the comments with the bike measurements, I discovered trends – for example, the shorter the rear of the bike and longer the front triangle, the faster they went. Lower bottom brackets added to stability over jumps. The steeper the steering head angle, the better the bike would turn.

Using this information, I drafted the design for my first frame. It was the lowest bike on the market, with a long front end with a 74-degree steering head angle. The distance between the bottom bracket to rear axle was as short as possible.

At the time, most bikes were made out of steel. I looked into titanium though found it difficult to work with, too springy for track with a tendency to fracture. Aluminum was another possibility. At the time there were a handful of frames made from it, though most of low quality. I found out I would be able to get some high grade, aircraft-certified material, which was light and strong. It meant segments could be layered much thicker than steel frames, increasing their strength but not their weight. I also found out about flat oval tubing designed for the Lockheed space shuttle, but never used for its intended application. This would allow for a thin profile with enough strength to keep the bottom bracket stiff.

I created the first prototype with the help of Hall of Fame and Bonneville salt flats legend Tim Rochlitzer. When we test rode it on the track, we found it was much smoother than other bikes, the aluminum actually helping absorb the vibration from the track surface. We did make some adjustments though, including increasing the wall thickness in parts to increase the strength further. Yet when it was done, it was as much as eight pounds lighter than some of the other cruiser frames.

In 1980, the Nomura Racing team rode the bike to victory in all six of the US National Bicycle Association Cruiser classes from age ten to the 27 and over category, ridden by myself. This had never been done before, or since.

We went into production, with me machining parts. As we built the frames, I would machine some of the parts that needed to be lathed or milled and fit the frame tubes into the fixtures Tim built out of steel stock. I would then take them to a welder and another facility for heat-treating.

After that, I hand polished them to a chrome like finish. It was a real chore, but necessary since after we outsourced this a number of them went 'missing'. We would then send them out to be anodized in a variety of colors. Once the production was complete, Wendy and I would box them up and send them out. Most ended up going to cities in the United States, but we did have a few frames go to Germany, England and Australia.

They were the first and probably one of the only exotic BMX bikes ever built, since there isn't a broad market for them.

Wade leading the race with the national number 1 plate.

Nomura racing team members in red and white outfits, Wade on right hand side.

They cost more than double the average BMX frame price, since they were handmade and in limited production. Demand was far higher than we could match with supply.

I also designed a chrome moly steel frame later in my career to cater to larger riders, manufactured by the CW Racing Company. These frames were bigger, had a slightly taller crank height, and I used the chain stay material to create a boxed in rear drop out. The six-foot tall members of the Nomura Racing team, Turnell "Tuni" Henry and "Insane" Wayne Croasdale, rode these in competition with success.

14. The Pro

As an amateur BMX rider, I became one of the most successful racers in the history of the sport, winning eighty-five percent of the races I entered. In 1981, I was at the peak of my amateur career. I had already won a few national titles in my age group and I had gained a Number One National plate and title.

It was time to start thinking about the future. People started telling me I should turn pro. This would mean competing against the best in the world. I had raced many of these riders at a local level, so knew how tough it would be. But I had managed to hold my own against them though, plus pro level would increase the media coverage of myself and my brand.

About that time, we also started hearing rumors the Olympic committee was considering including BMX as an exhibition sport in 1984. Pros weren't going to be eligible, which would mean the best of the sport would be unable to compete for spots. I could have a good chance at being an Olympian, if I was competing against other amateurs.

Not only that, I could even have a shot at a medal. Since BMX began in the United States, we had a decade old racing scene, with the chance to compete almost any day of the week somewhere in California against other nationally ranked racers. BMX riders elsewhere in the world would be well behind. So, I waited, to hear the Olympic Committee's decision.

The news came in – BMX was not chosen for inclusion. With the encouragement of friends and family, I decided to turn pro. I made the submission for my professional license in 1983, months before my thirtieth birthday. At the time, I was the oldest racer to ever turn pro.

I found out immediately pro racing was much tougher than being an amateur. My competitors were bigger, faster, stronger. They were in their early twenties but had been BMX riding for most of their lives.

The challenges of making a main event were increasingly difficult. There were very few races when at least one racer didn't crash, since we were all taking risks to try and place. I was pretty much always nursing an injury of some sort. Here my age was against me again, since the younger players healed and recovered much faster.

One race the track was so drenched from rain we were all riding through deep mud, with the track lined with deep ruts. I got caught in one and went down, only to have my foot run over by my own bike. Afterwards, I went to the doctor to have it checked out.

The doctor asked to have both my right and left foot x-rayed so he could compare the two. He brought me the print outs looking puzzled. "You've broken your foot. Actually, you've broken both of them." I was equally confused. "But only my right foot was run over?" It turned out I'd broken the left foot probably around two or three months prior, based on the healing that had taken place.

A far greater challenge was the mental stress I had to cope with. I lived life on the road for the most part, travelling from race to race, seeing little of my family. I could hardly sleep for days before a race, worrying if I would get there in time, what the conditions would be like, if my injuries would set me back, knowing I needed to place high enough to get a paycheck to continue on and hoping not to get injured bad enough to not be able to drive home. I continued to compete on tour in the hopes there would be a breakthrough moment, and everything would fall into place.

Producing a first-class bike wasn't the only way I went about securing an edge. I instituted a grueling workout regime, and at some point, exercising sixteen hours a day. Back then we did not have trainers as knowledgeable or specialized as today, so I came up with drills that would strengthen my body and mind.

I drew on my experience in other sports to create workouts honing my strength, speed, technique, endurance and flexibility. I drew upon a lot of my experience in other sports such as Judo and high school track, constantly evaluating my weaknesses and adapting my training to compensate. I worked on my endurance using Cross Country running techniques, however I soon found this affected my speed. So, I added in speed workouts onto the end of every endurance training session. I also practiced stunts like wheelies and jumps, to further hone my control and capabilities on the bike.

Being a perfectionist led me to internalizing more than was healthy. If I failed to win, whether it was from a bad start, a small misjudgment, or crash, I would hear comments, "I'd lost my edge". I was even harder on myself.

There were a lot of perks, though. As I was handed a trophy, all the difficulties evaporated for a while. The media started following me more, with local television and radio stations asking for interviews. Fans would come up to me for autographs. It was my first taste of fame; the buzz was exhilarating. I can definitely see how it could go to your head, especially if you were a young person.

The beginning of the end came during a prerace in Las Vegas, when I spotted an opening at the edge of a track over a jump. I went for it, however caught some soft sand and was launched sixteen feet into the air. I broke my collarbone, shoulder blade and two ribs, as well as punctured my lung. At the hospital, the doctors were concerned my lungs had collapsed. Miraculously, overnight they re-inflated and I was taken off the list for surgery.

I didn't help myself by taking only a week off to recover before starting racing again, leading me to fall on my shoulder and do more damage. After taking a longer break – a month – I set out training again for a competition at the local track in the Azusa area of Southern California. I figured the competition was not that strong so it would be a good way to ease back into competition. But I crashed on the first turn and broke my shoulder again.

I looked at my options. With so many injuries, it was unlikely I would ever make it back to top condition and I didn't want to hang around a shadow of my old self. So, I chose to walk away from the sport.

In five years of racing, I had won over a thousand trophies. My record as an amateur competitor was impeccable. Amongst my wins were five national titles, including two National Bicycle Association and two National BMX Association titles. It's been 35 years since I retired from BMX racing, yet rarely a week goes by without me hearing from someone reminiscing about those days.

On Saturday March 4, 2000, I received an unexpected recognition of my legacy in the sport. One day, I got a call from Roxanne's cousin, Grace. She asked if my son Ryan would be interested in participating in a display at the Japanese American Museum of Los Angeles on Japanese American athletes. I was thrilled Ryan had built up his reputation as a professional golfer enough to be considered. However, Grace said he may not be selected, as they were giving preference to athletes who had been national champions. As a proud parent,

I mentioned Lisa had been a BMX national champion in the same year I won my second national. Later that day, Grace called back to say the chair was interested in my career and to send her more information.

I ended up being one of forty-two athletes chosen for the More Than A Game exhibition, including professional, amateur and Olympic athletes from baseball, football, basketball, bowling, surfing and more. They borrowed some of my racing memorabilia to display, including some of my winning bikes, racing gear and trophies.

The opening of the exhibition and induction to the Japanese American Hall of Fame was hosted in a huge hotel in downtown Los Angeles. At that stage of my life, I wasn't used to such large-scale events, and was somewhat overwhelmed. There were more than a thousand people in attendance. Each inductee was spaced out between the sponsor tables; I was surprised to find I had been seated with none other than Lew Abe of Carpinteria and his family, who had been my boss and mentor before I got married and went off to college. He had no idea I was being inducted that night. It nevertheless felt meaningful to me he was present, since he had given me such important guidance which had made many of my achievements possible.

At one point in the evening the Emcee, television sports commentator Rob Fukuzaki, boomed out my name and it was time to get up on stage, with a big screen behind me lit up with photos of me racing. I stood with other inductees in a line in front of everyone, truly humbled to be honored with such company. I was able to speak with some of my fellow athletes afterwards, finding we shared many parallels in life, not only in our sporting challenges but in the discrimination we had to overcome to succeed.

Television film crews were there, capturing the event and interviewing all the athletes. They asked all of us the same question, "What do you attribute your success to?"

The answer didn't immediately occur to me. I started thinking about all the challenges I faced, the many broken bones and injuries, countless hours of working out, tight budgets and driving enormous distances across the country. Yet none of this would have been possible without the endless support from my family. It was my family and friends who celebrated my successes and encouraged me to continue. It was all those that had influenced me and motivated me to succeed no matter what I did, to make them proud.

So, I gave my answer: "My success came from those who believed in me and shared my dream. It was my wife, family and friends who believed in me and sacrificed so I could succeed".

Despite many invitations, including being asked to participate in a Legends of BMX series around the world, I have never raced again. I have however maintained contact with many BMXers and attended various reunions, including in Melbourne Australia. I still hear from my past racers, some thirty years later. Many have told me racing with me was one of the highlights of their lives, thanking me for being there for them when they were at their most troubled. Some even said I was their role model, a good example in a world of bad. I never had any idea of the impact I was having at the time. Many are now coaching their own kids in sports, working on the same principles of good sportsmanship, discipline and respect for themselves and others.

Tim and I wrapped up making Nomura frames on my retirement. However, I was approached by Kawasaki to design a 'Nomura' bike. I declined; on the basis I would not have any say in how my name was used after I was paid.

In subsequent years, Nomura frames have become highly collectible amongst enthusiasts. When I visited Sydney in 2018, a collector wheeled his Nomura frame across the city, all the way to the Sydney Aquarium I was visiting, so I could sign it. I've had some impressive offers for some of my personal bikes. I declined, since they are irreplaceable, but it's nice to know my creations and career is still appreciated. I was called at one point the 'Grandfather of the modern BMX bike' for my innovations which were replicated in the decades that followed.

Many people have asked if I would consider starting up production of my own frames again. I have considered retrofitting new features into our timeless classic at some point in the future.

15. BEHIND THE LENS

My first camera was a Kodak Instamatic, one of those cheap disposable types. Even as a little kid I remember being fascinated by the ability of photos to freeze a moment in time forever. But I remembered also being disappointed with the results of my efforts. When the photos came back, they were a pale reflection of what I originally saw, flat and lifeless.

My Uncle Joe was interested in photography also, and would go through my photos with me, explaining how I could improve each shot. I learned proper photography was far more than just clicking a button. I needed to learn principles such as how to balance the objects in the image to enhance the subject and how to capture the light.

Uncle Joe also suggested I get a better camera, since improved equipment would help with capturing more dynamic images. When I was about twelve, my father brought home a proper camera for my brother and I. I would take photos on our adventures, action shots of us doing sports as well as the natural wilderness we explored.

I have continued to upgrade my cameras over the years. There have been a lot of changes, most notably the transition from film to digital. I mostly now use professional standard equipment, though this means lugging around a seven-pound camera sometimes for hours at a time.

My photography skills have ended up overlapping with my community service work. I've lost count of the number of times I've been asked to be the photographer for events from Rotary conferences to Boys and Girls Club fundraisers. Photographing people is very different to landscapes. Posed shots are nice but

I prefer capturing spontaneous moments.

Recently I used my telephoto lens to capture some candid shots of people in a crowd of Rotarians. A friend of mine, Dick Elixman, spotted me taking photos and as I panned over to him he beamed and waved. A few days later, he passed away, with this photo the last of him ever taken. His kindness and energy shines bright in the shot, an unplanned moment preserving a glimpse of his spirit forever.

I'm often asked what my favorite photo is I have ever taken. Truthfully, I don't know. Some I like because they are artistically and technically correct. Others are special to me because they take me back to a time and place, evoking wonderful memories. I appreciate the ability of a visual image to translate multi-layers of meaning in an instant. One photograph I took in Moradabad, India, for example, shows the stark contrast between those living in slums alongside open sewage flowing, and looming in the background, a highway and bridge under construction, representing the approaching modernization and development.

I'm most grateful for photography teaching me to find the beauty in everyday life. I've learned to focus on the unique attractions of all the places I visit. Even in mundane scenes there are slices of unique beauty ready to be discovered.

I've also spent time in front of the camera. This began when our neighbor Dana, a photography student at Brooks Institute, asked my family and I to model for one of her assignments. Later, she put us forward for a paid modeling gig for Coleman Outdoor Equipment. The set was a staged campsite in the mountains. The director asked us to sit around an unlit campfire in folding chairs, in front of a tent.

We were also asked to bring our dog Herbie who was excited by all the new sights and sounds. The kids complained they were freezing and asked to get inside the tent out of the cold wind while they were waiting, since the staged camping heater had no fuel or batteries; like everything else it was a new item straight out of the package.

Soon the wind came up even more and started blowing the empty chairs away. The props fell over one by one, having to be reset for each shot. Herbie started getting bored and wouldn't sit still. Meanwhile, the director was losing his mind as one thing after another went wrong.

The final shot that made the magazine advertisement, Lisa and Ryan were standing in the doorway of the tent with the screen down, Herbie wandering off set, with Roxanne sitting in her campfire chair with a forced smile on her face, and me cracking up at the chaos of it all.

Dana also asked us to pose for some stock photos for her portfolio. A publisher asked to use one of the photos of myself, Lisa and Ryan in a park playing baseball. I had the bat over my shoulder, tossing a ball to Ryan.

I didn't know this, until a friend of mind asked me if I was still married to Roxanne. I answered, "Yes, why?"

He opened up a magazine he had with him, revealing our photo printed underneath a large title, 'Family life as a single parent.'

It was a more popular publication than I realized, with Roxanne and I suddenly receiving letters and cards offering condolences, asking if we were planning on getting back together, and how the kids were taking it...

Some of Wade's favorite photos:

The slums of Moradabad, India with highway construction approaching.

Ryoan-ji Temple Gardens, Kyoto, Japan

Koi Pond landscape reflection, Hawaii

Carpinteria Beach, California

Through exposure as a BMX racer some more modeling gigs came my way, this time going solo. On one memorable occasion, I was asked to be a model for a new line of Ralph Lauren menswear at a newly opened Nordstrom, to fill their minority quota and help appeal to the Asian customers. At the time I was considered the perfect model sizing with 30" x 30" pants, 15" neck and 30" sleeves and size 8 shoes.

The clothing was summer wear, with shorts, sandals, and polo as one set, and a casual business look with slacks, loafers, button down shirt, and sports coat as the other. I thought this would go more like a normal photo shoot, where I would stand there and pose – boy was I wrong.

When I showed up, I realized it was a runway assignment and the audience was 100% women. I'd never done anything like that before. I would have been way more comfortable jumping 50 feet on a bicycle. Not only would I have to walk, the clothing change time was set to two minutes.

When it was my turn, I walked out trying to pace myself to match the upbeat music, finish within my assigned runway time, while looking poised and friendly.

I have never felt so awkward in my life. Yet the women seemed to love it. I was asked to stop and strike a front and back pose by a number of women in the audience, their eyes roaming all over me. I also happened to be the only model subjected to this 'closer inspection'.

Then came change time behind a curtain to the summer outfit, which I pulled off just in time to go back out. The second time around I was asked by the same women to stop and pose. Then I was back out on stage for the finale.

My payment for the assignment was in the way of merchandise and a generous amount Nordstrom credits. Despite this, I vowed never to do a runway again. Even though I was asked multiple times to reconsider, nothing was worth that kind of embarrassment.

Sometime after this, Roxanne came from work and told me I had been asked to consider another modeling assignment, but she'd already declined it for me. Since she had never done that before I was curious what this assignment had been.

Apparently, they had been looking for an Asian male with young, athletic build. The client had been a personal security company producing blow up dolls for women able to be placed in the passenger seat of a car so they would not appear to be alone. Roxanne laughed, "Can you imagine all my friends saying they kept seeing you with other women?"

It is comforting I am able to say, "No, I have never been a model for a blow-up doll."

16. SMALL TOWN CHARM

Carpinteria is a special little town. Even people who have lived in Southern California their whole lives often pass it by, knowing it as nothing more than the name of a place along the highway. Hidden away are lots of exceptional people and the traditions that have popped up in our little haven away from the rest of the world.

As I mentioned previously, Carpinteria is unusual in the number of people involved in community service. More than 1% of our adult population are members of Rotary clubs, and Lions International also has a strong presence. On the Fourth of July the Lion's Club hosts a barbeque with hundreds from the local community gathering to dance to live music played by local bands comprised of locals throwing off their everyday guises to become eighties rock stars and country western crooners.

We have a year round colony of Harbor Seals who raise their pups on one of our golden beaches. A dedicated group of volunteers oversee the seal rookery, taking shifts to watch the colony from the bluffs above to ensure they are not disturbed by people or wandering animals during breeding season, as well as carefully monitoring their numbers and health. The sight of mothers and pups lazing in the sun, occasionally playing in the shallows and barking with excitement, is a scene Carpinterians take pride in protecting.

Photos:
1. Carpinteria beach sunset.
2. Carpinteria Bluffs with Harbor Seals gathered in foreground.

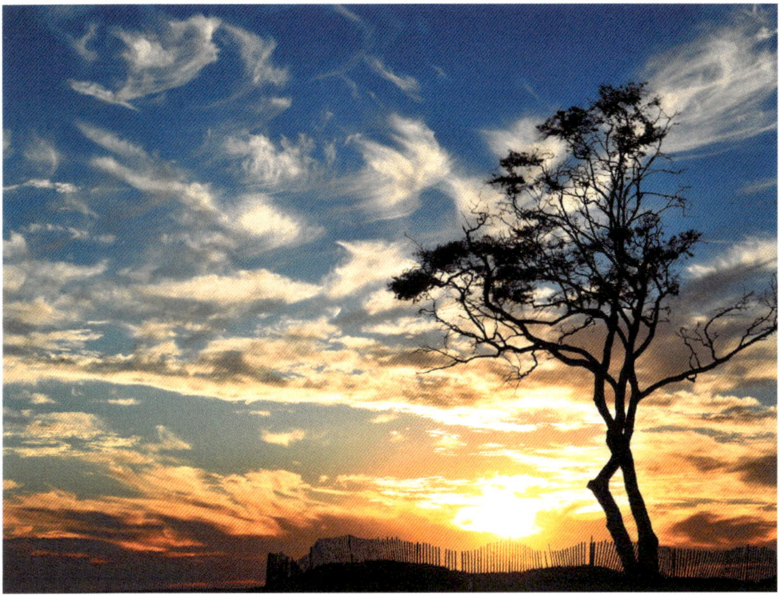

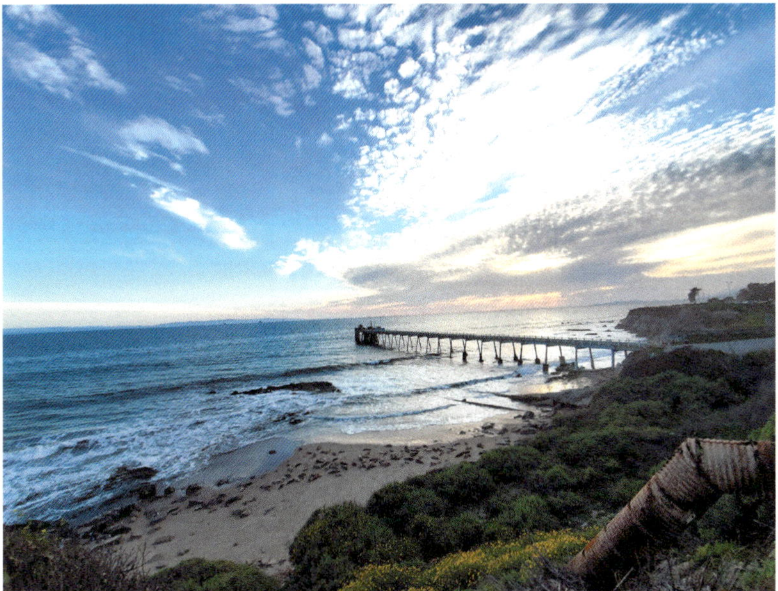

Every year Carpinteria recognizes the contributions of local volunteers at an annual awards night hosted by the Carpinteria Valley Chamber of Commerce. The event honors individuals from local service organizations, who each put forward a Volunteer of the Year for recognition. There are also awards for small and large businesses notable for their community involvement. The night is capped off with the naming of the Junior Carpinterian and Carpinterian of the Year, who carry the honor for life. There is always a huge crowd, including locals as well as representatives from city, county, state and federal government.

Emily Calkins was last year's Junior Carpinterian of the Year. She began community service early in life, founding a Girl Scout Troop in Carpinteria when she was only in First Grade. This she continued through her school years to achieve a Girl Scout Gold Award in 2018. She additionally served as Student Representative of the Carpinteria Arts Center and on the Cate School Activity Board and Student Alumni Association. Emily represented her school at an international conference in South Africa, was an exchange student in Lima, Peru, and as well, has many academic achievements including a National Scholastic Art and Writing award.

Sixth generation Carpinterian Curtis Lopez was named the 2018 Carpinterian of the Year. There are very few organizations in Carpinteria that have not benefited from his generosity of time, money, energy and talent. He has served as a passionate board member and volunteer for the Carpinteria Education Foundation, Carpinteria Valley Chamber of Commerce, Carpinteria Boys & Girls Club, Girls Inc, Site Committee for the Carpinteria Unified School District and the Carpinteria Lions Club and the Carpinteria Lions Community Building Association. Curtis is also a performer with two local bands,

The Rincons and the Dusty Jugz who perform at many local occasions and fundraisers at no charge.

We have many events raising funds for local charitable causes, the largest being our annual California Avocado Festival which attracts more than 50,000 people over a three-day weekend, supporting the local economy, boosting tourism and raising money for local non-profits. Locals Debbie Murphy and the late Fran Puccinelli came up with the idea, based on the number of avocado growers in the Carpinteria community. As Directors of the Chamber of Commerce, they presented the concept to the rest of the board and rallied community support. A few months later, the first California Avocado Festival was held in 1986.

The festival closes our main street, stretching along four city blocks. It includes local food vendors selling everything avocado: avocado chocolate, avocado beer, avocado ice-cream, avocado pie, avocado brownies, avocado oil, deep-fried avocado, and traditional dishes like guacamole. Many merchants gather to sell arts and crafts, clothing, home décor and more, also with many avocado themed goods like avocado soap and avocado print t-shirts. Plenty of these are run by local non-profits as a way to raise funds, supporting their activities throughout the year. Three bandstands feature live music throughout the festival, with local talent and youth groups joined by headliners from other regions. There is also traditional fairground fun like a Ferris Wheel and museum-style tents displaying local history.

A yearly competition for designing a logo for the event gives visual artists a chance to showcase their skills. This logo finds its way onto caps, poster and other memorabilia. Many Carpinteria businesses have a collection gathered over the years on display throughout the year, demonstrating local pride.

A local is selected as the Honorary Chair, another way to recognize locals who have contributed to our town. In 2019, Betty Brown was chosen, one of the first people in the valley to grow avocadoes on her ranch in the early 1960s. She is well-known as a tireless advocate for children's education and welfare, volunteering and fundraising extensively for the Children's Home Society, Rainbow Girls and Girls Inc of Carpinteria. She's credited, along with her late husband Ralph, with spearheading the $2.46 million fundraising program to build the farm style Girls Inc campus on Foothill Road.

There is a VIP reception where the Honorary Chair of the event and logo designer are honored by the Avocado Festival Association, with all proceeds going to local charities and youth scholarships for higher education. In the typical Carpinterian way, there is a group of volunteers behind the scenes, making the event happen, with heavy weights Mike Lazaro and Gary Dobbins leading the charge.

The Great Canoe Races of Carpinteria were an especially memorable event on the town calendar for me. In 1769, the Spanish Portola expedition happened upon a large village situated on the land point now known as Carpinteria Beach. They noticed the villagers building canoes, inspiring the soldiers to name the place *La Carpinteria* meaning 'the carpentry shop'. These canoes were made from wooden planks sealed with naturally occurring surface asphalt. Petroleum seeps are still visible along the beach bluffs at Tar Pits Park.

Photos:
1. Avocado Festival in the main street of Carpinteria
2. Fourth of July parade - High School tractor entry.
3. Annual Rods and Roses car show.

In 1985, Carpinteria celebrated their 20th anniversary of becoming a city. Because of our history, the promoter thought it would be a great idea to include a 'canoe' race down the main street of Carpinteria. The canoes were made out of cardboard and wood, squeezing in six people with their legs hanging out the bottom. The first to finish the race with the canoe intact would win.

Roxanne wanted to enter and asked me to help out. She had recruited a bunch of coworkers to join the team and talked her real estate broker into sponsoring us. There were about a dozen other entries, including the high school football team and cheerleader squads – in other words the field was stacked with others far more athletic than us.

I never do anything half-way, so I started strategizing ways to give us the edge. I knew how fragile the canoes were and decided to use this to our advantage. Since there was very little room for our feet and legs, I knew it would be worse for the big, muscled types. I told my team to run in stride, matching our right and left feet as we ran. I also knew the other teams were going to be very competitive so I told my team the first thing to do when the starting gun went off was to push the canoe forward as far as we could without moving our feet to give the illusion we were lightning fast off the gate. The other teams thought we were out in front and would try and match us.

It worked. Half the canoes blew up right on the starting line, so they were out of the race. It was difficult running with canoes held around our hips, so we lifted it over our heads to give us more legroom. To everyone's surprise we crossed the finish line way in front of second place.

Three years later, the canoe race came back, this time with ply board canoes running on trash dumpster casters. The team had to sit inside and use oars to row down the street. I was talked into entering the race as 'defending champion'. This time I knew it would take some muscle to win this race, so I recruited the strongest and lightest guys I knew. I wanted to get a huge lead off the start, which we did and never looked back. It was a one-block race and we won by nearly a third of a block.

In 1990, Carpinteria celebrated their 25th anniversary, with calls again for me to defend my title. I'd hung onto my canoe from last time, which I started polishing up early. I lightened the wooden plank 'oars', reshaping them for greater leverage, adding grip tape to the handles and neoprene to the ends so they would not slip on the asphalt. I shaved down the sides for better leverage and hand polished the bearings and races to mirror smooth, before repacking them with racing grease.

To reduce friction, I replaced the axles with high polished stainless-steel bolts, smoothed the bearings and races – just like I would on a racing bicycle and added nylon lock nuts so the tension would not change once I set them. The difference was amazing. Before, I had to turn the wheel as I would a knob, but once I had them set right, they would spin for nearly a minute by themselves.

At the start of the race, the promoter pushed each canoe behind the starting line, so none were further ahead than the others. Normally this took a good shove. When he came to our canoe, he nearly fell face first onto the street, since ours could literally be moved with one finger. He looked at me and laughed, "Only you could figure out how to put an engine into that thing undetected."

When the gun fired and we started out and immediately took a full canoe length lead that kept growing. Unlike the other races, this one had a 180 degree turn around the last section of the road. I gave instructions to slow down and drag our oars on the inside of the turn, as you would do in water. But nothing happened, since we were going so fast. We flew by the turn.

Further down the road we were able to stop the canoe and by slowly turning the canoe around with our oars, get it back on direction. We could see the other canoes way out in front, making the turn to race back to the finish line. As we gathered our speed back, we flew by two canoes almost instantly. But the lead canoe was nearly to the finish line.

As we approached the finish line, I lunged forward, striking the bow support with my shoulder in the hopes it would thrust us past the other canoe. It worked – though it also propelled me so far forward I almost fell out. We were going so fast bystanders had to help grab us to stop us flying off into the next block.

Tom came over immediately and declared us the winners. He said we had won by a head length – mine. Sadly, that was the last time Carpinteria ever held a canoe race, as the promoter and organizer of the event moved to Oregon shortly after that. I've been in a lot of races in my life and though many were much more dangerous, and the stakes were higher, I remain extremely proud of my title as a three-time undefeated champion of the Great Canoe Races of Carpinteria. I hope we'll be able to reinstitute them someday.

A great gift to my life has been what is known as The Breakfast Club, a group of locals who meet up at the famous Jack's Bistro to share a cup of coffee and 'solve the world's problems'. It's not an official club as such, with anyone welcome to join in with the regulars, and Jack's owner Doralee often drops by. Usually four or five of us show up sit around and chat about what's going on in our lives, work, politics, friends and family, and everything else. We've been mentioned in the local newspaper even for causing a ruckus. Because passions can run high, and probably because a few of the members are hard of hearing, we can get loud enough for the whole place and maybe the whole block to hear.

The group is composed of quite the cast of characters. There is the lawyer, Gary, who first invited me along to the group when we met through Rotary. It turns out we went to the same school nearly 50 years ago, though we didn't hang out back then. He is deeply knowledgeable about corporate law and politics and together we have established a number of non-profit organizations. Another member is Les, who was a priest that left the church to marry his wife. He is energetic, sincere and ready to help anyone. I have roped him into just about everything I get involved in.

Will is our senior member and a real character. He is a past collegiate athlete in two sports, runs an avocado business, and now coaches sports at the girls' high school. He lives an extremely active lifestyle, and that's probably how he stays so young. Joe is a former successful greenhouse grower and does a lot of travelling around the world now he is retired, enjoying the fruits of all his hard work. Andy is another avocado grower and chair of the School Board who we call 'Grease Monkey' because of his passion for and huge collection of tractors and cars.

If anyone in the group needs help, we band together to make sure they get what they need. Their friendship has been an outlet from the pressures of daily life and a source of never ending camaraderie.

17. INTO DARKNESS

Roxanne lived for volunteering at events. One morning in 2015, we were set to help out with the Rotary Club of Goleta Noontime's annual Easter Egg Hunt. I was to shoot photos for the local newspaper and Roxanne was to be a registrar and organizer.

When she woke up that morning however, she complained of a backache and said she would have to take it easy that day. During the event, she told me she was now having chest pains, too. We rushed to the hospital; afraid she was having a heart attack.

They did a variety of tests, narrowing it down to possible kidney stones. After further testing however we were told to go to the UCLA hospital to see a specialist, and to "expect the worst." A month later, we were handed the news she had pancreatic cancer. However, they believed she was young and healthy enough to have what is known as a Whipple procedure, which removes the head of the pancreas, first part of the small intestine, the gallbladder and the bile duct. The remaining organs are then reattached, allowing for the digestion of food after surgery.

It turned out the procedure almost killed her. She spent over two weeks in hospital, and as her condition got worse, was told she might not recover due to sepsis. After another surgery to remove some of the excess fluids, she pulled through, and we headed home with a positive prognosis.

Over the next two years we lived on a roller coaster of ups and downs as the cancer came and went. We lived day to day, checking off things on her bucket list or just planning for things we would do in the future, when she was better. Yet Roxanne made me promise I would find someone to be with if she was gone. I said I would, not really meaning it. I was always hoping for the best.

The Nomura family, celebrating Roxanne's birthday two months after her surgery in 2015. Front row from left: Wade's mother, Roxanne, Lisa and grandson Tyler. Back row from left: Weldon's wife Ann, sister Wynne, grandson Zach, sister Wendy, brother Weldon, Ryan and Wade.

Roxanne's condition continued to deteriorate. Yet she told me when she started losing strength to continue doing what we started out to do, helping others. Even though she was in constant pain, and needed help with many simple tasks, she insisted I continue on with Rotary work because that was what we had invested in over the years and it was too important to walk away from.

On my trip to Maryland to serve as a Rotary International President's Representative which she insisted I go on, she was very weak and, in the hospital, having fallen while getting ready to go home and breaking her hip. She was so excited when the doctor said she could go home and in such a hurry, she tripped while putting her clothes on. When she was told she had to stay in hospital after her fall, she was crushed. She seemed to give up after that. I never saw her excited again.

On my last day in Maryland, having just finished my assignment, I got the call from the doctor it was time to give my directive to not resuscitate. I couldn't wait to get home.

When I got to the hospital Roxanne awoke at once, stared at me, then went back to sleep. I could see from her glazed eyes she was on heavy pain medication and not really aware who I was. I spent most of the day by her side, with her sleeping the entire time. Eventually, I decided to go home and get some sleep myself.

The next day, I got a call early in the morning from her, and in a strong voice, asking where I was. She told me I needed to hurry over as fast as I could.

I rushed over to find her in a coma. I sat with her that entire morning and watched as she struggled to breathe, with an occasional twitch or groan of pain and when I touched her, her hands were cold. I was scheduled to do my TV show that afternoon, and I decided to go ahead and do that since she had been sleeping the entire time.

That afternoon she passed. I had spent almost all my life with her, and now she was gone.

I had known the loss was coming but that did not lessen the pain. Roxanne had been in my life for nearly half a century, and we lived as one for most of that time. Life had suddenly changed into something unrecognizable. It was hard to know where Roxanne began and I ended. I felt like I had half of myself cut away.

The local high school offered to hold her farewell service there, due to our support of many youth activities over the years. It seemed fitting, given Roxanne's passion for community work it should be a place she had contributed to in life. Over four hundred people attended, honoring her life and recognizing her tireless work in the community.

After her passing, I was never alone during a meal; my friends and family would take me out to lunch and dinner every day. I found out later Roxanne had made people promise her they would make sure I ate regular meals after she was gone, knowing my tendency to skip eating when I was busy, or depressed. She was watching out for me even after she was gone.

Yet after these hours with companionship, it was time to go home to a dark, empty house, with no lights and no sounds.

18. A Second Chance

I threw myself into my Rotary and community work, to keep up the vision that had been so important to Roxanne and, in hindsight, to mask the loneliness. I went to Atlanta for the Rotary International Convention in 2017, only a month after Roxanne passed away, before she was even interned, just to get away from the dark silence. The following year, I travelled to Toronto, the location of the convention for that year, where I had been given a number of speaking spots. I didn't realize my life was about to change forever.

While in Toronto, I was asked to assist a good friend of mine, Mike McCullough as a Sergeant-At-Arms for the Peace conference, helping VIPs and doing odd jobs to ensure all ran smoothly. I spent a lot of time around the registration area with Mike's wife, Sheri, who told me of a lady from Australia who was thrown into presenting the day before. Then Rotary International President Ian Riseley had commissioned six Rotary International Presidential Peacebuilding Conferences throughout the world during his term. Each needed a representative at the Toronto Peace conference to report back on their event. The Chair of the Sydney conference scheduled to speak was delayed after her flight was cancelled. She spent over two hours sitting on the plane with the other passengers, only for it to be announced they would have to all get up and leave to fly another day. It turned out the navigation system program had not been updated and expired. The plane lacked the correct cable on board to update it, meaning it was grounded. Whoever was responsible for that blunder might not have been in their boss's good books that day, but whoever they are, I owe them dearly for what happened next.

Debbie was the only key committee member involved in staging the conference held in Sydney able to present in Toronto at the time, so she would need to take the Chair's place. With the short notice, Debbie needed somewhere to hurriedly make notes before presenting, and Sheri kindly allowed her to sit at the Sergeants' table.

After she presented, Debbie came to see Sheri to tell her how it went. I saw a lady with a big smile and looking very professional heading towards the Sergeants' table. The three of us talked for a while, before I had to leave for an assignment.

That evening we ran into each other again. I was going out to dinner with some members of my Rotary District and had asked a friend of mine, Catherine, from Australia who was in an e-Club I had established to join us. Then along came Debbie, and I asked if she would like to come too. Debbie had no dinner plans but was on the way to meet with some Rotaractors from Europe, so we had to see them first. Rotaractors, are the young adult segment of Rotary.

Catherine and I sat in the hotel foyer while Debbie chatted with the Rotaractors, who were presenting the following day at the Rotaract conference. Their presentation was on corporate responsibility, advising Rotaractors to consider partnering with corporates in their projects. Debbie was providing them with various resources she had on the topic to assist them, as this was an area she was passionate about.

I watched their interaction with interest. Despite their youth, she treated them with absolute respect, recognizing the quality of what they were saying while providing them with some extra information. It was like looking in a mirror. It is just the way I strive to treat young people, treating them as equals with something to learn, rather than inferiors.

There was something about Debbie that was different. It was natural to be with her.

Debbie and I chatted continuously throughout dinner and I found out later a number of my friends spotted what neither of us had seen at the time. One friend Sandi, the Governor Elect sitting opposite us, Debbie noticed giving her odd looks. Watching the two of us, she told me later she was certain we would end up together.

Debbie and I were both busy at the convention. I was speaking a couple of times for the Rotary Foundation and Debbie was keen to attend as many sessions as possible. I made a point to ask her to come with me on a cruise my District had organized. Debbie later told me she agreed to come as she had fun at dinner, and thought I was probably a bit lonely being on my own having found out that I had lost Roxanne only a year ago. She was amazed to see hundreds of my friends come up to talk to me on the boat.

Due to other engagements, I was flying home early from Toronto, meaning the only other time we could catch up was the night before I left. Debbie had booked to go to Niagara Falls in the afternoon with a friend and we agreed to have dinner together after that. Due to unexpected traffic the bus trip arrived back very late. I waited patiently for hours to see her that night, and it was only then she realized the level of my interest in her.

I very much wanted to see her again, but she was hesitant to get involved with anyone, given a prior, nasty divorce. Even after I left that dinner and headed back to my hotel to pack, I had no idea what was to come. Undeniably there was a connection we both felt strongly. We agreed to stay in touch as we parted to return to our home countries.

Suddenly, text messaging, phone calls and emails took over our lives. I became expert at knowing Australian time and her routine so we could catch up at every opportunity. This was amusing to my friends, as they would watch me cut short our time together to go and talk to Debbie, or she would be on speakerphone conversations with them too. Jokes were made in both hemispheres we were like a pair of love-struck teenagers.

Others started asking me what had happened in my life, seeing me start to smile again. Everyone noticed the difference in me. It made me realize how sad I had been, the extent of my grief.

We decided to meet again in Hawaii, a place around halfway between the two of us we both loved. We got on so well, I asked her if she could extend her trip to come and visit California. With my level of community involvement, it would be difficult for me to move away, so I was hoping Debbie would like California – and me – enough to consider moving here if things worked out. It was a good plan, since I was also able to give Debbie insight into my everyday life. She met my family and friends, accompanied me to events, visited a few of my worksites and explored Carpinteria. The time went by quickly. When it was time for her to return, we found it very difficult to part ways.

We decided for the next meeting we should do the reverse – I would travel to Australia to meet her family. I remember Debbie running to greet me with true joy in her eyes. It was then I knew for sure she was going to be a major part of my future.

I had been concerned her family might take issue with my ethnicity and our interracial relationship, but they didn't even appear to notice. I seemed to have a strong bond with her daughter Danielle from our first encounter. Since Debbie had to go to work, she kept me company over my first couple of days, taking me to see interesting sights like black swans in the large central park in Sydney and the aquarium. I also met Jesse, their beloved Jack Russell who was the third member of their family and was celebrating her seventeenth birthday.

Debbie's mother flew down to meet me from Queensland. I could tell that she was making sure I was right for Debbie, asking pointed questions to test my character and the sincerity of my interest.

The trip was soon over and once again, we had to part ways. Separation was becoming harder. We made plans to see each other a month later for the Christmas holidays. Even though the time between these trips was short, it seemed like an eternity.

When Debbie and Danielle arrived in California, we had plans on her staying for the month and traveling back to Australia, however both Debbie and Danielle came down with an awful flu. They couldn't possibly travel, so their flights had to be delayed. I spent weeks taking care of them as they recovered, since they were almost bedridden – proving, if nothing else, my commitment. I became an expert at making British-style tea. Debbie and I grew more attached than ever, dreading the day she would fly away. Neither of us wanted to live apart again, so we decided to get married.

I wanted our ceremony to be somewhere special for both of us, and was delighted when Debbie suggested we marry at one of my landscaping projects, my signature Japanese garden she had seen me make the finishing touches to on her first visit to Carpinteria. My clients were delighted to oblige. We were married in a small garden ceremony in March of 2019, with my friend Les, a former priest, officiating.

Debbie entering my life has been a true blessing. My friends and I have fun learning this new language called "Australian" and its many colorful sayings, like 'sticky beak', 'dog's breakfast', and 'spitting the dummy'. Australians speak British English and I have been told multiple times by Debbie and Danielle you cannot argue with the English how to pronounce and spell the English language, since they were the ones who invented it.

In our first year of marriage, Debbie and I got the chance to explore many regions of the United States. She travelled with me to Rotary conferences and events in New Orleans, Nevada, Alabama, Chicago, Indiana to name a few, with every trip being an adventure filled with new experiences and memories to last a lifetime.

On one occasion, I had to be in Long Beach for the annual League of California Cities Conference then fly directly to Bend Oregon for a Rotary event. Debbie was dreading the condensed travel schedule but went along with it for my sake. When we finally arrived in Bend, she was surprised how beautiful the area was. I was the keynote speaker and as I stood up to speak, noticed a light dusting of snow falling through the glass wall in the back of the room just behind where Debbie was sitting. I tried to get her attention, but I couldn't.

When I finished, I told her about the snow and could see the disappointment in her eyes she missed it – the few places in Australia that receive snowfall are remote, meaning it is a spectacle many don't experience. After the event, one of the participants, AJ asked if we would like to tour the area as he was willing to drive us around. We eagerly accepted and off towards the mountains we went. About an hour into the trip we encountered the first snow of the season. Debbie was excited by seeing the white form on trees, "Like in the movies".

Debbie and Wade in the snow in Bend Oregon, 2019.

Courtyard garden off the bedroom built by Wade for Debbie, with carved named bricks gifted by Goyo in the foreground.

Spurred on by her enthusiasm, AJ drove us to a beautiful meadow surrounded by trees with a stream flowing nearby. Even though I was still in my suit, AJ insisted we get out of the truck and he helped Debbie make a snowball she could eat made of freshly fallen snow. She was like a child, so happy and laughing, a memory I will forever treasure.

Another memorable journey was a road trip from California all the way to Denver for a Rotary event. A couple of months before we had flown to an event via Denver, where we were delayed on the tarmac while we waited for tornadoes to move out of the area. For most of the return flight, we were weaving around tornadoes through mountain ranges to minimize turbulence. To say the least, Debbie, who is already fearful of flying, did not enjoy this experience, and vowed never to fly into Denver again.

I invited my Rotarian friends Scott and his mother Jan, to join us on the road, and we all set off in my Mercedes van seeing the sights along the way. We spent the trip enjoying music, sharing stories and touring small towns. A dinner at Vail, Colorado, was memorable for a couple of reasons. The town itself is like a postcard, so picturesque, and the evening was perfect, with the sun coming out following a light rain. We decided to eat outside at the base of the summer ski slopes to enjoy the sunset and our wonderful meal. Towards the end, Debbie suddenly started shrieking. A wasp had flown towards her and she started running around flinging her arms. It was an amusing end to a beautiful evening, with no Australians or wasps harmed.

Since the pandemic grounded us, Debbie has had me working on our very neglected house. I was always traveling and working and left most of my housework until when I had time to do it, which never happened. Debbie insisted I make our house not just a place to drop off stuff and sleep, but a home.

Debbie always wanted a vegetable garden where she could harvest food for dinner, which was one of the first new additions I installed. She picks fruit and vegetables, and her face lights up every time. She loves passionfruit, so rather than a hedge I planted vines on our property fence. The passionfruit love the area and every weekend I have to trim them so they don't take over the whole yard. At this moment, we have about four hundred passionfruit ripening on the vine.

Debbie says one of the best presents I've ever given her is the courtyard garden I built for her, with a new fence design I created along with a combination of her favorite flowers – a mixture of Japanese, English, and French combined, with a beautiful red maple, together with hydrangeas, stephanotis, gardenias, geraniums and more.

Goyo, a good friend from Mexico brought us hand carved bricks with our names on them which are proudly displayed there, too. Every morning Debbie wakes up, has her tea and walks outside to admire the gardens, appreciative of its continual transformation.

We still have more to do but a lot of progress has been made. I had forgotten how nice it is to have a home where we can relax and have friends over for meals or just to visit. This would not

Photos:
1. Rotary District Awards event where Wade was presented the Rotary Foundation Distinguished Service Award, 2019.
2. At Notre Dame for a Rotary District Conference. From Left Heather Goralski (then President of the Rotary Club of South Bend), Debbie, Notre Dame Leprechaun and Wade.

127

have happened had Debbie not 'cracked the whip' and after much grumbling, I can now see why she did. Debbie and I take walks every afternoon through Carpinteria, down to the beach, meeting many friendly faces along the way and often stopping to have a chat. Through her fresh eyes, I appreciate my home now more than ever, where kindness and community service are a way of life. Debbie calls Carpinteria our paradise.

My new daughter Danielle is the bookworm child I never had, sharp and clever with a passion for the arts. I very much appreciate having her in my life and taking on the role of being the caring father she never had. Toru, the little Maltese I inherited from my elderly aunt has adopted her, following her whenever she moves anywhere in the house. He used to spend most of his day motionless, either sleeping or lounging around by himself seemingly moping from the loss of my aunt, then Roxanne. Now with a new life and companionship, he goes on walks for hours, with all his steps developing muscles upon muscles beneath his snowball fluff. One of the things I truly love about Debbie is how she accepts the wonderful life I had with Roxanne. After Roxanne's passing, I take flowers to the cemetery every week and with Debbie's support this has continued. Of course, I always buy Debbie flowers as well. I never imagined I would be given a second chance at love. I believe it was fate Debbie came into my life, with all the chance happenings that took place for us to come together, and I have honored my promise to Roxanne to continue living a full life.

Debbie has brought me the strength and desire to continue with the mission of helping others. She motivates me, supports me, and helps me think things out. Together, I feel we can change the world. For my once again happy life, I am profoundly grateful.

Mayor Wade as Celebrity Judge at the C-Dog Halloween Dog Costume event, with Debbie, Danielle and Toru, 2019.

Wade helping Danielle create wall art in the Carpinteria Chalk Art event encouraging everyone to Mask Up during the pandemic. 2020.

Giving

19. MY HOUSE IS YOUR HOUSE

My house has become an impromptu home for dozens of different people over the years. When I was racing, team members would often stay with us, sometimes for months at a time. Ryan and Lisa's friends would also stay for extended periods. Most of the time, these young people were trying to get away from their own households, which were fractured by issues like financial troubles or divorce.

I knew how vulnerable children were to long-term effects from this kind of trauma, so I was happy to offer a safe haven of sorts. Some would stay a few days; others would be around for months. We only asked they help out in the household during their stay by contributing to chores, just as if they were members of the family.

One of these kids was a teenager, Billy, who asked if he could come home with us after a race in the Bay area. At first, he refused to eat anything other than McDonald's hamburgers even when Roxanne had cooked up a hearty family meal. I told him he would have to work to pay for the hamburgers; after a few weeks when he realized how much it cost him to buy take out, he started trying a little of our food here and there. By the end of his stay, he was eating everything and begging Roxanne for new Japanese dishes to try. Billy's passion was cars and he helped me work on one of my trucks. We swapped out the engine to a larger more powerful one and added a stereo system, creating a much more comfortable ride for driving across country for races. His skills came in handy more than a few times when we were struck by mechanical problems on the road. He was able to get us up and running every time.

Another very different boy came to stay with us thanks to a

client of Roxanne's real estate business, who lived in Japan. His son, Isamu, was enrolled in a nearby private high school for the next school year. He asked Roxanne if he could come and live with us beforehand, to help him adjust to the American way of life.

It was immediately apparent Isamu had lived a sheltered life in Japan. He wore his pants high up on his waist, attracting attention to his penny loafer shoes and striped socks, with large round lensed glasses. My children, still in grammar school, called him a nerd, telling him it meant he was a, "Cool dude". Isamu believed them at first, and would proudly tell others he was a nerd, until my children's mischief was explained to him.

The next time we went to the shopping mall, Isamu followed me around without me noticing. Everything that caught my eye, he quickly grabbed in his size. When we left the mall, he had three giant bags of "Cool clothes". He then went to the optometrist and bought some new "cool" wire frame glasses. Now dressed in one of his new outfits, he asked the kids, "Now do I look like a nerd?"

He was shocked when they answered yes, learning it wasn't just the clothes that make you cool, you have to act cool too. They instructed him not to sit with his legs crossed and walk slowly and casually. The next thing I knew I had a shadow following me everywhere, with Isamu copying the way I walked, picking things up I had just set down and sitting on the sofa next to me in my exact position, determined to mirror my every move.

Isamu decided part of being a cool American was owning a cool car. The coolest car, he was told, was a Porsche sportscar. He came from a very affluent family, so he could easily afford such a car with his pocket money. He asked Roxanne to take him to the local dealership. He picked one he liked the color of and asked the salesman if he could test drive it before buying. Isamu was straight away allowed to jump behind the driver's seat of his five-speed dream car. He turned it on and began to drive, the car immediately jerking, heaving and stalling. It then happened a second time. It turned out not only had Isamu never driven a sportscar, he had never driven any kind of car at all. It was literally his first time behind the wheel in his life. Unfortunately for the Porsche salesman, he did not end up making a sale that day.

Of course, our home was also always open to family as well. Lisa had her first child while still studying at college. From when Zach was around four months old, he stayed with Roxanne and I for a week every month, to give Lisa some time to concentrate fully on her studies.

After Lisa graduated, they moved in with us so Lisa didn't have to worry about being home when he was finished at school or Boys club. I remember him asking Lisa, "How come Grandma and Grandpa never go home?" believing our place belonged to him. I spent a lot of time with him playing sports, just like I did with Ryan and Lisa.

My house remains open. Shortly after Debbie and I were married, an old friend of mine from Mexico and his family wanted to stay with us as they had fallen on some hardship. We welcomed them without question, enjoying each other's company for around six months. When they left, there were tears all around, as we had become family.

In Mexico there is a saying, "My house is your house." It comes with the understanding you are invited anytime and will treat the house as if it were your own. I have lived by this saying, and welcomed people seeking a safe place for whatever reason. When they stayed, I usually got to enjoy watching them slowly improve from whatever issues they were facing. I still hear from many of them, grateful for the stability we were able to offer during a tough time, which helped them get their life back on track. I am hopeful all of them spread the same kindness to others given the opportunity, creating a broad safety net in our community for people in need of a place to stay during difficult times in their life.

20. WHAT'S ROTARY?

In 2001, Roxanne came home from a dentist's appointment with Dr. Janice Sugiyama all excited. Janice and others in the town wanted to start a second Rotary club with morning meetings and the idea had gained a lot of traction. Roxanne was planning to join and wanted me to do so also.

"What's Rotary?" I asked, bemused.

When Roxanne explained it was a service organization working together to help the community, I said thanks, but no thanks. I was too busy to take on something like that. This wasn't an empty excuse – I was involved in eight different organizations at the time, including many youth athletic programs, the Japanese American Citizens League and the Carpinteria Architectural Review Board.

Roxanne asked me to reconsider, as they needed 25 signatures to start the club. I said I would, but only if they were short on signatures. A few weeks later, she asked again, telling me they'd been stuck on 24 for a long time. I looked over the list and was impressed by the business and community leaders who had signed on, thinking the opportunity to network with such people would be of benefit to my business. So, I put my name down, as number 25.

I discovered the list was submitted to Rotary International that afternoon, with 32 signatures. Roxanne had one upped me again!

Admittedly, I started out as far from being an exemplary Rotarian. At Rotary meetings, I felt like I didn't fit in. I would sit at the back of the room and put in my one hour eating my breakfast, thinking more about the day ahead rather than projects and events the others were enthusiastic about. I was there in body, but not in spirit.

Two years after joining, the club President announced he would have to step away from organizing a trip to Mexico to complete a water project due to business obligations. He asked if anyone in the club would be willing to take his place?

I raised my hand. Since I'm fluent in Spanish, had been installing irrigation systems as part of my landscaping work for years, and studied organic chemistry and microbiology in college, I figured I had the skills to get it done. Plus, I had never travelled out of the United States on a plane before. Secretly, I thought this was a great opportunity to have an all-expenses paid Mexican holiday.

Getting on the plane and taking off was an adventure. Yet when we were walking across the tarmac after landing my colleagues brought up how I would be picking our project, getting the contracts signed with the government, and getting the community to buy in to our idea, and much more. This was news to me, and my head in the clouds swiftly plummeted down to earth. I asked how long I had to do all this? Five days was the response.

We were greeted at the airport by the President of the Rotary Club of Patzcuaro who was to escort us to our hotel in Patzcuaro. It was only about 50 miles but took us hours to get there. The roads were terrible, covered in paving stones and there were speed bumps in every town. Drivers were impatient, in cars barely running. Smoke filled the air, with many people burning their trash on the side of the road. In contrast, I saw massive cathedrals and grand statues of historical figures from the liberation from Spain.

Patzcuaro was an old colonial city made up with city squares filled with large trees. The streets were filled with market vendors and live music, from radio rap to traditional Mexican songs, being performed all over. I saw many historical plaques dating back to the 1600s. We were taken to the central plaza, which featured a magnificent fountain of Don Vasco de Quiroga.

The municipal building was located there, where we met with the directors of the region including the local water agency. Hydrological engineer Bernardo Ramos shared his expertise of the water quality in every region and where it was needed. We identified three project locations and decided to help the one in the worst state first.

I was put to work negotiating with the government for assistance, engaging the community to assist with construction and then dedicating themselves to maintaining the system. We also needed to institute hygiene education programs in schools for children living in the area.

The first site visited was Colonio Miguel Hidalgo, a small agricultural village of 120 people who had recently suffered an outbreak of cholera. Many of the young residents left to seek employment opportunities elsewhere leaving behind women, children and the elderly. I was surprised to hear music coming from many of the houses indicating there was electricity, but no water.

I asked where they got their water from. They pointed to a small hole about three feet wide and two feet deep in a field where cattle were grazing. I was also shown a water spigot in the center of the village which apparently had water directed from a water tower. I opened the spigot and out came mud and clumps of algae.

With the agreement of local Rotarians, water engineer Bernardo and the local people, this was selected as the first system to fix. Thanks to Bernardo, government workers came to clean the water spigot system, including the piping to the town and the water tank. The well was also drilled to a deeper aquafer, and a new pump installed.

The community agreed to grant the land used for the water system to the project and assist us with some of the work, like cleaning out the water tank and flushing out the pipes. We asked that they commit to maintaining the system once installed, which would also require collecting a small monthly fee for maintenance and filter replacements.

A local contractor installed the filtration system and community volunteers built a structure to house it. This was to protect the equipment from the elements and prevent the possibility of vandalism. Bernardo offered to organize the government to work on the well, including replacing the pump and any bad pipes in the distribution system and providing materials for the tank sealing. He kept us up to date on their progress and within the year, the system was complete. We had made plans to return to the project site when finalized to evaluate it and to celebrate its success, so we went back for the inauguration.

I remember the excitement and gratitude expressed to us by the locals. Then the local leader came out dressed in his very best. "Thank you for bringing us water. For us, water is life. Thank you for bringing us life," he said.

I was overwhelmed with emotion. I date this as the moment I truly became a Rotarian. It was rewarding beyond words to know I had been able to deliver the gift of a better life to so many.

Wade with the water committee discussing options for a water project in Colonia Miguel Hidalgo, Mexico, 2007.

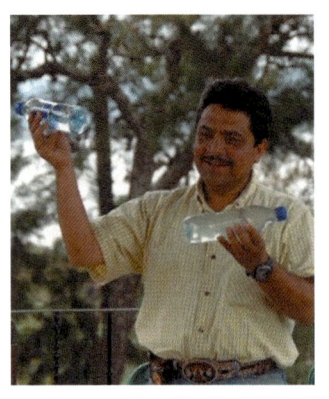

Left: Patzcuaro Water Engineer, Bernardo Ramos, celebrating a successful project on the Island of Yunuen, showcasing dirty water versus clean water, Mexico, 2008. Right: Installing a solar water pasteurizer at a school in Colonio Don Vasco de Quiroga, Mexico, 2008.

21. GROUNDWORK

Not all humanitarian projects are a success. In my travels I have seen many well-intentioned projects in disrepair and disuse. When I've asked locals for details as to why, their answers have included everything from "The system broke and no one could fix it", "People left the area," "We did not need it," and "It was too expensive to run." They also talked about the projects as 'their' project, belonging to the people who put them there, not 'ours'.

The second project site we visited on the trip to Mexico was a prime example of this. It was a small indigenous village situated on the island of Tecuena on Lake Patzcuaro.

I had gathered as much data as I could on the island and its people before going to the site. This included population demographics and local infrastructure such as medical facilities and schools. But there are a lot of things these sorts of facts and figures don't reveal about day to day life. These can only be revealed through engaging the people themselves.

With the help of a translator who spoke ordinary Spanish as well as the local dialect, Purapecha, I asked as many questions as I could. I wanted to know the kinds of jobs they did, their average weekly income, how often people around them fell ill, how often they went to the mainland, the age young people left school and more. The goal was to gain as intimate understanding as possible of their lives as I could.

They let me explore, giving me the chance to see for myself what daily life was like. I inspected first hand their homes, the kinds of sanitation facilities in place, what vehicles they drove, their pets and livestock and agricultural sites. I find all this on the ground engagement vital, not only because official data can be incomplete or outdated, but also because it lets you really feel and understand what life is like to a person living in the community. You have walked a mile in their shoes.

When they showed me their water system, they told me they preferred the polluted lake water, since filtered water tasted weird and made them sick. Instead, they wanted our help getting insulin, since a quarter of their community had diabetes and the government was not filling their prescriptions. In order to get any medical care, they went to an adjacent island called Janitzio with ten times the population. I offered to talk to the health minister and see if I could assist with the shortage of insulin and if they could schedule staff to stop by the island on a monthly basis to check on the residents, but also told them I was there to assist with the water situation as my primary mission. I remained unclear on why they were so certain they disliked filtered water.

It turned out the government had installed a filtration system twenty years before, which had long been abandoned. When I went to take a look at it, I quickly realized the problem. The chlorine injection system had been calibrated to inject fifty times the required dosage. This perfectly explained their comments that filtered water smelled and tasted bad and led to sickness. Mystery solved.

Because I took the time to get to know them well, I developed a level of trust with the community. When I explained in detail how greatly their village would benefit from a properly installed water system, they gave the project their blessing.

We installed a new water system with the government supplying a contractor to install the necessary electrical connection, with a complimentary education component on the equipment usage for the locals. A job well done – or so I thought.

A year later, we went back to check on how things were going, only to find the filtration system had been abandoned yet again. It was hard to hide my frustration. When I asked what had happened, they told me it was costing them more to run the filters than it was to buy bottled water. On inspection, I found the contractor had installed a 220-volt single phase electrical system which used twice the power required by a standard 110-volt system and cost the community ten times more. We had this fixed and the villagers promised to start using the filtration system again.

The water system has been in use ever since. I've been back a number of times over the past ten years to do checkups and see how the community is progressing. Because of the water project, health, education and living conditions have all dramatically improved since my original community assessment. Families were also more cohesive, since income earners were able to stay on the island rather than be forced to the mainland to work thanks to the newly thriving economy. The issues with insulin had been resolved for the best of reasons: they no longer needed it. Previously, many people had bought sodas and other sugary drinks, since they were half the cost of bottled water. Now water was nearly free they were drinking it instead, resulting in the diabetic rate reducing by fifty percent.

Over the years, I have landscaped thousands of gardens for clients. Before I start any project, I assess everything that could impact the garden – the soil, sun or shade, wind factors, plants, the background and proximity of existing features and the resources available. I also consider my clients needs. How will they use it and how often? How many people live at the premises and what are their ages? Children have different needs to the elderly. What garden styles do they prefer? What is their budget? While I may prepare the design, the client's needs and wishes are always at the forefront of my mind. No matter how beautiful the landscape I create, unless the client is catered to, they will never take ownership of the end product.

I've found the same approach is what works best with humanitarian projects to truly address the community's needs. Without a thorough assessment beforehand, humanitarian initiatives can become something like buying presents for people based on your own preferences or what you think they 'should' want, rather than what they would actually desire.

Taking the time to do proper groundwork can be the difference between success and failure. In the case of the Tecuenan filtration system, the community assessment upfront gave us the opportunity to understand the village and their issues in detail, get their support for the project, and later on measure its impact once we finally had it up and running successfully. Ultimately, it helped us find out how to truly help them and gave them the pride of ownership. In addition, we learned valuable lessons towards helping others in the future.

22. WATER WORKS

When our club organized a second water and sanitation mission to Mexico, I was the first to volunteer. I was accompanied this time by Roxanne, as well one of the club members who was on the first trip. We focused on Colonio Don Vasco de Quiroga, the third site we had identified during my original trip, a village near the first project.

We had a solar pasteurizing filtration system with us purchased previously by another Rotary club in our district. It had been left unused as it had taken literally years to arrive from China after it had been ordered. We decided to install it on top of the roof of a local school.

To take the crate apart which housed the filter, we had to borrow tools from the locals. It was then I realized how poor the people were. The homes we managed to source the tools from were only the most basic shelters, with dirt floors; even though the people who lived there dressed so clean.

A twelve-year-old girl named Angela helped us in gathering up tools and ladders. She told us she helped take care of her little brother while her mother did her chores. When Roxanne asked if she was going to high school next year, Angela said no, because she could not afford the uniform required to attend. Roxanne was deeply upset by this and we decided to sponsor her school supplies.

As we disassembled the packing crate, I noticed the local people picking through the dirt to salvage the nails as we pulled them out from the sides. They also salvaged all the wood from the crate itself. It humbled me that even the packing we consider disposable could be considered a treasure.

After realizing the government only supplied water in the lines for four hours each day, we decided to install a water holding tank on the hillside above the community. This would supply water when the domestic lines were not pressurized. Eventually we got it working, much to our relief and the joy of the locals.

One year later we went back to the school to check the system out and make sure it was still working as it should be. As we drove in, we saw Angela standing at the bus stop with a high school uniform on. She told us clean water had changed her family. Her little brother had stopped getting sick and could now go to school, allowing her mother to work in the city. Not only did they have more money, both Angela and her brother would have many more opportunities in life thanks to being able to get an education.

I've continued with my passion for water projects over the years, and either in my own right or mentoring others, have implemented systems in many communities needing help.

Recently, I've become involved the Haiti National Clean Water, Sanitation and Hygiene Strategy (HANWASH), initiated by Rotary International President Barry Rassin at the 2018 Rotary convention in Toronto. It is Barry's personal passion to bring water and sanitation systems to the entire nation of Haiti, where the majority of infrastructure is non-functioning. The aim is to create an umbrella organization uniting government sectors, donor agencies from around the world, grassroots groups on the ground digging wells and building toilets, with Rotary's systemic, technical driven approach to collecting data and creating sustainable community driven action plans.

I was fascinated by the sheer scale and vision of such a project, jumping at the chance to become involved when Barry and his aide John Smarge asked me to join the steering committee, as well as manage a team to implement grant projects under the HANWASH banner. It will take an estimated $2 billion and more than a decade to fully realize the entire initiative, with a dedicated team working towards this goal. It is our hope HANWASH will function as a blueprint for implementing water and sanitation infrastructure in other developing nations in the future.

Through my work in Rotary, I have come to realize clean water is fundamental to lifting education and health standards and fostering economic development and peace. Clean water is absolutely integral to prevent the spread of disease. This helps save lives, as well as lift the health of the entire community, improving educational and economic outcomes. Children stay healthy and in school, building skills for the future. Adults are able to work, without resources and time spent caring for family members who are ill. Standards of living rise across the board, leading to less conflict internal and external. I know when I am working on filtration systems and pipes what I am really doing is helping to save lives and build a better future.

23. Playground of Dreams

Shortly after our Rotary club formed, we began looking for large-scale signature project. Jim Heth suggested we build a playground, based on the success of a similar project by his former Rotary club in Texas.

The club liked the idea and in 2003, we hired New York architect firm Leathers and Associates, specialists in building playgrounds, to develop plans. They sent one of their staff, John Dean, who was an expert in facilitating design, pre-project planning and coordination to Carpinteria. We held public meetings with parents and students of three local grammar schools he helped facilitate. He asked what they would like in a park and the children were quick to pipe up with answers such as "A water slide that lands in water!" John politely and tactfully managed these less feasible requests by asking the children to consider the drawbacks. "If we have a water slide, what could happen if someone who cannot swim falls into the pool? And what if your mother gets wet watching you?" Even if they couldn't have everything on their wish list, the children were all excited at the prospect of a great new place to play.

The next step was to meet with volunteers, with John providing a model of how to structure the project organizationally, breaking it down into committees and appointing captains to manage their sections. The community was now invested in the idea and to our delight both Rotarians and non-Rotarians stepped up to take on roles. John's approach deeply impressed me. I had never before seen someone come all the way from across the country and in a few days create such excitement and buy in. I took note of all he did and use many of his techniques in developing other projects even today.

It was anticipated the build would take five days with the assistance of the community volunteer force and cost approximately $128,000. Our Rotary club started a foundation in order to raise funds through events and donors. We also set up an appointment with the Parks Department to see if we could use a grassy spot, we had our eye on close to the beach. We were informed this would not be possible as Californian State Parks do not allow playgrounds on their land, however our attention was drawn to an area running alongside the railway. It had just been acquired and was not yet within the State Parks General Plan. If we finished the playground in the two-year timeframe we had planned, it would be left standing and be maintained as an existing amenity.

We got tentative approval from the Director of the California State Parks and our efforts shifted to fundraising the $128,000. The process proved to be slow however and a year later, we were told that doing the proposed design, which was basically a wooden structure, would not be approved. State Parks engaged their landscape architect Barney Matsumoto to develop a plan that would conform to their guidelines focusing on education and historical significance. They came up with a concept of an interpretive play area including a Chumash theme in honor of the people that populated Carpinteria before the Spanish explorers came. It was a beautiful design encompassing a replica Chumash village, however the estimated cost for construction was now $650,000.

By now, we were three years into the project and everyone in our Rotary Club was understandably disappointed. The scope of the project had changed, our club was no longer the steering force and we would now have to come up with another half a million dollars. Yet Roxanne was still set on the idea of creating the playground and wanted me to continue the cause with her.

Of course, I couldn't say no. The rest of our Rotary club moved on to other projects, agreeing to contribute the $128,000.

Roxanne and I continued in our efforts to secure more funding, which now increased to close to $1 million with the time delays and increased amenities. The City of Carpinteria agreed to match the Rotary club's contribution providing $125,000 towards the project. State Parks were now committed and offered $245,000 to the project. We then secured a Federal Government grant of $400,000. This meant we only had $100,000 left to raise. When the local community found out we had almost reached our target, they came out in force to provide the extra dollars. Some paid for certain playground items, like a seal, *tomol,* or hut statue. The city allowed us to develop the sidewalk with commemorative bricks to recognize donors, including individuals, families and local businesses.

Everything seemed to be on track until in 2007 we were advised by State Parks the site had been adopted into their General Plan. We had not been fast enough installing the park and now it was officially part of State Parks land. The construction of a playground would not be allowed.

Roxanne and I were understandably devastated all our hard work appeared to have been for nothing. We reached out to the Director of California State Parks Ruth Coleman. "You keep working. The project will go on," she assured us, determined to fix the issue internally.

She was successful in negotiating an exclusion for the play area, on the basis of its educational and cultural aspects. It would not be an ordinary playground but an opportunity for children to learn about indigenous history in an interactive way. We are to date the only play area built on California State Parks property.

We officially began construction on September 7, 2010. Roxanne and I ceremonially broke ground together, tears welling up in her eyes as we drove the shovel into the dirt. After so many years of struggle, it was hard to believe we had finally reached that moment.

City of Carpinteria Parks Director, Matt Roberts, and I were charged with implementing the project. Local excavator Pete Lapidus was awarded the contract to do the heavy equipment work on the site since his bid was almost forty percent less than the others. I asked him if he knew he was priced so much lower than his competitors. "My wife would have killed me if I didn't get this job," he replied with a smile. They had young children and were very enthusiastic about the project. Graders and loaders were used to move boulders and a retaining wall functioning as our mound elevation support. Rotary Club of Carpinteria Morning members June and Rene Wingerden offered us stones they had on their ranch. Pete hauled them down to the site to be set in artful and strategic locations, doing over forty truckloads back and forward.

We created a variety of climbing structures including a replica of the Anacapa Island Arch Rock. The pathway into the park is made of colored concrete and blue glass beads representing the Santa Barbara Channel created by the Channel Islands off the coast. In the play area this transitions into blue rubberized, bouncy material for safety. Crossing overhead is a multicolored bridge, representing the Rainbow Bridge Chumash legend holds connected Santa Cruz Island to the Carpinteria coastline. It is said those that fell off the bridge crossing the channel did not drown, instead transforming into dolphins and living on as people of the ocean. Life-sized concrete dolphins, as well as seals and traditional Chumash dwellings known as *aps* were custom built by a specialist company in the Midwest. There is also a large replica *tomol,* a plank board canoe after which the park, and Carpinteria itself, derive their name. The City Hall parking lot was the only place we could store them before it was time for their installation creating a strange sight outside a government building.

The children of the community were passionate about having a slide, so we had a big one put in the center of the play area. With a bit of inventiveness, we were even able to put in a second slide. The second spot lacked the slope required for a traditional slide, however we figured out a design made out of rotating tubes like a conveyer belt could work.

The more you weigh, the faster you descend, meaning smaller children slide softly and average size children move faster. Our Parks Director wasn't entirely convinced on the design, concerned it would be too slow to enjoy and so decided to give it try himself. The rollers propelled the weight of a fully-grown man six feet away, with him landing unceremoniously on his posterior to a chorus of laughter. Needless to say, he was satisfied it was fast enough to keep.

We tried to make the park as attractive yet safe as possible. Since the site was close to the railroad tracks, we had it fully fenced with only two entry points, and high visibility so parents could watch their children from just about anywhere within the play area. I designed a unique railing on top of the retaining wall, made of galvanized tubing, which was in the shape of the silhouette of the Channel Islands.

This was a more unique alternative to a standard chain link fence. The metallic vertical tubing blends into the scenery, making it almost disappear while still providing the necessary safety features. The fabrication involved was time consuming, but I felt the visual improvement made this worthwhile.

Various images of the Tomol Interpretative Play Area in Carpinteria, Ca.

1. The rainbow bridge in the background with the Portola Sycamore story tree and amphitheater in the foreground.
2. & 3. A dolphin and tomol climbing structures.
4. Wade and Roxanne Nomura being recognized as the 2011 Carpinterians of the Year.

I planned to do much of the cutting and drilling myself with a small team of volunteers, however when I scheduled the work, I was told it had already been done.

The City maintenance crew had volunteered during their break and lunch times to install them.

Once the major landscaping work was complete volunteers came in to help grade the site and do the planting. Hundreds of locals came to help, very young children to the elderly all working side by side, with our Rotary Club members. The plants we used are all indigenous, with significance to the Chumash culture. Some were used for food, such as the acorns of the Coast Live Oak, which were ground up and used as a meal to make bread. The Catalina Cherry and Toyon were harvested for their fruit and the Juncus rush for material to weave baskets.

Storyboard plaques were incorporated to explain the history and significance of many of the design elements in a child-friendly way. Matt had overseen this part of the park and when they arrived he insisted on showing them to Roxanne and I personally. It turned out he had a surprise in store. He directed us to one of the boards asking us to see if we could find anything special. Roxanne and I were perplexed. It was certainly a lovely design but we weren't sure what he was talking about. Finally, he pointed to a *tomol* floating on the ocean background of the scene. There was Roxanne and I sitting inside, the image lifted from a press release photo taken for a local newspaper. It was a secret tribute to our efforts creating the park we appreciated far more than any public spectacle.

On June 10, 2011, the Tomol Interpretive Play area was finally completed. At the entry to the park there are three pavers bearing the insignia of California State Parks, City of Carpinteria and the Rotary Club of Carpinteria Morning, recognizing the basic partnership that made the park happen. I pass by the park multiple times a week, with the sight of children playing making all the years of hard work worthwhile. It's not only locals who enjoy the space, with families coming in on the trains to spend the day enjoying the play area. It is also a major attraction for the children of campers and tourists who stay at the State park campgrounds in Carpinteria. It is one of my proudest achievements, and in January 2012, Roxanne and I were named Carpinterians of the Year.

Tomol Park stands as a testament to Roxanne's kindness and determination to bring joy to the lives of others. Last year, the Rotary Club of Carpinteria Morning installed a handmade bench and plaque honoring Roxanne's memory. It overlooks the play area that brings joy to so many, that would never have happened without her tireless spirit and determination.

24. THE MOTIVATOR

Roxanne became involved with everything she could in Rotary from the very beginning. Because of her enthusiasm and outgoing personality, she was asked to serve as the club's first female president. I had no idea at the time how much commitment this would entail. Presidents are elected two years in advance, acting as President Nominee and President Elect beforehand.

I offered Roxanne my help so she could do a good job and have fun doing it, instead of stressing out about keeping pace with all her responsibilities. I also attended all her training sessions, including those specific to incoming presidents like the seminars, retreats and the Rotary International Convention, that year in Chicago celebrating Rotary's Centennial. I had never been to one before and was in awe realizing how huge Rotary is worldwide. I met with world leaders and Rotarians working all over the globe on diverse efforts improving lives.

About a year after Roxanne was selected, our then president, Ed Van Wingerden, called me and asked if I had any recommendations for the president to follow her. Since the nominating committee was made up of past presidents, I hadn't given it much thought. "Why're you asking me?" I asked, confused. Ed answered, "Because you are the one we want!"

After reflection on what a rewarding experience all the training and duties had been for Roxanne even before she had begun her term, I decided to accept nomination as our club's fifth president.

When my presidential year was approaching, I was told by the district staff I should come up with a project I was passionate about and enlist my club members to make it happen. I wanted strong engagement and participation from everyone, to channel their energy to help the community in the best possible way. So instead, I focused on my fellow members and what was important to them. I sent out a questionnaire asking everyone to tell me any community efforts they were involved in outside of Rotary. I called the members who didn't respond, making sure I had answers from everyone. The responses were interesting and sometimes overlapping.

It was clear helping youth organizations was a common theme. Quite a number volunteered with the Boys and Girls Club, Boy Scouts, Girls Inc. and High School Boosters. I pledged to bring our club into partnership with such local groups where possible, adding Rotary support to their projects and causes. One project called Computers for Families had the goal of purchasing computers for disadvantaged students who did not have access to them at home, handicapping them compared to their peers who did. Roxanne and other members volunteered to be on the committee and one million dollars of computers were provided to young people in the surrounding community. We also provided English and Spanish dictionaries to all third-grade students in Carpinteria and Summerland, personally delivering them to classes and helping them to write their name inside the cover. We still do this project to this day and I have heard back from a few students who are now grown that this was the very first book they ever owned.

Another project led by June Van Wingerden was to fundraise enough to build a $100,000 barn at the Carpinteria High School, supporting Future Farmers of America training students for agricultural roles. The effort meant a lot to June, as she worked at the school as a teacher before her retirement and was married to a greenhouse and field nurseryman.

One of our fundraisers was a calendar featuring pictures from throughout Carpinteria. Anyone could submit a shot, which were all considered and winners selected by a panel. A tide chart was also included, distinguishing our calendar from others and appealing to the beach loving local community, the bright idea of a member Rick Joy, who is an avid surfer and photographer. That year we made $10,000 and the project has continued every year since. To date it has raised over $150,000, with all proceeds directed towards local charities and school funded programs.

We assisted with the Carpinteria Boys and Girls Club Annual Auction. That year's auction netted $115,000 and our club played a major part helping with participation, donations and managing the event on the night.

One of our more entertaining projects assisting the Cancer Teddy Bear Foundation was to help entertain the children at an outdoor beach restaurant. I recruited some of my Junior Golfers to participate, helping them to gain community service hours for school requirements. The chair of the event showed up with a teddy bear costume and asked if one of the kids could wear it. Most were too shy but a boy, Dodge, was game, especially since he figured no one would know who he was. He was great at dancing and performing for the children, however found the costume was incredibly hot. We had to tell him to

Photos:
1. Dodge Ward as the bear at the Teddy Bear Foundation fundraiser event for cancer.
2. Happy third grade Canalino School recipients of the dictionaries with Rotary club members (from left) Kelly Morman, Steve Bunting, Jim Heth, Art Fisher with the teacher on the right.
3. From left to Right: Hans and Barry Brand, Roxanne and June Van Wingerden organizing the distribution of Dictionaries.

Webster's Dictionary Students
Webster's Dictionary
Webster's Dictionary Students

stop as he got so tired and overheated, he almost couldn't stand.

We started out with 31 members and with all the activity, another five joined during the year. A total of sixty-four projects and events were completed, fundraising independently and through helping other organizations nearly four million dollars. We ended up being recognized as Best Small Club in International Service, Community Service, Vocational Service, and the Overall Best Small Club in our Rotary District.

Most importantly, club members were enthusiastic and proud of the new work we were doing for the causes that truly mattered to them.

I feel a test of success is how long it lasts. Often after a leader steps down, the changes they have initiated disappear. Projects that continue to thrive do so because others share ownership. I am pleased to say many projects I spearheaded continue within our club because members were working on the causes that mattered to them. We have been awarded best club three more times in our district, and in 2012 were one of 34 clubs recognized by Rotary International worldwide for our hard work.

Yet the greatest satisfaction of that year was seeing how involved and engaged the members became. Everyone took on projects and worked hard to make them succeed. In the end, they all thanked me for an outstanding year. I reminded them it was not me but their passion and effort that had made it possible; I think they were all just having too much fun to notice how much work they had all done towards creating our success.

25. Joy of Service

There is nothing quite like seeing the impact of humanitarian work firsthand. In Rotary we call that joy a Rotary Moment – where you realize you have changed someone else's life forever through an act of kindness.

I felt compelled to let others experience the same joy in service through what I called Project Safaris. I would invite Rotarians from my own club and others to travel with me to see projects implemented on the ground. I started offering annual tours to our Rotary district's sister district in Mexico and then a second trip around the time of their annual conference. I would coordinate with the Mexican Clubs optimal timing and a tour of projects for Rotarians to see. It became an opportunity for Californians to meet their counterparts in Mexico as well as become better familiarized with the projects, region, culture and community. They could meet in person the people they were helping, working back home on international projects.

From left Savi Bhim, Scott Phillips, Wade Nomura being hosted by Juan Maho Ochoa and his Rotary club in Patzcuaro, 2018.

Early safaris were planned around my own projects. More recent ones have started through project fairs we organize in Mexico where local clubs show their project ideas to members from our district, hoping to gain partnerships and to begin to develop friendships prior to the work. There is no better way to do international projects than as friends helping friends, with Safaris creating this working environment.

I believe it is important these friendships to be true friendships going both ways. I encourage Mexican Rotary clubs to reciprocate any assistance they are given. This may include helping with fundraising and promotion. Travel has also taken place in the opposite direction, with Rotarians from Mexico now visiting Californian clubs as guests. Successes have come out of every Project Safari I've organized. Not all projects are eligible for Rotary Foundation funding, and my job, besides translating when necessary, is to make recommendations on how to make it eligible, or to offer alternative solutions such as local resources or funding from other organizations working in their area. I love being part of helping facilitate new projects and matchmaking Rotarians with a shared passion for helping others. On one of these trips I took a small team, including a member of the Rotary Club of Lompoc, Rob Klug, who wanted to get involved in international projects. We ended up visiting eighteen clubs in six days, seeing many new projects and cities. We also had the opportunity to meet many local dignitaries thanks to our host, District Governor Ubaldo Lara.

One stop was the Rotary Club of Patzcuaro 2000 and one of their projects, a house built by their members to house a needy family, including elderly grandparents and a child with Downs Syndrome called Angel. She was unable to walk and was blind as a result of acute cataracts.

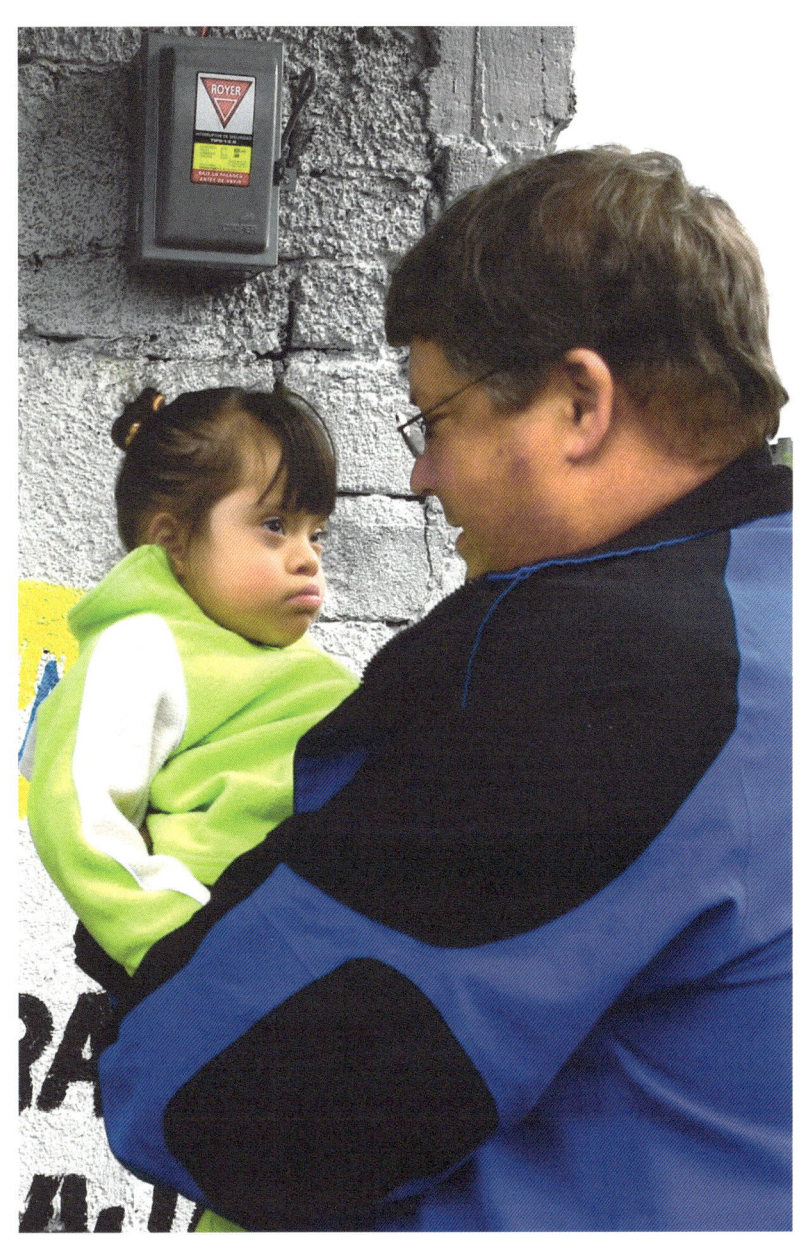

Rob Klug with Angel, the recipient of eye surgery from his generous donation.

The club was fundraising to pay for surgery to restore her vision, with US$1000 needed per eye. She had to be carried around by her family, as even though she was five years old, she could not walk. Rob asked if he could help, and as he held her, he started talking to her, trying to cheer her up. Eventually Angel gave him a smile and tears came to Rob's eyes. He looked over at me and said, "Tell them I will pay for the surgery." This was Rob's Rotary Moment and one he, nor I, will ever forget.

We were present during the ceremonial handing over of the keys to the front door of the donated house. Angel's grandfather held the key in his hands, staring at it. He then inserted it into the lock, turned it, and opened door. He then shut the door, turned the key again, locking it. This he repeated over and over again. Rob noticed this little ritual and through the translator asked him to explain what it was he was doing.

The grandfather explained in his eighty years of life very few of the houses he had ever lived in had a front door, and he had never before had a lock and key. To him they represented safety for himself and his family that he had never known before. He kept using the lock to prove to himself it was real.

Angel had her surgery on both eyes, with the hospital donating half of the surgery costs. Rob has since gone on project trips to Guatemala and been back to Mexico many times, a regular on my Project Safaris as well as assisting and participating on other projects himself through the network of new friendships he has established on these trips. We saw Angel and her family a year later, thriving. Angel no longer in need of constant assistance, thanks to the efforts of the Rotary club and Rob's generosity.

26. INDIA

Like many people in developed countries, the scourge of polio had faded into a memory – though naturally my memories were rather more potent than most given I had experienced the disease firsthand as a boy. Widespread vaccination had seen cases in countries like the United States hit zero. Yet when I learned about Rotary's major efforts towards polio eradication, I discovered this was not the case in developing regions like India, Asia, Africa and the Middle East.

In February 2010, Roxanne and I set off to India on a National Immunization Days program, which are mass campaigns to deliver oral poliovirus vaccine under direction from the World Health Organization and Rotary.

India was like nothing I had ever seen. As we started on our descent, I could see from the plane window hundreds of thousands of low-set houses, constructed from cardboard, concrete and metal, and arranged chaotically over the vast, dusty land. When we were out on the street the noise was deafening, people were shouting and horns pumping everywhere. People on foot, bikes, cars and carts crisscrossed everywhere with street dogs, chickens and goats weaving everywhere in between. Cows on the other hand, being sacred, were accorded the utmost respect. Even if they decided to lay down in the middle of the street, no one would move them. Instead the traffic weaved around, one of the few signs of cohesive order I could see on Indian streets.

When we attended a briefing in Delhi the first thing said was, "Who was assigned to Rampur? You have been re-assigned to the city of Moradabad in Utter Pradesh." I confess I was a little relieved after what I had read about Rampur – until someone sitting next to me said she had been in Moradabad a few years ago and had sewage dumped on her when she walked through the slums. All I could think of at that time was at least my jacket was waterproof and had a hood. We were advised to not eat any local food or water, and hotels were scarce and poorly maintained.

The next day my team of five and I were off, with the journey itself certainly an experience. The roads were shared by everything from oxen-pulled carts, to scooters carrying families of four plus a calf, to trucks so overloaded they looked like mushrooms on wheels. Road rules did not seem to exist. When we came to a highway stopped with traffic, without missing a beat our driver took off through the center divider, splitting the oncoming traffic while roaring along at 70 miles per hour, our safeguard was nothing more than a car horn. All I could think of was at least going this fast, death would be instantaneous.

The slums of Moradabad were like many others I have experienced in the world, only with ten times the number of people. There were thousands living life as best they could. One woman I spoke to told me her family shared a house with two other families. Each family rented the house for an eight-hour shift, after which the next family would come in, then the next. The other sixteen hours they had to spend on the streets.

We were concerned we would be treated as outsiders, or worse – a past team had actually been chased out of the neighborhood. Yet we were greeted with cheers and chanting, and many came and thanked us for being there. This was due to the efforts of the local Imam, who had converted the Muslims of Moradabad to believers of our mission to immunize their children against the deadly disease. He was one of the humblest and soft-spoken men I had ever met, yet clearly a force to be reckoned with. He invited us to his house for tea and cookies, which was very pleasant until local police appeared and called our guide over to speak with them. When he returned, he told us with a concerned face we were all to go to the Police station.

When we arrived, the police chief addressed us himself. He asked us where we were going and asked for our itinerary. He looked over it in detail and we started to worry something was seriously wrong. Eventually he said, "Thank you. I wanted this because you are our guests. We want to make sure all is well. I will have a policeman with you at each of these locations." We were escorted into the next room where they had tea and desserts set up for us to enjoy.

The next day, we were greeted by a team of physicians. One introduced himself as the Minister of Health for the Country of India, who was also a Rotarian. He told me he came to meet me after hearing I was not only a Rotary governor, but also a polio survivor.

He invited me to the polio team report meeting, where all the teams of Moradabad detailed their progress and numbers of children vaccinated. He also organized for a media team to record our journey for local and national coverage. At the train station, we met with three cameramen and media staff who followed us around to capture us in action. We vaccinated children as they were held out the train windows, since it was so crowded it was almost impossible to walk through and could leave without warning.

Word got around I was a survivor myself which made a great impression with the locals, especially because I had come from so far away to help their children from ever experiencing the same affliction. I gained a deep appreciation of polio workers in India for their unselfish fight against the disease.

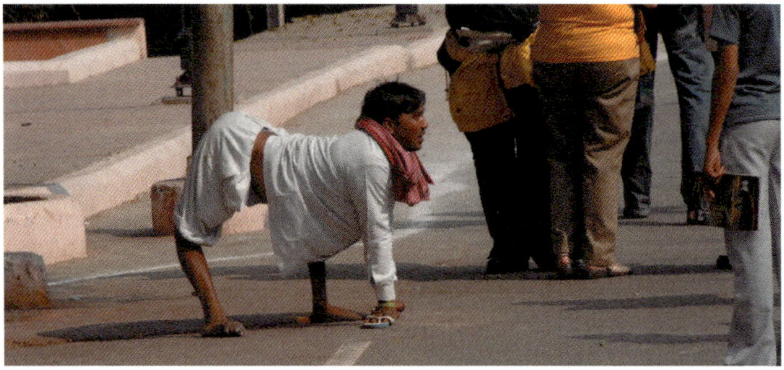

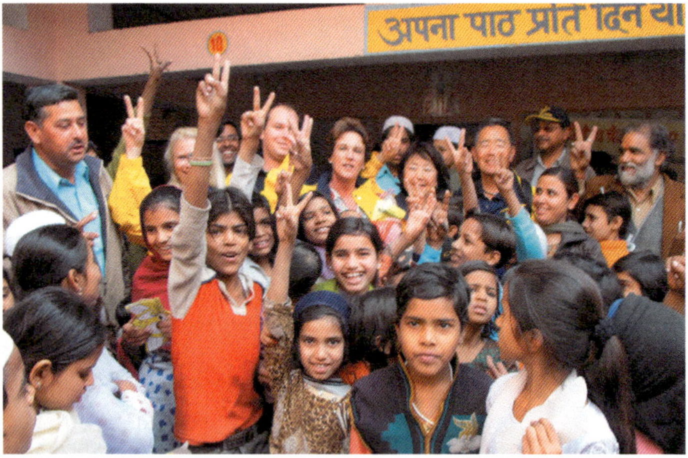
अपना पाठ प्रति दिन

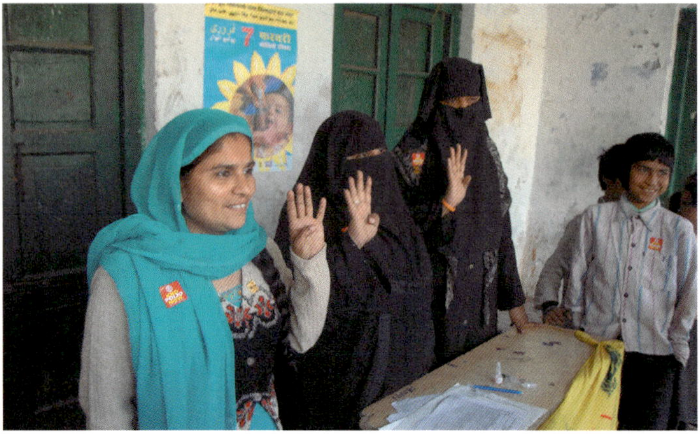

We were there for five days, but many of them had undertaken the process every day for the past twelve years, some without any payment, but driven by the knowledge they were doing something to protect the future of the children of India. Seeing the gratitude in the eyes of those we worked with and the mothers and children we immunized was deeply moving. At one stage in our journey we visited a neighborhood polio station where three women were working. I was awed by how efficiently they worked, moving at a pace ten times faster than we could manage. They had immunized four hundred children that day alone by the early afternoon. Parents were not given a choice to opt out, though everyone I saw was happy to participate. Citizens would even offer to help however they could. In the five days of the immunization program, 916,000 children under the age of six were immunized in Moradabad alone.

I could have written an entire book on just this trip. It was a privilege to work with the wonderful people we met, who welcomed our efforts as the only foreigners in their city to help with their mission to ensure no one again suffered the affliction of that terrible disease. That year in 2010, India recorded its last case of polio. However, as it still exists in some countries, Rotary is determined to fight until polio is absolutely wiped from the planet. I hope it happens in the very near future, so I can know that no child will ever again experience the horrors of the disease like I did, suffer the life altering disabilities, or death that can result.

Photos:
1. Polio victim on the streets of Agra, India.
2. Community health camp with some of the Rotary National Immunization Day team members.
3. Neighborhood Polio Immunization Station, Moradabad India, with the women holding up 4 fingers indicating the 400 children they had immunized so far that day.

I still keep in touch with Rotarians there, in recent years assisting efforts to provide Rotary Foundation grant funding of over $1.2 million to projects in India. These were an across the globe collaboration between the Rotary Club of Bakersfield, California, and the Rotary Club of Gandevi, India, spearheaded by members of each club Jim Damian and Amrat Patel - Rotarians living on separate sides of the world united in their desire to help improve the lives of some of the poorest people in the world.

One grant enabled over ten thousand people to receive free medical checkups and treatments in Gujarat. Another provided three thousand children in ten rural village schools with playground equipment, clean water filtration systems and hand sanitation stations, as well as technologies including smart boards, iPads, and computers. Gender specific toilets were also created, with free sanitary pads now provided to girls, since lack of facilities related to menstruation is one of the leading causes of young women leaving the education system.

27. THE WADENATOR

In preparation for becoming President of our Rotary Club, Roxanne was expected to attend a series of training sessions organized for all the incoming presidents in our district. I went along as her spouse, allowed to sit in on sessions if I wished. One of these sessions was a class on becoming a District Governor delivered by Past District Governor Jock McKenzie.

We knew each other from previous Rotary events and he immediately singled me out. "Nomura! What are you doing here? Just because you're a good speaker doesn't mean you're governor material!"

He proceeded to tell us in detail about the role, which entails an enormous range of duties, including helping clubs with their projects, managing budgets and reporting, promoting Rotary's public image and hosting annual district events.

Despite his jokes, Jock seemed to decide I had the potential to be a District Governor one day. However, I would need to hone my skills and make some changes before I was ready. After my year as Club President, we started meeting up once a month for lunch, where we would talk about the happenings in our District and how I could start to measure up as a leader.

Jock was a retired Marine Colonel and never held back. To start with, he told me flat out I didn't dress properly. I used to attend Rotary meetings in shorts and a golf shirt - that had to change. According to Jock, proper presentation commanded respect. As I built a more professional looking wardrobe, he would tell me if anything wasn't up to his standards, noting if my shoes were scuffed or my shirt wasn't pressed with military precision.

The next year, Jock put me forward for my first District position as Vocational Service Director. My job was to encourage Rotarians to use their professional skills and educational backgrounds to help Rotary. The year after that I was appointed as a Group Representative, essentially an assistant to the District Governor, assigned to assist a cluster of Rotary clubs in my areas. Jock monitored my progress, mentoring me as well as motivating me with his high expectations.

I decided to get a head start, hosting a Christmas social a year before I officially took office. I wanted to get to know everyone on a personal level, to encourage good relationships and get to really know the ins and outs of the clubs I would be helping. After that, every meeting I attended, I spent half the time focusing on working with the Rotarians to apply their skills, and the other half hanging out casually. Often these times spent in a friendly way led to new ideas as well as made clubs more receptive to my suggestions.

Five years into Rotary, I decided to apply for District Governor. When I told my mother, she reacted with horror. "Why? Don't. You will only be disappointed."

"Why?" I asked her, shocked.

"Because you are Japanese."

I told her plenty of people from minorities had held the office, and I didn't see why this would make such a difference.

"America never put any of them in a camp," she replied, shaking her head.

I decided to apply anyway. I was told three others withdrew their applications in my honor. I was unanimously approved, the first time in the district's history this had happened. When I heard the news, the first thing I did was call my mother. She promptly burst into tears. She never believed it would be possible for her Japanese American son to be chosen.

Jock was pleased, of course but told me that I still had a lot to learn before taking office during the two years I would spend as Governor Nominee, then Governor Elect, before taking on the governorship myself.

By the time my term was approaching, Jock's health was failing. A month before my governorship was to begin, he told me he didn't think he would make it but he was proud of me and he had no doubt I would be the best governor the district ever had.

When he passed, his wife gave me his Rotary pin and first ever Paul Harris fellow pin. He had wanted me to have them because they meant a lot to him and he was sure I would appreciate them more than anyone else. They remain two of my prized possessions.

When I began my governor term, I wanted focus on my district's club presidents rather than developing my own projects, in a similar way I served the members of my Rotary club as president. I prioritized having one on one time with every club president, as well as asked them all to send me their goals for the year. I made it clear myself and other district staff were there to support them achieving their goals.

Over the year, I visited all 72 clubs in our district which covers roughly 40,000 square miles and includes Santa Barbara, Ventura, San Luis Obispo and Kern counties. Roxanne and I attended a vast array of events, from festivals to golf fundraisers, making many lifelong friendships.

With our busy schedule, it was common for us to attend back to back events held by different Rotary clubs. We were guests at the Rotary Club of Nipomo barbeque and auction event held at the Hearst Ranch. There was a western theme, and Roxanne wanted to dress the part, dragging me to a Western store filled with boots, hats and clothing. She quickly went off browsing, instructing me to find a 'cool shirt'. I finally found one I liked and shouted to Roxanne to come and look. She emerged from the dressing room wearing the same shirt I had in my hand. "We can be twins!" she exclaimed. I was ready to go back and find another shirt, when I saw the disappointment in Roxanne's eyes and had to just suck it up. When we arrived, we had to pose for more photos than I could keep track of, including for photographers from the local media. At least Roxanne was thrilled how "cute" our outfits were.

After that, we had to rush to the Rotary Club of Paso Robles Wine Cook Off. This featured twenty wineries creating food dishes to match their wines. Thousands were in attendance, with fundraising proceeds exceeding $50,000. We were told it would be Western themed also, so we went over wearing the twin cowboy outfits we already had on.

However, when we arrived, I saw everyone was in summer casual. I jumped back into the car in horror. Not only was I the only Asian cowboy, I was the only cowboy in sight. Thankfully we found some clothes in the trunk so I could change. A twinset of Japanese cowboys was spectacle enough without being literally the only people dressed in costume out of thousands.

Another fun event was a bowling fundraiser for polio eradication – 'Bolio' – held by the Rotary Club of Simi Sunrise. I was bowling at the time in two leagues, though slowing down due to my Rotary commitments. I brought along all my own equipment, including custom made shoes and an arsenal of high-end bowling balls. Roxanne had her own equipment too and so when we arrived and unloaded the car everyone stared, with no idea what to think.

When all was said and done and the awards were being announced for the best one game score, one of the members friends who was brought in as a ringer to win jumped up to claim the prize, with a 217 high score. It was then my host announced I shot a 234. The prize was a coffee mug with 'Bolio Top Score' written across it I have displayed on my mantle.

One of my highlights was selecting the district staff. I selected Sharon Girod as my right-hand District staff member given her efficiency, creativity and positive attitude. I relied on her to manage communications with Rotarians and district staff, oversee events, manage my calendar and more.

Since the Rotary International Convention was going to be in New Orleans, she suggested the annual president's retreat could be themed after Mardi Gras and we could carry that theme throughout the year, creating a festive, upbeat feel. Sharon and the committee took over the organizing and, on that night, I was only told to show up wearing a purple shirt and wait outside.

When I was allowed in, there was colorful decorations, lots of sparkly beads, music and cheering. When I started focusing better, I noticed everything from the centerpiece alligators, balloons and banners all bore a strange logo with the words, 'Krewe of Nomura – Let the Good Times Roll'. Sharon explained to me 'krewe' is the Cajun term for the team who put together floats at Mardi Gras parades, each of which is led by a captain.

They decided 'The Krewe' was a fitting name for our year

group and the designation followed me throughout the rest of my governor year. I also got a special name badge with the title 'Ragin' Cajun Asian'.

During my governor year, I also ended up with other nicknames. When Arnold Schwarzenegger became Governor of California, he became jokingly known as the 'Governator'. With this inspiration, I started being called the 'Wadenator', Sharon making up yet another name badge for me bearing this honorary title. It was something I encouraged as it showed I was not above being poked fun at.

The fact our Rotary International Convention was in the United States that year meant a big contingent from our district could attend given the minimal travel costs. We had over three hundred people from our district sign up, the second largest district in attendance behind the local New Orleans clubs.

Sharon's family was from New Orleans, so she knew her way around better than anyone. She booked the four thousand square foot rooftop of historic Jax Brewery overlooking Jackson Square for a district reception. I also invited another hundred friends and acquaintances from around the world. Since I was the only one who knew all the guests, Sharon had me stand on the sidewalk outside to direct people up the private elevator, wearing an enormous, comical alligator hat.

Photos:
1. Wade's visit to Cambria Rotary Club with members dressed in cycling outfits to recognize Wade's passion.
2. Wade as the greeter for guests to his event at the New Orleans Rotary Convention, wearing the infamous Alligator hat.
3. Some guests from Mexico participating in the Rotary District Conference parade.

NEAL JENSEN
CAMBRIA ROTARY
CHAPTER 432
VETERAN

END
POLIO
NOW

Another event we were responsible for was our annual Rotary District Conference. Every year, the District Governor and Executive committee organize the event, featuring educational topics and opportunities to make inter-club connections. Roxanne suggested we hold it in Carpinteria, since it is a tourist town well able to host visitors and we could use our local connections to make it a top-notch experience.

We wanted to involve the local community as much as possible. We received approval from the City to hang Rotary banners from the light posts along Linden Avenue. Clubs and Rotarians could sponsor a banner to have their name on it, which they could keep after the event. The City also declared the week as Rotary Awareness Week, which later evolved into the Community Service Month we have currently. We spoke with local businesses regarding offering discounts to Rotarians for that week, as well as created a passport style stamp contest, with the winner having the most stamps from local merchants receiving a prize.

We held a dinner serving food prepared by local restaurants at the local Boys and Girls Club with a donation given to them to fund their gymnasium. The only thing we overlooked was providing servers for food. When I announced there would be a wait for staff to be found, many people stood up. I thought for a moment they were leaving, too hungry to wait, until they came forward all volunteering to act as servers. It was a small but touching moment of Rotarians being willing to help others, no matter when or where.

On the final day of the conference we organized a parade and car show down the main street, finishing at the State Park where they were set up for Rotarians and the public to view. There was also a place for clubs and partnering nonprofits to set up expo booths to show off their projects and products, a bandstand and food vendors. To entice more attendance, we decided to hold a Crab Feast based on the success of similar events on the West Coast.

We found a supplier from the Bay Area in San Francisco from whom we bought a hundred pounds of crab. A lot of buzz was created when we began marketing and based on presales, we were looking like we would easily break even.

A Rotary contact was happy to pick up the crab for us in his refrigerator truck to save on costs.

Our conference was scheduled on what was the driest weekend of the year in Carpinteria according to a century of data. Of course, it rained on the Crab Feast day and we ended up with only half of the crowd we originally anticipated. This still meant over two thousand visitors, but it wasn't enough to move our enormous pile of crustaceans.

We started to sell at a loss, just so we wouldn't be left with a mountain of rotting crab. Fortunately, a number of local residents, including the local Jack's Bistro purchased the leftovers, creating 'Jack's Crab Omelets' so at least nothing went to waste. I was embarrassed we ended up in the red – apparently, I hold the record in our district for the largest loss at the conference. However it was also most attended conference in our district's history. I take solace in the fact it gave lots of Rotarians the opportunity to discover my town, including sixty international guests with representatives from our sister Rotary districts in Mexico and Korea and exchange students from around the world. It also attracted many members of the public, opening up what is usually an insular Rotarian-only event to the broader community.

Keeping with my theme of supporting others to realize their goals, I closed my year as District Governor by taking the year-end award budget and using it to create special yearbooks for all the club presidents and staff. This featured photos of projects, events and meetings, highlighting every club and their good work for the community and the world. I also created the Robert 'Jock' McKenzie award for leadership through education to honor my mentor and sorely missed friend.

My time serving as a Rotary District Governor was exciting, but in the end, it was all to benefit Rotary members striving to make their communities and the world a better place.

28. CAMP KEEP

During my term as District Governor, I visited the Rotary Club of Bakersfield to present on district matters. After my talk, they had scheduled a presentation on a new project still in the planning stages. It was based in Camp KEEP (Kern Environmental Education Program) located in the coastal area of San Luis Obispo near Morro Bay. Local students spend a week away from home experiencing the outdoors and studying flora and fauna in an intensive immersive program.

Their original focus was removing an old World War II trailer being used as the kitchen facility and installing a new kitchen and office space adjacent to the Dome. A large geodesic dome covered in a tarp was used for dining, as a classroom and for displays such as on native wildlife. The Rotary Club of Bakersfield had expanded their original concept to include adding in a new outdoor classroom area and native botanical garden. They announced this would be called the Wade Nomura Native Plant Garden in honor of my contributions to Rotary. I was caught completely off guard. I was surprised they would choose me, since their club was one of the oldest and largest in the district, with surely many local members worthy of recognition. Much to my surprise, they had no idea I worked professionally as a landscaper. I offered immediately to draft a design of the garden as well as assist with fundraising and organizing a volunteer workforce for its installation.

I traveled out to the site soon after to get a sense of the area. It turned out to be just near the Montana de Oro, an area my mother had spent a lot of time as a child. She and her sisters would travel there to gather abalone, sea snails, fish and seaweed to eat.

Volunteers in action, building the native gardens and outdoor classrooms at Camp Keep

Completed amphitheater, with downlights under the benches and at walkways, to minimize contaminating night sky.

Photo of the waterfall, stream and pond, to attract wildlife and create a more natural setting.

Signage representing completion of Camp Keep Landscape project. Wade with Camp Director Elizabeth Roberts.

My family had later camped at the State Park to enjoy the untouched wilderness. The beaches are pristine, with plentiful deer and wild turkey throughout the secluded forests.

I completed my design soon after. My idea was to create a network of walking paths through groves of indigenous plants. A water feature created an inviting place to sit, and as well, would attract native animals. The goal was to create a naturalistic, relaxing space, sparking curiosity about the local environment.

Once the installation of the new kitchen and outdoor facilities had been completed, including a new dining and gathering area and classroom, we started on the garden. A retaining wall was built to level an area, after which I took some workers from my landscaping company to do layouts and other initial phases. After this, the Rotarian volunteers came in to lay blocks, fill in soil and gravel and other aspects of the design. Among these recruits were Roxanne and my grandson Zach. We all had great fun and there was a strong sense of camaraderie at these workdays. Everyone ended up with nicknames, project lead Dave Morton dubbed 'The General', myself 'The Gov' and Zach 'Little Gov'.

The team from Camp KEEP also put in a lot of hard work, continuing the landscaping after the Rotary volunteers left. Thanks to all the volunteers and the generous discounts and donations from material suppliers, the costs for the project ended up being minimal. Many of the volunteers from Bakersfield would come in a day before so they could start work early, staying at the camp or at a hotel on their own dollar. The project stands as a testament to the commitment and support of young people's education. Everyone involved takes pride in what we did to enhance an already beautiful place.

29. CONNECTING THE DOTS

Many people around the world are forced to live in darkness once the sun sets. They may have the option to use kerosene and other open flame lanterns for illumination, however these emit toxic fumes and are responsible for many household fires. In response to this problem, Unite to Light was founded to manufacture and distribute low-cost solar lights for people in need.

I became involved with the initiative after attending a Rotary Club of Montecito meeting where by chance a Unite to Light board member, Claude Dorais was presenting. I could see his passion, the profound impact the lights could have in developing regions.

After the meeting I asked Claude why he was not part of Rotary, since both had the same mission and he could potentially tap into Rotary's international network through strategic partnerships with Rotary Clubs. Claude responded with "No one ever asked me to join." Claude joined the E-club of One World and I joined the board of Unite to Light. Within the first year of our collaboration Rotarians moved around 4,000 lights and the relationship has continued ever since.

My role as a director of Unite to Light lead to my first real personal experience with a corporate responsibility project, which opened for me a whole new world of possibilities. In 2011, we began communications with a large company in Japan called Daiteki Electronics, a subsidiary of Mitsubishi's chemical division, who were interested in collaborating on a humanitarian project in Bangladesh. They recognized the value of utilizing Rotary's wide network and project implementation processes to execute their corporate responsibility activities.

Essentially, they had the funding but lacked the connections and, on the ground, experience implementing a humanitarian project. Working together, they knew we had a much better chance of achieving success.

I became friends with Bangladeshi Rotarian Syed Abu Sayeed, when he led a Rotary Group Study Exchange team to California three years previously. I contacted Syed and asked if he could scout out areas in need of light in his region. He found eleven schools with students who did not have safe lighting at home to use, meaning they were limited in the hours they could read and study in the evenings. Daiteki's budget allowed for the purchase of two thousand lights. Such a simple gift had the potential to literally change their lives, through enhancing their access to education and leading to long-term improvements in their life trajectory.

I was asked if I could meet with Daiteki in Japan to figure out all the details. It worked out I could stop over with Roxanne on our return from the Rotary International Convention, hosted in Bangkok that year. We had never been to Japan before and were jumping with excitement to do so. We had always been called and thought of ourselves as Japanese, but we had never been to our homeland.

When we arrived in Tokyo, I immediately wished I'd practiced speaking Japanese more. I was more than rusty, only getting by because a lot of Japanese people spoke at least some English. It was ironic though, as I looked like I fitted perfectly into Japan but I was actually a disoriented tourist. Conversely, while in Mexico I obviously stuck out, but was able to communicate perfectly.

Tokyo was amazingly clean and orderly, even though there

were swarms of people everywhere moving in orderly lines. We were told before we arrived there was plenty of signage in English and people would show us the way if we needed help. However, I had trouble seeing any such signs and found people were walking so fast it was almost impossible to get their attention to ask for directions. Everyone moved as if they were inside their own personal bubble, neatly moving around us and rushing on their way without seeming to see us at all. Roxanne and I were used to standing out because of our Japanese ancestry; in Tokyo of course we blended right in, making us basically invisible. Yet we were outsiders, the language, culture, and even the clothing foreign to us.

I set up to meet with Mitsubishi Chemical the second day of our stay in Japan. I provided a detailed plan of how the light project would be implemented, including my contacts in Bangladesh who would ensure implementation and provide reports. They advised they would get back to me and promptly called while we were on our way back to the hotel, to advise they wished to proceed with the project as presented.

Now we had completed our assignment, we were free to spend some time exploring Japan. We met up with Tomoko Karasawa a former Rotary ambassadorial scholar who studied in Santa Barbara, who I advised during her time in California. She and her parents travelled to Tokyo from Iida, near Nagano to spend time with us. They acted as our guides through Tokyo and Shinjuku for an unforgettable day. We drove around much of the area with Tomoko's father Katsumi, who was a college professor, pointing out landmarks and sharing their interesting histories. We explored a famous Buddhist Temple, where they explained to us the traditions and the daily rituals held place there. Roxanne and I both found it moving to experience our heritage first hand.

The next day, we took the bullet train to Kyoto. It lived up to its reputation as incredibly smooth and quiet with luxurious seating and services. While Tokyo was a bustling, modern city, Kyoto preserved many aspects of traditional Japanese culture as it had existed for hundreds of years. It matched up to my childhood fantasies of what Japan was like with people dressed in kimonos and women with their faces painted white. I was fascinated to walk through many landscapes I knew from books, such as the famous Ryoan-ji and Daitoku-ji temple gardens.

A schoolboy using a light to read in Bangladesh; a recipient of the project between Unite to Light, Daiteki Electronics and Rotarians.

I found my language skills rapidly improving, my childhood memories of my grandparents speaking regular Japanese revived by daily exposure. The only problem was the Japanese I knew had been imported to the United States almost a century ago. I was speaking the equivalent of Victorian formal English. The people I interacted with were too courteous to let on they thought it was odd, but I imagine they thought I was quite eccentric.

Japan was a grounding experience. I felt connected to my heritage in a new way. My ancestors had lived there for thousands of years, walking through the same places I now walked. It was a feeling of 'fitting' I had never quite experienced in the United States, where my differences were so often highlighted growing up.

However, at the same time I realized Japan was not my true home. I had the expectation before I went that I would suddenly blend in seamlessly, however there was no escaping I was a foreigner even though I looked like everyone else. I was a Japanese American, with a Japanese cultural background – but truly an American. It was a complicated mixture of belonging and not-belonging, being home and not-home.

When I returned home, we coordinated the shipment of lights to Bangladesh. Syed began distribution the day after they arrived into the hands of schools and families. He kept thorough documentation for our Japanese corporate partners, ensuring all the intended beneficiaries received the lights and understood their function. The project was so successful that Mitsubishi Chemical immediately offered to replicate the project to assist further schools and families. Once again Syed was happy to assist, and the second round was carried out even faster than the first.

30. SHOWTIME

In 2014, my friend and Rotarian, Gary Dobbins asked if I had time to talk about an idea. He and Michael VanStry are the publishers of our local newspaper, Coastal View, and Gary was also on the advisory board of TV Santa Barbara. The paper is supportive of charities in the region, dedicating at least a page every week to highlight their activities. In a similar vein, he suggested a weekly television show focused on Rotary, given how active the many clubs are throughout our region. It could help grow awareness of our organization and our many community causes and charity partners. When I asked who he had in mind to be the host, Gary replied, "You of course."

I was taken aback. Like lots of little boys, I dreamed of becoming a movie star. I was actually offered a few parts back in my BMX days, but since they didn't fit in with my competition schedule, I had to turn them down. I had long put any ambition of being in front of the camera to bed. Despite the appeal, I didn't think I would be able to manage the time commitment involved with shooting and organizing a weekly show given my schedule.

Gary suggested we could prerecord two shows, twice a month, which could be finished in less than two hours. It seemed possible, so I said yes.

Photos:
1. Wade, assisted by summer school class, interviewing the 2018-19 Best Rotary Club Presidents from our district: Sherry Sim (Rotary Club of Cayucos); Terry Moerler (Rotary Club of Westlake Village Sunrise) and Doug Halter (Rotary Club of Ventura).
2. TV show on Habitat for Humanity build in Carpinteria with Rotaract Club of Santa Barbara President Boris Grodzovski, Governor Sandi Schwartz and fellow Rotaract Club workforce members.
3. TV show on the Botanical Gardens built by the Ventura Clubs after the Thomas wildfire and the ribbon cutting at the spectacular Ventura Rotary Clubs Plaza.

191

I went home still not quite sure what had happened. Once I got over the initial shock my face would be on TV, it hit me I was also going to have to come up with program ideas and get people lined up as guests.

We named the show Rotary Serving Our Community. Filming takes place nearby at the studio for TV Santa Barbara. The funding for shows come mainly from Community Access grants, with semi private funding to assist the station with its overhead. Production costs are kept low through using mostly students and apprentices for staff, which helps them gain career experience. I have also had help from TV Santa Barbara's summer program for eleven and twelve-year olds teaching them how television is produced. They have helped in the filming of a number of programs, including manning the cameras. As thanks for their hard work, I let the kids come on stage, for most their first ever experience being on television.

My good friend Scott Phillips offered to help with the marketing and technical work, setting up a website and YouTube library of past shows. This means past episodes can be used by Rotary Clubs to promote their project, or to watch at club meetings for training and inspiration. We are now into our fifth season with close to one hundred and fifty shows covering peacebuilding, education, youth, fundraising, and interviews with inspiring people from Rotary International Presidents to Interactors, one of Rotary's youth movements.

I am always amazed by the variety of fundraising events Rotarians put on. I have covered a Cajun festival, Spaghetti Western dinner, Pints for Polio and Cioppino Feast, naming only a few.

We've also taken filming to project sites. We showcased the botanical gardens in Ventura, created through a collaboration of local clubs after the Thomas wildfire wiped out a lot of the county. The project was the vision of members Bruce and Kathy McGee who also set out to install a plaza within the gardens to host events, weddings and lectures. The clubs worked together to transform a vacant hillside into a vibrant outdoor area, showing what can be achieved when people join together with shared passion. During our program we were able to showcase the green spaces and the spectacular views from the Rotary Plaza overlooking the city and the channel.

We also filmed at a Habitat for Humanity build of affordable units in Carpinteria. I interviewed Club President Boris Grodzovski, and you could see the passion in his eyes as he shared the experience of working side by side with his fellow Rotaract members and the future tenants who were helping as part of the buy in process. Boris and I became great friends after that, which is one of the reasons this show stands out for me; it has given me a lifelong friend. The international assignments I do for Rotary have given me the opportunity to film projects firsthand, including Mexico, Guatemala, Honduras, Belize, Ecuador, Chile, and Puerto Rico. It allows me to share views of projects created with the support of Rotarians and the faces of people they have helped that many never get to see firsthand.

My goal is to showcase what Rotary is doing beyond the club. The show also reaches many non-Rotarians, as the show is aired on local television six times a week. It is especially rewarding when people outside Rotary mention they've tuned in and tell me, "I never knew Rotary did so much".

We continue to evolve the show which started as a talk show, then we added photos to the production. We are now including video clips taken on location and live internet feeds to talk to guests around the world in live time.

31. COMMUNITY

I became involved with local government over twenty-five years ago, when a friend of mine asked me about taking over his role on the Architectural Review Board. This Advisory Board included locals with backgrounds in construction, architecture and engineering who volunteer to review building and garden project applications. My friend Kip Omweg was looking to retire and thought I would be perfect to take over his role advising on landscaping. My primary role would be to review landscape proposals based on practicality of plant choices, suitability for the location regarding size and scale, and aesthetic considerations. Since there were no other applicants, I was soon appointed by City Council.

With all design guidelines, there is latitude in making decisions. We as the board had a responsibility to strike a balance between an applicant's personal preferences and our duties, such as ensuring the design conformed to the neighborhood and observed City regulations and guidelines. It wasn't always easy. Some people were very attached to features that needed to change, or neighbors would have strong opinions. The role gave me the opportunity to see firsthand how to work out these sorts of issues, as well as pick up a lot of architectural know how from my co-members.

An extension of my role was helping with efforts like the revitalization of Carpinteria's streetscapes. The intention was to create an inviting outdoor environment people would enjoy walking through. I became the volunteer landscape consultant for the City, advising on features such as trees and gardens. The City removed an amount of street parking and installed landscape planters, replacing the walls of cars with greenery.

The result was a much less urbanized, pedestrian and bicycle space more in line with Carpinteria's small town charm.

Another aspect of this was bringing art into the city, with murals and mosaics proposed to beautify public spaces. We formed an unofficial partnership with the Carpinteria Arts Council to establish submission guidelines. We now have some vibrant murals on walls throughout downtown and colorful mosaic features. Original concerns that they might be vandalized proved unfounded; none have ever been touched, showing how much they are loved by the community.

In 1995, I was asked to serve with then Public Works Director Dave Durflinger, on my first large scale project. Highway 101 was being expanded to three lanes in the north and southbound lanes, including the stretch from Ventura to the north side of Goleta. Each municipality it would cross through had two representatives and we were appointed by the City to serve in this capacity. When presented with the conceptual design, the first thing I noticed was the lack of greenery. The center divider was planned as just concrete walls, paving and gravel with sound walls installed along the entire corridor. In most areas, concrete traffic dividers created a walled in driving environment.

I suggested we plant trees in the center median and alongside the roads, as well as remove or lower sound walls wherever possible to allow in views of the ocean and mountains. Where possible, concrete walls could be swapped for chain linking fencing or railing with enough separation to allow drivers to see through. This proposal was adopted and trees and other natural features can now be seen nearly all the way from Ventura to northern Goleta, including the spectacular oceanic views of Rincon beach.

Unfortunately, only part of the expansion was implemented due to lack of support in the Montecito corridor and the expiration of available funds. The result was a traffic bottleneck, which almost twenty years later sparked a new expansion from Carpinteria to Montecito as the original plan had intended. This time I also had input at the planning stages. Since they wanted to install an overpass wide enough to have an additional lane in the future, I suggested they install a center planter box on the Casitas Pass overpass. The planter could be removed at a later date exposing the additional lane without requiring construction of a whole new bridge, an idea that was readily accepted.

My time on the Architectural Review Board was priceless, teaching me many new design concepts, how to implement the principles of facilitation and make fair decisions for all, skills I use regularly in all areas of my life. I served for nearly eighteen years, twice as Chair, until I was persuaded to run for City Council. I had been asked to consider doing so a number of times including by my good friend Bob Berkenmeier, however I had always declined, wanting to remain apolitical and secular in community work.

However, in 2011, discord within the council was affecting the community, with divisions increasingly evident between members. Bob, the Breakfast Club and others asked me to reconsider, saying my presence could help mediate the decision-making process and bring a more civil approach to deliberations.

I decided to run with a focus of protecting the rights of others, and making changes benefiting the community as a whole. I ended up winning with a record number of votes, thanks to the vigorous campaigning done by my friends and for my volunteer work within the community.

I was elected to City Council in 2012 and was later sworn in as Mayor in December 2018 for a two-year term.

One of my first projects when I joined the Council was to improve the relationship between law enforcement and our citizens. They were considered outsiders to the community, with a reputation, true or not, for bullying and general unfriendliness. I suggested we come up with a way to allow for more positive interaction. The first step was making a space on each city agenda for a police report and asking the police to come up with some ideas to better engage with the people.

From this came the Coffee with a Cop program, where police officers were available for casual chats over coffee with citizens so they could get to know each other better. It was also arranged for the same officers to patrol the city, to become 'regulars'. The police chief and officers further made a point to attend local events and get to know the community better. Now, I seldom hear negative comments about our police. In contrast, I'm told its comforting to see them patrolling and the officers are very friendly, always ready with a warm smile.

In 2019, the city approved budgeting a position absent for quite some time: A Community Resource Deputy to work within the Community, including schools, to help deter wayward youth, set an example for them, and be there for them in times of trouble. Our city has had some gang issues, though never a serious one. The program focuses on steering youth away from this path, as well as generally keep our number of troubled youth low. The efforts have paid off, with Sheriff Lieutenant Butch Arnoldi proudly reporting our crime rate had dropped significantly over the last year. I am proud I was able to be a small part of this transition, supporting the programs and trusting those in charge to create change.

Members of the City Council when Wade first joined the Council, 2012. From Left Brad Stein, Fred Shaw, Gregg Carty, Al Clark, and Wade Nomura.

Carpinteria Bluffs — a public preserve.

Wade Nomura (then Vice Mayor) speaking at the opening of the third lane completion on Highway 101 at Carpinteria, with Salud Carbajal (then Santa Barbara County Supervisor) and Steve Bennett (then Ventura County Supervisor) 2015.

Carpinteria Community Garden Photo credit: Robin Karlsson

I've also been part of efforts to make Carpinteria a place promoting a healthy life in the great outdoors.

In November 2018 we opened a bike path beside a re-forested creek now populated with indigenous flora and fauna including frogs and birdlife. A new addition of the scenic Coastal Bike Path has now also been approved, which is the final connection from the town to the beach and also forms part of a network stretching across multiple counties. This is sure to attract cyclists from all over the world.

Our Carpinteria Community Garden project was funded by a $300,000 State grant promoting healthy living, with an emphasis on educating the public of the benefits of fresh produce. We dedicated part of a city owned empty lot near the train station for its creation. Today the garden is 100% filled with 100 individual plots, all paying $10 per month for their use. It has become a wonderful gathering area for many groups and families, with gardening classes also on offer.

Carpinteria has become a City that prides itself on being at the forefront on environmental issues. We were among the first towns to ban plastic bags, to prevent them ending up on the beaches. Restrictions were also placed on Styrofoam, straws, food containers and cigarettes as these were all ending up on the beach, eyesores threatening our wildlife and tourism industry. The Council is constantly looking for new ways to reduce our footprint.

At the annual League of California Cities meeting in 2019, we were awarded the Institute for Local Governments Beacon Spotlight Award for Agency Electricity Savings of 36% placing us in the top ten municipalities in California. We achieved this through installing more efficient LED lights and reducing the number of hours lights were on in evenings where possible.

The largest environmental project would have to be the acquisition of the Carpinteria Bluffs, the land above the beach cliffs. Back in the 1950s, it was the site of the Thunder Bowl, a dirt racetrack, which attracted many famous racers to the area. When it closed, developers proposed everything from a convention center to an outlet mall. Locals considered many ideas incompatible with the town's character and newly discovered land faults put an end to the large-scale concepts.

A group of locals then banded together and formed the Citizens for the Carpinteria Bluffs to purchase the land to create a nature preserve. This was handed over to the City of Carpinteria to preserve for generations to come. A second parcel of land to the South East was recently purchased by the Santa Barbara Land Trust and given to the City to maintain. This will become a second preserve, with plans to reforest native plants as well as install walking paths and a small amphitheater for nature talks.

32. Fighting Fires

Most of my time involved in local government has been peaceful, as you would expect from a relaxed beachside town. However, I've also been involved in facing some enormous challenges.

The Thomas Fire, which ignited in December 2017, left Carpinteria under siege for weeks. Wildfires approached Carpinteria from the south, then the north, and finally the west – every side except the ocean. We were evacuated many times. Then debris flows cut off roads, leaving us isolated for five days. By the end, we were running out of food and water. However, the most unexpected shortage was money. Due to electricity being cut off we were unable to use credit cards or ATMs. Our small-town camaraderie came to the rescue, and stores set up IOU records to allow fellow locals to pay for their food and water once electricity was restored.

The Thomas Fire was the second largest fire in California history at that time. Together with the subsequent debris flows, it claimed over a thousand structures in the Ventura and Santa Barbara Counties and the lives of twenty-four people, including some friends. Another wildfire hit us in January 2018, in what was the worst fire season in living memory.

Two years later we are still dealing with the effects of this disaster. Reforesting of the mountainsides are underway, debris dams have been cleaned out and our rainwater flows have been modified to better handle debris in the future. We learned from it the need to establish communications and protocols to streamline efforts in times of need. Vulnerable areas have been identified for pre-emergency evacuation notices in the event of oncoming peril. The City is also working with the community to educate on disaster preparedness.

In 2018, a lawsuit was filed against the City of Carpinteria by a private law firm, who had also sued a number of other cities on the premise it was unconstitutional to not have voting by districts. They argued this was necessary to create fair representation, especially for minorities. We thought the small size of Carpinteria, which has a 2.5 square mile footprint and a population of 14,000, would exempt us from this action however this was not the case. During the hearings it was evident there was a push to include more of the Hispanic community in city operations, which I was definitely in favor of. However, I took issue with the arguments supporting minority representation did not represent all minorities and classified the council as 'all-white'. I pointed out I was a minority, even if it was only a single digit minority in our area. Their consul did all they could to sidestep this, I believe to their detriment, since truly inclusive representation would mean fighting for all minorities, not just the second dominant ethnicity of our region.

At the time, eleven cities had fought the lawsuit and all eleven had failed. We decided to pay the $25,000 settlement and agreed to create a committee to develop districts into ethnically representative blocks following the 2020 election. However, attempts to draw the lines of these districts have repeatedly shown Carpinteria does not actually have areas specific to Hispanics. No matter how they draw the lines, the percentages remain virtually the same. The final outcome remains to be seen. The need for true equality does exist, but a one-size-fits-all approach won't necessarily achieve the desired results.

One of my goals as Mayor was to take action around inclusivity. All city council information, including reports, our website and telecasts of our meetings are now provided in Spanish. Free English and Spanish classes are also provided at our local library.

In a unique approach to building interracial community ties, Council approved a public art display by artist Patricia Houghton Clark *Facing Ourselves* showing the positives of multiculturalism. She previously had held such an exhibition in Europe, and wanted to bring a similar project to her hometown. Portraits of locals of every age and heritage were displayed on large outdoor canvases around downtown, myself and my wife Debbie among them. It was a way of showcasing and encouraging Carpinteria's diversity as well as creating an interesting attraction for all to enjoy.

Photos:
Some images from the Facing Ourselves Public Art Exhibition by Patricia Houghton Clarke in Carpinteria showcasing the many different nationalities that make up the Carpinteria community Photo Credit: Patricia Houghton Clark

FACING OURSELVES
CARPINTERIA   OCTOBER 16 - NOVEMBER 5, 2019

ALBANIA CHEROKEE NATION PAKISTAN
COSTA D'AVORIO DANIMARCA ECUADOR
FRANCIA GERMANIA GRECIA INGHILTERRA

Irlanda Italia Jamaica Nigeria Romania Mexico Sudan Russia Serbia Spagna Syria Stati Uniti Uganda Austria Canada

"We know what it's like to carry a suitcase…"
"Noi sappiamo cosa vuol dire portare una valigia…"

Facing Ourselves: Carpinteria
Patricia Houghton Clarke

Another enormous challenge arose when cannabis was legalized in California. Previously our region was one of the major flower growers in the USA. However, the rise of the import industry wiped out many growers, who could not continue profitable operations. When cannabis was legalized, many rented their vacant flower glasshouses at premium rents to growers.

Legalization has created jobs, as well as increased public revenue thanks to the taxes paid by cannabis operations. Additionally, many growers generously provide donations to a variety of non-profits and other community programs. Unfortunately, initially the legalization legislation failed to fully anticipate some of the problems resulting from the industry including the instantaneous growth and development within the valley. The most common complaint was the smell, which is something like the stench of a skunk. Some neighborhoods close to growers experienced this for many hours every day.

Winds also spread the smell a great distance. The installation of improved air filter systems can reduce it, but since initially it was not legally required, it was up to the grower to decide whether to go to the expense or not.

There were a lot of complaints as a result and the City of Carpinteria organized a public forum in 2019 on cannabis. On the day of the forum, our chambers overflowed with people and local media including John Palminteri, a reporter and anchorman for KEYT TV news. Three hundred people wanted to have their say, on the positive and negative side of the spectrum. Everyone was allowed three minutes only, and for hours myself and the other council members had to ensure each person's opinions were heard and noted.

It was challenging not to take some comments personally, not to mention exhausting, but this is exactly the role government should play, mediating and providing balance. A month after our cannabis forum, the County decided to also hold a similar event. I had to present a summary of our City's issues on Cannabis again to a packed house. Fortunately, they allowed me as the Mayor to be one of the early presenters, in what was an all day and late-night event.

It has been good to see a group of growers working together over the last year, focusing on community concerns and creating a model for responsible growing. They have been addressing the smell by introducing new technology and also created better business practices for their industry as a whole. I look forward to the day the gap between the industry and community concerns is resolved.

In 2020, the global coronavirus pandemic has spared no place in the world, including Carpinteria. In response to this unprecedented crisis I realized that it was imperative to protect our community in terms of health and the economic fallout of isolation orders. There was no such thing as a weekend for City Manager Dave Durflinger and I, who continuously attended State, County, City and committee meetings to receive the latest information and coordinate responses.

On my recommendation to the Council, we instituted a communications committee to keep everyone up to date on the latest information and a second focused on economic recovery. I made sure to have a broad array of representatives including from the Hispanic community, law enforcement, religious organizations, the not-for-profit sector and Council members and staff. Many of these people are on the ground, assisting people in need during these difficult times. We also started up a weekly newsletter with State and County updates and how those translate into our local plan.

I am always impressed with the Carpinteria community spirit. Millions of dollars have been donated, as well as donations of goods and volunteer hours, to help others get through these tough times. Local service clubs worked side by side with other local volunteers and City staff to help feed up to two thousand people every week. This included purchasing the food, manning the event with up to thirty volunteers, packing the food and gathering donations. Local flower growers even donated flowers for the food recipients and volunteers to lift spirits. My Rotary club, as well as helping with food distribution, posted flyers on the windows of closed businesses as a morale booster, reading, "We are thinking of you and look forward to when you open. We will be here when you do." They have subsequently established a discounted gift voucher portal, providing local businesses with necessary sales now. The cannabis growers really stepped up, providing generous donations to the Carpinteria 93013 Fund established by the Rotary Club of Carpinteria Sunset for struggling locals. Many others followed their lead with close to $200,000 donated and still counting.

In the midst of the pandemic, we faced the tragic death of George Floyd, with an up swell of determination to abolish prejudice and create true equality. A group of high school students organized a protest and peace march in Carpinteria, for which we closed the downtown main streets. Hundreds turned out in support, myself included. I was proud to walk alongside people from all walks of life and every generation in a peaceful show of Carpinteria's united wish for equality for all.

Our City representatives could also not stay silent on this matter and in June 2020 we passed Resolution 5981 condemning the unjustified use of force and brutality against Black People and people of color. In July 2020 we then went further.

Foodbank distribution in progress on Palm Avenue, Carpinteria. Photo Credit: Robin Karlsson

From Left Kim Fly, then president of the Rotary Club of Carpinteria Morning working with Jaime Diamond, Founder of the Carpinteria Foodbank program. At the Boys and Girls Club providing food packages during the Coronavirus pandemic.

Despite discrimination not being prevalent in our town, we wanted to ensure absolute equality. This led to two new committees, one focused on reviewing and suggesting changes to governing documents and written policies to eradicate any possible discrimination. The second includes a mix of council members and public participants working to identify issues within the community which may be considered offensive, insensitive or discriminatory to minority groups. The feedback to these actions was strongly positive. One email I received told me it made them, "Proud to be a Carpinterian."

I, too, am proud to be a Carpinterian. I believe the greatest asset we possess is kindness and compassion. The willingness of the community to help one another provides a soft landing for people struggling in tough times. Whether we're facing wildfires or a pandemic, our unity makes us resilient.

Photos:
The peaceful protest and walk organized by Carpinterian High School students in support of Black Lives Matter in June 2020. Mayor Wade Nomura walking alongside Carpinterians of all ages and ancestry supporting racial equity.

211

33. The Tournament of Roses

Every New Year's Day since 1890, a convoy of enormous floats pass down the streets of Pasadena, California, for the Tournament of Roses Parade. Uniquely, it is a requirement for floats to be covered entirely in organic material. This constitutes mostly flowers in every shape and variety, but also vegetables, seeds, bark and nuts. Marching bands, horses and dance troupes join the floats, featuring everything from dragons to astronauts, in a dazzling display of color and activity. Nearly a million people line the streets, some camping out overnight to secure the best positions. Over 40 million people see the event live or televised throughout the United States and the rest of the world.

The parade itself runs for around two hours but it is a year in the making. Preparations for the next event begin almost as soon as the parade ends. After the float design is finalized, a metal skeleton is formed over a recycled truck chassis. This alone takes around three months to complete. Foam is sprayed over the top to give the final form, which is then painted as a guide for decorations.

Hundreds of volunteers turn out to cover the floats in organic materials. Lasting materials such as seeds, dried flowers and bark can be added weeks earlier. Fresh-cut flowers however, which are expected to form the centerpiece of the display, can only be placed a few days before the parade, meaning volunteers work around the clock to have entries dressed in time. Every inch must be covered, with judges awarding significant penalties if any manmade part is visible. Students through to grandparents work shifts in the float barn, engaged in meticulous tasks like pulling petals carefully out of carnations, so the petals and stems can be used, and gluing brussels sprouts up on ladders to imitate scales on a crocodile's face. It is commitment to meticulous detail that wins in the end.

All entries are expected to link to the annual parade theme announced each year by The Tournament of Roses Chair. Awards are given for a variety of classes, with twenty-four sought after trophies up for grabs. The judging actually occurs before the event in the float barn, with all riders and walkers dressing in full costume and waving to an imaginary crowd as the judges inspect our efforts. The judging is taken very seriously, with a timekeeper signaling the bell person when to officially start and stop the judging and all interaction with the judging committee is forbidden.

The Rotary Club of Pasadena first entered a Rotary float in the parade back in 1927. In 1979, the float organization was taken over by a committee of Rotarians from throughout California. I first joined in the effort in 2010. I had fond memories of the parade, as it was where Roxanne and I had our first date long ago.

The behind the scenes work is long and hard. Every year we must raise $160,000 in funding. This comes from Rotary Districts, Rotary International, clubs and individuals around the country as well as people who would like to ride or walk with the float who contribute for the privilege. When I started on the committee, longstanding member Frank Griffith took me under his wing. He was key in educating me on the hows and whys of the project. Frank is a fascinating man, multifaceted in his experiences in life and business, and we have become great friends beyond the float committee work. When we talk, he frequently surprises me with the answer, "I did that," in regard to many things. He has a seemingly endless network of people to call on in just about any situation.

As I learned the model they were using, I came up with ideas for some changes that would help promote the Float. The first of these was to invite the Rotary International President to ride on the Float, which I believed would result in an increase in publicity and support. When I asked incoming president Kalyan Banerjee from India if he would like to take part, he asked how many of his predecessors had done so. He was thoroughly surprised at my answer, "None." It has since become a tradition for international presidents to take part, keeping up with the 3 am cold morning start and grueling schedule which does not allow anyone who leaves the parade route to re-enter, even for bathroom breaks.

On the day of the parade itself I work behind the scenes as I am part of the support team who ensure everything runs smoothly.

Decorating the Rotary 2019 float entry in the Rose Parade is the 2018-2019 Rotary International President Barry and Esther Rassin, with 2018-2019 Optimist President Rebecca Butler Mona, husband Mike Mona and children Amanda and Alex Mona.

Rotary float entrant for Pasadena Rose Parade on January 1, 2020. From Left: Optimist President Adrian Elcock and his wife Ann, Gay Maloney, Wade Nomura, Rotary President Mark Maloney and Melody St John. Other riders, walkers and officials in background.

We have everyone in place for the parade including transporting all the participants to the event in the early hours and ensuring they have everything they need to enjoy the experience. I also help with recording extensive promotional video and photographs for internal Rotary distribution and a kit we hand out to media, which means racing around Pasadena backstreets to get the best shots of the float in action.

Others actually begin the day far earlier. Since floats can only move at a speed of around five miles per hour and most are constructed in areas around ten miles from the starting point, it can take over two hours to get each into position. Drivers actually sleep with the float overnight.

The parade officially starts at 8 a.m., with a stealth bomber flying over Colorado Boulevard. When it reaches the end of the parade route, it veers off to the east and opens up its jets. I've heard it moves so fast it reaches Arizona within minutes. Walkers and riders comment on their shock facing the sea of people as they turn onto the parade route. Taking part in The Rose Parade is on the bucket lists of many and I can see why. There is something extraordinary about the excitement and grandeur of the parade and its pure sense of celebration.

There are a host of other events that occur around The Rose Parade and it has been a privilege for the Committee, and everyone involved to spend so much time with the Rotary Presidents. The participation of the Presidents not only increases the spotlight on the parade and Rotary's involvement, but also gives Presidents the chance to interact with a vast variety of Rotarians and Rotaractors directly, hearing their thoughts and experiences of involvement in our organization.

The Tournament of Roses also presents the opportunity to interact with other service organizations. The Rotary Rose

Float Committee organizes an annual meeting of the Presidents of Lions, Kiwanis, Optimists and Rotary International during the festivities at the historic Huntington Library. During this time, they discuss their successes and issues with their peers, afterwards enjoying breakfast with members from all four organizations.

In 2016, Rotary International President K.R. "Ravi" Ravindran challenged me to strengthen Rotary's relationship with Optimists since I was friends with their President Dave Bruns. After many discussions, the Optimists agreed to be part of the 2020 Rotary Rose float, coinciding with my second time as chair. Optimist President Adrian Elcock and his wife Ann rode on the float with Rotary President Mark Maloney and his wife Gay. We were fortunate to win the volunteer trophy for the best interpretation of the theme 'The Power of Hope' resulting in plenty of media attention.

For a number of years, the Presidents have discussed bringing their organizations together to work on joint humanitarian projects. However, since The Rose Parade takes place halfway through their one-year terms, this was difficult to arrange. In 2019, Rotary International President Mark Maloney came with a pre-prepared agenda based on information from his predecessors, organizing further meetings between the Presidents, the Presidents Elect and the CEO's or equivalent to make this concept a reality.

Subsequent meetings have now resulted in the official announcement of a global partnership between all four service organizations to help fight the effects of the coronavirus pandemic. Linking our organizations together will help create global humanitarian impact like never before. I hope it is the start of many such collaborative efforts using our combined membership, resources and desire to help others to change the world in large scale ways.

The coronavirus pandemic means sadly the 2021 parade will not go ahead, replaced by a virtual telecast showcasing past events. Whatever the future holds, I believe our history of bringing recognition to Rotary with our creative entries, as well as joining together the four service organizations as one, is an extraordinary legacy of which all Rotary Rose Parade supporters and volunteers can be immensely proud.

34. CLEAN AND SAFE

The Rotary Foundation provides grants for Rotary Clubs to implement humanitarian projects around the world. Additional support is provided to Rotarians in a number of ways, including through the Cadre of Technical Advisers, who review, monitor and evaluate projects as well as provide practical suggestions to ensure project success. Cadres are Rotarian volunteers with expertise in areas such as engineering, health, finances, and implementing a wide variety of projects of their own.

Jan Lindsey, a friend of mine who passed away a few years ago, was in the Cadre and told me he enjoyed the opportunity of seeing interesting new projects and meeting Rotarians in different places. After my work implementing water projects in Mexico, he suggested I would be a good fit. After researching the program further, I applied and was accepted to specialize in Water and Sanitation and in Community and Economic Development.

It took a while for me to be selected to evaluate a project – however it turned out there was a shortage of Cadres that spoke Spanish and when I mentioned I was bilingual; I was quickly assigned to analyze the feasibility of a Haiti water project. The plan was to distribute water from a mountain spring to eight communities below with a budget of $200,000. This was a desktop review, meaning I did the evaluation remotely. I made recommendations mostly regarding the implementation and long-term sustainability of the system.

After that the assignments started coming. My first opportunity to travel came with a project in Guatemala helping indigenous villages raise their own food crops with enough excess to sell for profit through a developed cooperative market. This was to assist with growing the local economy as well as malnutrition in the area, with studies indicating villagers were only growing 85% of what they should have been. The one aspect I noted was missing was addressing the supply of clean water. The community's limited water source was grossly contaminated, resulting in dysentery spreading amongst the people meaning malnutrition would continue even if fresh food was available. It was motivating to meet the people being assisted firsthand as well as feeling like my knowledge could help make an important contribution to the project's goals. The following year I was sent to Guatemala again, and Honduras twice, this time to evaluate water and sanitation projects.

To ensure donations to The Rotary Foundation are safeguarded, there are tight controls in place surrounding grants. These include requirements for progress reports tied to future funding. Cadres evaluate any project where The Rotary Foundation has contributed $50,000 or more, and also step in if they have any issues or concerns during the project.

I was called in by Rotary Foundation on the fourth year of a project in Honduras, which involved drilling twenty-one wells in an area without existing water sources. I found that only thirteen wells had been drilled and of those, only eight were producing water. On top of that, the funds were nearly depleted. I started analyzing exactly what went wrong. I found some location sites where water could obviously not be reached, such as upper locations near tall cliffs. In other areas the drilling company had gone down the contracted depth, however this was thirty feet short of hitting water. I met with those involved with developing the project. It turned out the Rotary Club had partnered with another organization, with their responsibility to ensure installation. The other organization agreed they had made mistakes, including appropriate safeguards in drilling contracts. As a result, we successfully negotiated they would cover the entirety of project costs and Rotary would withdraw.

Despite everything not going as planned, the wells that were installed provided very positive results. In one village where infants were dying from dehydration and waterborne diseases from the polluted water available, the death rate had reduced to zero. I recommended to the Rotary Foundation future projects should require a hydrology study performed and drilling contractors to have performance-based contracts in place. I was pleased when this was made mandatory on future grants, as prevention is better than a cure.

While it might sound glamorous to be in the Cadre with all the travel involved, it is very hard work. Once the assignment is accepted, travel logistics including meals, hotel accommodation, ground transportation, meetings with partners, Rotarians and beneficiaries, and visits to project sites must be worked out. It also requires weeks of going through reports and correspondence with project organizers, as well as researching the region to gain a better understanding of the people and government. Understanding local culture, such as courtesy and the way officials go about authorization, are vital in regard to efficiency and creating lasting partnerships ensuring sustainability of a project.

Once at the project country and location, there is usually only a few days to complete the physical evaluation meaning work starts immediately with very little down time. In order to save the Foundation money, I usually do multiple grant evaluations on each trip. On one occasion, I traveled to Ecuador to look at a septic system, then to southern Chile to evaluate an ambulance project and finally to northern Chile for a pre-project evaluation, all within a week.

I also have had to face political unrest and violence on the ground. Sometimes my trips have been cancelled entirely. On other occasions, I went with travel advisories in place, creating challenges in planning. I even had to undertake training with Homeland Security who taught me how to identify, manage and minimize threats.

Many of the places I've been are very different to the relaxed atmosphere of California. In Honduras I remember seeing McDonald's parking lots filled with security guards armed with shotguns stationed at driveway entrances. I was told not to go anywhere without a local Rotarian escorting me.

I'm currently serving a three-year term as a Technical Coordinator of Cadres in Water, Sanitation and Hygiene where I oversee all Cadres in this area of focus globally. I am also serving on the Rotary Foundation Long Range Planning Committee of Cadres with Rotarians from India, Uganda, Brazil and other parts of the United States. Our goal is to make Cadres a greater resource for districts and clubs, available to assist club and districts in preparing grant applications as well provide mentoring throughout project implementation.

Recently, the Rotary Foundation has restructured Cadres, organizing them globally into seven zones. I have been asked to take on the new role as the Coordinator for Cadres in North America, Canada and English-speaking South American and Caribbean countries. It is my hope to develop, build and promote this program to better help Rotarians reach their humanitarian goals. My involvement with the Cadre program has been one of the most rewarding aspects of my Rotary service work. I have witnessed lives changed through the provision of clean drinking water, giving safety and good health to people who suffered for generations.

Evaluating an agricultural production project in a Mayan Chorti Village in Guatemala, 2015 where Wade at 5 foot 7 inches towers over other community members given their stunted height due in part to malnutrition.

Evaluating a new water well project in Escuintla, Guatemala, 2016.

No longer do they live in fear, wondering if their next drink will hold a fatal disease. I have seen their eyes shining with happiness, looking forward to life beyond facing the daily challenge to survive. Being a part of this has been transformational and inspired me to continue forward dedicating my life to serving others.

35. TRANSFORMATION

In September 2017, Hurricane Maria devastated Puerto Rico, with the eye of the storm tracking right through the center of the island. Widespread destruction and disruption led to many villages being cut off for weeks. With the majority of the island's food imported, this created a major humanitarian crisis. Aid organizations did what they could however until access was restored to more remote regions, they had no choice but to survive on their own.

After the initial troubles had passed, plans were made to try to find solutions to prevent the situation occurring in the future. Farms in Puerto Rico were predominately large commercial operations raising coffee and cane sugar for export. Only around 15% of food consumed was grown locally resulting in a limited supply of fresh fruit and vegetables. Another issue was the low nutritional value of the imported processed foods being consumed by Puerto Ricans. As a result, it was recognized the country needed to start homegrown food operations to support the population, decreasing dependence on imports.

In January 2020, I was asked if I could fill an unexpected cadre role the following week to review a new project in Puerto Rico. With a bit of juggling, I managed to free up the time. The Rotary Foundation had approved a $300,000 grant centered on economic development of remote areas to develop small independent farms. They would grow crops selected specifically to provide maximum nutritional value for the community.

The project had been launched by a local organization called Para la Naturaleza. They originally focused on preserving items and locations of cultural significance, however had since grown to other initiatives helping the community. They were taking a page out of the history books and helping establish a network of small family farms. Many families still owned fertile farmlands previous generations had cultivated in the past. There was also available labor, after an exodus of coffee and sugar cane companies following the Hurricane Maria left many workers unemployed.

Para La Naturaleza had arranged classes in crop selection, site preparation, production techniques and installing infrastructure. There were also components involving care of the environment through sustainable growing techniques, natural pest control, reforesting to prevent erosion. Once completed, the farmers were officially certified, with the more successful students given the bonus of becoming paid instructors in the future. The organization also conducted monitoring of farms and provided support where necessary to help the farmers best succeed.

This idea caught the attention of the Rotary Club of San Juan, who helped them develop a plan to receive Rotary Foundation support and grow the concept further.

The club president, Gerry Cumpiano, drove me to the project sites, driving past a shipping dock. Gerry pointed to the two enormous 250 feet tall cranes used for offloading. They remained largely intact, but the winds had literally stripped off the paint covering their steel frames. The wind gauges sitting on top of them had been ripped off and found some distance away, recording gusts of 185 miles per hour.

Gerry also mentioned supplies had recently been found there stored in a container, donated by well-meaning but misguided charities. They had failed to consider the damage to the equipment used for moving large crates, compounding the problem for the limited local volunteers. Once these were accessible, nothing had labels meaning tedious hand sorting was required, with hardly any manpower available to do so in the aftermath of the disaster. Most had simply been abandoned during the crisis and subsequently forgotten. It was a lesson in the need for humanitarian aid to be planned and implemented properly, so it actually helps those it is intended to assist in their time of need.

The project we were working on was based on consultation with the locals who operated the farms. Applicants were asked to outline a specific item needed for the farm, which would give them the greatest return on capital. Requests included cooler boxes to store harvests, mechanical equipment such as tillers and tractors and electric fences to keep out feral pigs. There were also requests to help fund expansion plants, such as provision of fruit trees to expand their product line and funding to lease more land. More unusual requests included native trees to provide shade for chickens and funding for the purchase of cats to eradicate rats. It is safe to say the program organizers would not have thought of many of these items without asking the farmers directly what they needed.

I visited around half of the thirty-four farms benefiting from the project. These farms were mostly small family owned properties passed down from generation to generation, in remote mountain communities connected by dirt roads. The small houses were nestled among rainforest, with donkeys, chickens, ducks, geese and pigs wandering everywhere. The people came out to greet us, full of smiles. Over and over they told me they had left their land, because they had lost hope for Puerto Rico's future. When they heard about the program, they had decided to return, with the benefit of some having completed higher education when they had been abroad and understanding different ways of doing things were possible.

I was able to share with them a lot of useful horticultural knowledge gained through many years of my professional life. I advised on pest control such as beneficial insects like ladybugs and wasps and plants with bug repellent properties like marigolds and chrysanthemums, soil borne pest species to look out for as well as microbiological pathogens. I was also able to help with farm layout advice, such as soil, bed and furrow cultivation, irrigation system designs, implementation of nutrition injectors, and newer technologies in plant and seed germination.

Beyond food production itself, the project had another hurdle to overcome. Many locals had become so accustomed to eating processed foods they no longer knew how to prepare meals based around fresh produce. Knowledge in regard to nutrition was also extremely limited. The program was expanded to provide elements such as cooking classes and nutrition education. Aside from providing funding to grow the project, Rotary is working with Para La Naturaleza to help spread the program across the island. There are currently twenty-seven Rotary clubs in all geographic regions of Puerto Rico. I helped develop a plan in which all of these clubs would work on new ways of promoting the project across the island.

Before I arrived, their model was to use organized outings to farms to gain support. The problem was, these farms were hours away from the cities, meaning for someone to sign up they would already have to be passionate about the project. I suggested for all of the clubs to work together developing an education program on nutrition and create community gardens at local schools towards creating further cooperative groups and demand for fresh fruit and vegetables, fostering production and sales.

Rotary grant evaluation trip to review agricultural project sites and participants in Puerto Rico. Project partners include Para La Naturaleza and Rotary Clubs in Puerto Rico.

I also suggested the creation of a recipe book. This would assist with promotion, fundraising and education on how to prepare nutritious meals.

I believe this project has the potential to transform Puerto Rico by increasing community sustainability, improving health outcomes, and generating growth of the economy. It also has the capacity to improve issues such as violence against women, through giving them a chance for greater income potential, when previously many were housewives dependent on their husbands.

This can also serve as a model for future projects globally as it addresses health, economic development, protecting our environment, and education at the lowest income level.

It is a prime example of what Rotary can achieve working with local organizations to create tremendous positive change.

36. THE ACCIDENTAL SPEAKER

When I was in school, I avoided public speaking and figured out how to bypass all my oral assignments completely. I was self-conscious and squirmed at the thought of my presentation skills coming under scrutiny. I avoided being the center of attention and never got involved any more than absolutely necessary.

That all changed when my father passed away in 1988. He was diagnosed with pancreatic cancer and within two weeks, he was gone. I spent every day with him during that time. He wanted to make sure the family was taken care of and we went over plans to put his estate in order. We talked about all the good times we had together and all the great places we had gone fishing, hiking and riding.

At the memorial service, I felt it was only proper I speak, as daunting as I found the prospect of addressing such a big crowd. As I walked up to the lectern, my stomach was rolling with nerves. Two hundred people sat below, looking up at me. I thought of my father and felt the urge to do his memory justice. I buried my fear and spoke from the heart.

Harry, my dad's best man at his wedding, came up to me afterwards. "That was powerful. I never knew you could speak!" he exclaimed. A number of others thanked me for sharing the stories that reflected his life. After that with new courage, I did a little speaking here and there, such as the Gardeners Federation and Japanese community events.

Then, in 2003 Roxanne and her good friend Janice were undertaking a six-week Rotary District program called Potential Rotary Leaders Seminars and asked me to join in.

When I graduated, the program director, Jock McKenzie, asked what I thought of the experience. I was honest: I found it too basic and lacking in participant involvement. He asked me if I would be interested in helping make improvements and so I joined the PRLS training team.

The curriculum was shifted to become more engaging and challenging. Many of the classes are not specifically Rotary centered, covering leadership, facilitation, project creation, management and more. These are cross applicable to many spheres of life, though of course are integral to effective humanitarian initiatives.

This was over fifteen years ago. I've since taught the program to thousands in my local district as well as other districts throughout the United States and Mexico.

I've come to present more broadly, on all sorts of topics such as how to prepare and utilize community assessments to identify needs and potential outcomes for community service work, how to gain buy in from beneficiaries and methods of obtaining financial support.

At first, it could feel a bit like showboating, talking about myself, my expertise and my projects. My perspective shifted when I realized spreading information about my service projects helped others to create similar initiatives of their own.

Sharing my stories, knowledge and passion to serve creates a sort of ripple effect where others can use my experiences to institute even more positive change in the world.

I've had the opportunity to speak at many memorable events and places, but a standout was being invited by Rotary District Governor Dan Ryan to deliver a keynote address and training sessions for his district conference at Notre Dame in Southbend, Indiana. I've watched football games played in front of an audience of eighty thousand there on television since I was a child. Never in my wildest dreams did I imagine I would one day walk on the field. My keynote took place in a huge room with glass walls built within the walls of the stadium, with views of the vast campus and landmark features. It was truly an experience of a lifetime.

I am now also heavily involved with training future Rotary club presidents. For nearly ten years I've been the curriculum chair for the Southern Californian and Nevada regions.

A couple of years ago, I was also appointed to the board of the organization which distributes the latest Rotary information to training groups similar to ours, throughout the United States. I hope to be able to also share Rotary training programs with these organizations, as well as expand our network internationally.

My Spanish language proficiency has become helpful in allowing me to present in Spanish speaking countries. When I was sent by past Rotary International President Ian Riseley as his representative for a district conference in Mexico, it was amusing seeing Californians who had accompanied me wearing headphones to listen to the English translation of my delivery of Ian's messages.

I am also a regular trainer in Mexico on how to do projects; including completing community assessments, finding partners, soliciting financial support and accessing grants from the Rotary Foundation.

In recent years I've begun speaking to groups as a Council Member and the Mayor of Carpinteria. This has meant engaging different audiences to those I've become accustomed to.

Recently I was invited to speak on a panel with two other Mayors at a gathering of the American Institute of Architects in New Orleans regarding how we handled natural disasters in our respective communities - in my case the Thomas Fire and subsequent debris flows.

One of the most challenging speaking assignments I've had was a class of six-year olds on Career Day at a local school. I was supposed to cover my role as Mayor for a full hour, though I could hardly speak on subjects such as the budgeting, policy development and staffing matters to children of such a young age. I winged it, starting out with what was a fairly easy question. "Who knows what a Mayor is and what they do?" "I know!" shouted one boy. "It's like the President only more important!" Some of the answers to my other questions were also highly entertaining. When I asked them to estimate what I was paid for my duties a little girl piped up with, "One trillion, billion dollars!" However, when I asked, "Who wants to grow up to be Mayor?" no one raised a hand. Tough crowd. I did make it the full hour, however.

Photos:
1. *From left: Speaking at the American Institute of Architects Grassroots 2020 National Conference. Peter Exley, 2021 National President interviewing Mayor Wade Nomura (Carpinteria, California), Mayor Quinton Lucas (Kansas City, Missouri) and Mayor Kathy Ehley (Wauwatosa, Wisconsin)*
2. *Participants from a Rotaract and Interact training program presenting Wade Nomura a T-shirt signed by all as a thank you for his Leadership training. Bakersfield, California 2018*

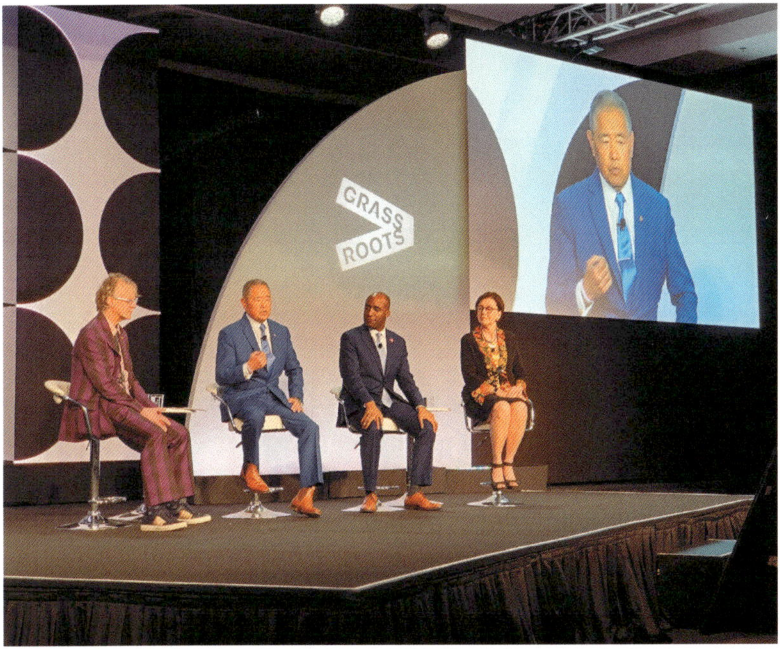
GRASS
ROOTS

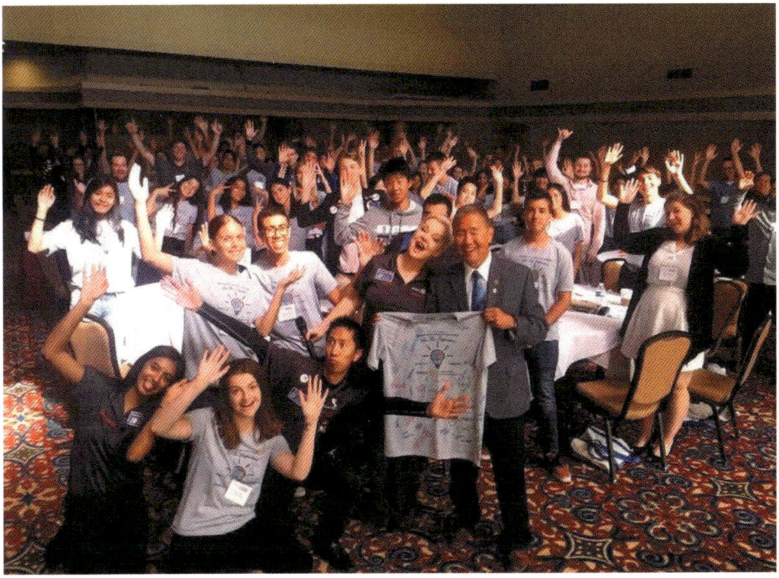

They say public speaking is something people are more scared of than death. My speaking engagements started late in life and I would say truly if I can learn to do it, anyone can. The nerves never go away, but with practice, I focus more on the people I'm talking to than myself.

Many decades after my father passed away, I was invited to speak at a Rotary conference in Korea to an audience of four thousand people. I was given an interpreter, and he asked me if I had ever been there before. I said no, but my father had during his wartime service.

When I rose to speak, the thousands stood up to applaud in a mass standing ovation. I was baffled by this fervent welcoming, until my interpreter explained they had spoken on my father's service in my introduction. They were thanking me on my father's behalf, as one of the Americans who risked his life to save their country.

It felt meaningful, it was in his name I started on my journey as a speaker, and now I was standing on stage in a massive auditorium filled with people celebrating his memory. I was never more humbled to be standing in someone else's shadow.

William Tatsuro Nomura 1950. (Wade's father)

Afterword

Debbie was the main reason this book has been written. I had considered one day writing memoirs for my family, preserving our personal history. When Debbie suggested we write a "proper" biography for publication, I was hesitant. I didn't think anyone would really want to hear my story, nor did I want to be seen as boastful.

Debbie changed my mind. She told me it was like I'd crammed three lives into one – very few people go from racing tracks to projects in the slums of India. She also said my story was not only the story of my own life, but also of the many people I had met, worked with and helped along the way. Her view was sharing about the different projects I've done could help others in their humanitarian efforts, by serving as blueprints for them to duplicate.

I began the process of digging up my memories and typing more than I ever have in my life. Debbie was tireless in working with me to plan, write and re-write this book over more than a year, for which I am immensely grateful. Danielle helped teach me the art of storytelling and writing. I am also thankful for my many wonderful friends who helped with the proofreading and printing process.

I never imagined my life would take the shape it has. I am from very humble beginnings and other than my grandfather, no one had any great expectations of me – in fact many thought the reverse given my heritage, including some who loved me most. Growing up Japanese in postwar America presented many challenges and I'm happy to say that in most cases I have overcome them, though we still have work to do towards creating a society with full racial equity.

Opportunities have presented themselves, in my case often in unexpected ways. If I hadn't befriended those kids at the housing project site, I would never have become a BMX racer. Volunteering to travel to Mexico for my club's project led me to creating water and sanitation infrastructure around the globe.

I titled this book Creating Destiny because I believe we can all be authors of our own story – though remember it might not be the story you thought you were going to write at the start. We can choose to take these paths and make the most of them. Even the darkest of days have taught me valuable lessons and an appreciation of what I have even more.

The coronavirus pandemic has brought new challenges for all of us, but it's also given me the chance to step back from my normal fast paced life and reflect, as well as spend more time with my family. I've been going to the park and playing catch with Lisa's seven-year old son Tyler, getting to appreciate his energy, intelligence and cleverness.

My family has also grown larger. I gained a new daughter when my son married lovely Nicole. When I first met her, Nicole caught me off guard when she started speaking Japanese to me. In fact, one of her grandmothers is Japanese, though it's not evident in her features. Ryan and Nicole recently welcomed a little son, Griffin, who definitely exhibits his Japanese ancestry. He reminds me of his father Ryan, at his age, very relaxed and easy going, and with chubby cheeks.

In the end, I believe people are what really matter. Connection and compassion matter far more than wealth, material items, or trophies. I consider helping others to be my life's passion and purpose. There has been no greater joy for me than seeing others grow, achieve and transform as a result of my efforts. The more you give, the more you receive, as they say – and

I have certainly received much joy from my dedication to improving other's lives.

If nothing else, I hope this book inspires others to look for the light in the darkest of times and seize the unexpected opportunities by helping others wherever they can. You're the author of your own story, make it meaningful.

Ryan and Nicole Nomura, with their son Griffin, 2020.